T0281771

Duck
Walk

Kathie and Ed Cox Jr. Books on Conservation Leadership

Sponsored by

THE MEADOWS CENTER
FOR WATER AND THE ENVIRONMENT

TEXAS STATE UNIVERSITY

Duck WALK

A Birder's Improbable Path
to Hunting as Conservation

MARGIE CRISP

TEXAS A&M UNIVERSITY PRESS • *College Station*

Manufactured in China through Martin Book Management

LIBRARY OF CONGRESS CATALOGING-IN-PUBLICATION DATA
Names: Crisp, Margie, 1960– author.
Title: Duck walk : a birder's improbable path to hunting as conservation /
   Margie Crisp.
Other titles: Kathie and Ed Cox Jr. books on conservation leadership.
Description: First edition. | College Station : Texas A&M University Press,
   [2022] | Series: Kathie and Ed Cox Jr. books on conservation leadership
   | Includes bibliographical references and index.
Identifiers: LCCN 2022016211 | ISBN 9781648430770 (cloth) | ISBN
   9781648430787 (ebook)
Subjects: LCSH: Crisp, Margie, 1960—Ethics. | Duck shooting. |
   Ducks—Effect of hunting on. | Fowling—Moral and ethical aspects. |
   Hunting—Environmental aspects. | Birds—Conservation. | Wildlife
   management.
Classification: LCC SK333.D8 C75 2022 | DDC 799.2/44–dc23/eng/20220411
LC record available at https://lccn.loc.gov/2022016211

A list of titles in this series is available at the end of the book.

For my mentors,
the duck dudes:
Bill, Andy, and Ken.
And in memory of the
duckiest dude of all,
 Jim Weisenhorn.

"Yes, yes, Billy! You go down that side of Long Pond, and I'll go this side and we'll get some ducks."

—John James Audubon's reported last words before his death, spoken to his brother-in-law William Bakewell, January 1851

Contents

Part IV: Hunting Season

Foreword

Among my earliest memories of growing up on the Texas coast is the sound of millions of geese arriving each year about the time of my birthday in October. Later, I used the first income I ever earned to purchase a shotgun and begin what would become a lifelong tradition of waterfowl hunting. Through all those many sunrises in the marshes and rice fields, perhaps the most enduring images are those of the myriad winged creatures, both game and nongame, that filled the morning skies and filled me with wonder.

Here in the pages of *Duck Walk: A Birder's Improbable Path to Hunting as Conservation*, award-winning writer and artist Margie Crisp captures the love of birds shared by those who hunt them and those who prefer to observe them, offering her reflections on the continuing dichotomy—and fluidity—between these outdoor enthusiasts.

Traditionally, these two groups have been identified as "consumptive"— those who hunt—and "nonconsumptive"—those who watch. During my years at the Texas Parks and Wildlife Department, we worked hard to increase our attention to the interests of nonconsumptive users, finding ways to enable them to contribute materially to the conservation of nongame species. In a wonderfully readable account of her adventures into the world of consumptive use, Crisp uses thorough research, humor, delightful anecdotes, and beautiful illustrations to portray the seeming disparity between birders and hunters, the joys and perspectives that bind them, and the successes and opportunities of each in improving wildlife conservation. Artfully and compellingly, she leads us to understand that there are no consumptive or nonconsumptive users. There are only users who care and users who don't.

In an engaging historical narrative beginning with iconic conservation figures including John James Audubon and Aldo Leopold, Crisp details the immense contributions to wetland and waterfowl conservation that have been made in America through the years by hunters. Given the drastic decline in songbird populations in the United States today, she thoughtfully contemplates how much healthier these avian populations might be if we could find a way for nonconsumptive users to materially contribute to wildlife conservation and wildlife habitat as hunters have done.

Duck Walk is a wonderfully readable narrative that explores the continuing cultural divide in the conservation community as well as the ties that bind all who love the outdoors and the natural world. The author captures the rituals of waterfowl hunting and birding as few have done and affectionately describes the congenial relationship of good friends and good dogs in the field.

This fine read is an important contribution to the Kathie and Ed Cox Jr. book series on conservation leadership and to the conservation literature.

—Andrew Sansom
General Editor, Kathie and Ed Cox Jr. Books on Conservation Leadership

Preface

I grew up with a bird brother as well as a human brother. One was a year older (human, named Chris), one was a year younger (bird, named Boris), and my sister was three years behind me. My grandmother bought Boris, a common hill myna, on my first birthday. From that day on, we shared our birthdays. I got cake; he got green grapes cut in quarters.

He learned to speak before I did, but I put together sentences and he never moved beyond mimicry. He refused to learn any of the phrases we repeated, instead picking up things at random. He coupled the standard avian "Hello" with "I love you," "Notify the state department," and the horrible screeching of the rusty oven door hinge. To my mother's mortification, Boris mimicked with stunning accuracy her heartrending groan of "I want a cigarette" during one of her attempts to quit smoking. No one knew how he learned the earsplitting wolf whistle that could be heard over a block away.

Boris had a beak of rich orange blending to yellow like a kernel of candy corn. Scallops of bright yellow skin decorated the sides and back of his head, the flaps moving as he tilted his glossy black head one direction and then the other to aim an intelligent brown eye at me. Vivid lemon-colored feet and legs contrasted with his silky black plumage that shimmered with green and purple iridescence. He lived in a cage and on rare occasions would nervously clutch my grandmother's shoulder as she wheeled herself through the apartment. But he was calmest in his birdcage. I remember him flying around the apartment, clutching onto curtains and pulling towels off rods, flapping and calling "Help! Help!" until he found his cage and slipped back inside to sit and rock and rock on his swing.

I'd watch Boris for hours as he preened, drank water, ate, and dozed in the sun. I pestered my grandmother to let me feed and water him and I even begged to clean his cage. To this day I remember how I folded the *New Orleans Times-Picayune* with sharp creases to fit the bottom tray.

Living with Boris led me to notice wild birds. I watched a fat robin tilt his head and peer into the blades of the overgrown lawn just the way Boris examined the contents of his food bowl. The robin stabbed with his beak and drew back a wriggling cricket. Black crows crossed the sky morning and night on their way to the grain elevators along the Mississippi River docks. Spotted starlings pranced through the park in front of our house and packs of blue jays rumbled through the neighborhood like hoodlums looking for trouble.

American robin and field cricket

Everywhere I've lived—city, mountain, desert, or woodland—I've looked to the local birds to center myself. Even a momentary communing with a feathered being is enough to relax me. Pigeons stroll up to me in Paris, just as they do in Italy, New Orleans, or my small Texas town. Their heads bob as if tied by threads to their red feet. Step-bob, step-bob, where is the food? My heart rate slows. A crow is a crow is a crow is a crow. Almost everywhere in the world there are large, social, gregarious black birds raising hell and never hesitating to make eye contact with the featherless two-legged creatures. In the desert, a parade of birds march, flutter, and scurry to drink from a ground-level birdbath. Are they aware of me as I watch them bathe, splashing water and tilting their heads back to slide water down their throats? I should be working. A roadrunner rattles at me from the patio, startling me out of my reverie and back to the blank page, the cold coffee, and the burned toast that scents the air. Regarding me through the screen door with her indignant crest raised, she eyes me and then lowers her head to pace off into the brush.

Birds are everywhere. They live and breed in nearly every habitat on earth from the equator to the poles. Our feathered neighbors share our cities, our farms, and our wild places. They are critical to defining our world yet remain essentially elusive and alien. Maybe my sense of self was skewed by having a bird brother. I don't know. What is certain is that my attention is constantly drawn to the fluttering of wings in my peripheral view. I lose track of conversations to watch a sparrow glean seeds. I root for grackles stealing French fries in an open-air café and shiver in icy Gulf of Mexico wind to cheer whooping cranes as they stalk blue crabs in salt marsh muck.

I can't imagine a life without birds. The news that we've lost nearly three billion wild birds since 1970 makes me desolate, but I am not surprised. For hundreds of years, especially in the last century, we've usurped our native birds' breeding grounds, plowing up grasslands, cutting down forests, and dividing open land into tracts with houses surrounded by sterile lawns, trees, and shrubs that provide no nectar, no fruit, no home. We've forced our feathered compatriots to dodge buildings with reflective glass that mimics the sky, installed turbines in their migratory flyways, and hidden the night sky with blinding artificial lights. We have introduced invasive species that prey on native wildlife, and then we turn a blind eye when our domestic cats decimate bird populations. We have systematically destroyed essential habitats for the winged migrations that happen each spring and fall and then wonder where the birds have gone.

Yet there is a glimmer of hope, a way forward. It is short necked, short legged, and waddles when it walks. Its voice would never be called melodious and is neither regal nor elegant. But the watery path of nearly a century of duck conservation could be the map we need to help us protect our remaining avian brethren.

After a life spent watching my neighborhood birds, wandering through sometimes remote habitats seeking out beautiful, unique, or simply new birds; after joining and supporting local and national Audubon Societies along with other conservation organizations—how, at an age most women are considering retirement, did I find myself crouched in a duck blind holding a loaded shotgun? And why did I believe that learning to hunt ducks was the next step in my journey as a conservationist, birdwatcher, artist, and bird lover?

Acknowledgments

There are persons whose desire of obtaining celebrity induces them to suppress the knowledge of the assistance which they have received in the composition of their works.

 —Introduction, *Ornithological Biography*, vol. 1

When I look back at the number of people who helped me on this journey, I am humbled. From the biologists who took the time and did their best to educate me in the ways of wetlands and waterfowl, to the many hunters, birdwatchers, friends, and strangers who helped me along the way—most of you know who you are. A few will never know the impact of their kindness.

Any mistakes are mine.

This journey wouldn't have been possible without the generosity and patience of my hunting mentors: my husband, William B. Montgomery; Andrew Sansom, PhD; Kenneth Sherman, MD; and Jim Weisenhorn. Andrew Sansom not only mentored me in a duck blind but has been a steadfast friend and a model conservationist. Not a word of this book would have been written without his enthusiastic support. Shannon Davies encouraged me on this journey as she did on my previous explorations of the Colorado and Nueces Rivers. I would not be an author without her belief in me, her friendship, and her guidance.

Red-winged blackbird

I owe thanks to the many employees of Ducks Unlimited, Ducks Unlimited Canada, the Texas Parks and Wildlife Department, the National Audubon Society, and the US Fish and Wildlife Service who generously gave their time to talk to me about birds, wetlands, and prairies. Special thanks to Ducks Unlimited's Rogers Hoyt Jr., Craig LeSchack, Joe D. Kramer, Matt Hough, Steve Donovan, Randy Renner, Taylor Absheir, Kirby Brown, Becky Jones-Mahlum, Andi Cooper, and Jennifer Kross. Dave Kostersky of Ducks Unlimited Canada suggested a number of places I should visit while in Manitoba. US Fish and Wildlife Service employees Neil Shook, Barry Wilson, and David Allen deserve recognition, as does the Texas Parks and Wildlife Department's Kevin Kraai. Marshall Johnson gave me valuable and inspiring insight into the National Audubon Society's conservation work and goals. Laura Chamberlin of the Western Hemisphere Shorebird Reserve Network kindly took the time to answer my questions. Matthew Mahoney of the Texas Department of Transportation, Maritime Division, talked me through the complexities of managing the Gulf Intracoastal Waterway and its spoils.

A number of private landowners across the country spoke with me and welcomed me onto their land so I could see their work firsthand. They include Laurance Armour, Andrew Armour, Steve Balas, Jeff Hershey, Brent and Cody Kuss, and Dr. Robert McFarlane. Stewart Savage and Scott Savage not only gave me a tour of their Matagorda County family rice farm but also let me ride along in the combine as they harvested rice (which made me the envy of all my friends).

The Colorado River Alliance and its former executive director R. Brent Lyles deserve thanks for inviting me along on their Colorado River VIP tour, where this project started.

Laura Raun, Scot McFarland, Aaron Sumrall, Bill Balboa, and Renée Blaine all went out of their way to help me. I hope I can return the favor someday.

Inspiration, honesty, friendship, and support are equally important in a project like this book. I simply could not have completed this work without my friends and family who have encouraged me, challenged me, and provided a haven when I have been assailed by doubt. Artist and writer Carol Dawson ran away from home with me to watch birds (more than once), listened to me mull over duck details, and is simply a terrific friend. She not only improved the manuscript but inspires me to be a better writer and artist. I am forever grateful to my dear friend Martha Cox for introducing me to her South Dakota duck-hunting cousin, Jim Weisenhorn. My sister Frances Sharp is one of the most perceptive people I've ever met. Her insights made this a better book. My stepdad, conservationist J. David Bamberger, continues to inspire me.

The amazing team at Texas A&M University Press took my sometimes haphazard work and transformed it into a book. Magic indeed. Special thanks to Jay Dew, press director; Emily Seyl, acquisitions editor; and Laurel Anderton, copyeditor. Mary Ann Jacob's design skills, once again, illuminate my art and words and make it all look better than I ever imagined. My heartfelt thanks go to Patricia Clabaugh, senior production editor, who shepherded the book from my unpolished manuscript to the finished edition.

None of this would have been possible without the support and companionship of my husband, Bill. He never told me I was out of my mind but cheerfully taught me how to handle a shotgun, hunt doves and ducks, and accompanied me on this journey as I challenged my rusty old ideas about hunters and hunting. He is the best.

Duck Soup

LIST OF ABBREVIATIONS

While I have attempted to avoid the use of acronyms in the text, it is nearly impossible when writing about the many government and state agencies that manage wildlife in North America. When I added the various nongovernmental organizations to the mix, I had to choose between paragraphs stuffed with either lists of endless program names or a veritable duck soup of acronyms.

This is not a comprehensive list of the laws, agencies, programs, and organizations I encountered. Instead, it is here to assist the layperson with the unavoidable acronyms that pepper conservation work across our continent.

CRP Conservation Reserve Program; a program managed by the USDA whereby farmers are paid to take marginal or erodible lands out of production. Lands are seeded with native grasses and often become wildlife havens.

DU Ducks Unlimited, Inc.

DUC Ducks Unlimited Canada

DUMAC Ducks Unlimited de México, AC

GIWW Gulf Intracoastal Waterway; the Gulf of Mexico portion of the Intracoastal Waterway, a shallow-draft inland waterway. The GIWW runs from Carrabelle, Florida, to Brownsville, Texas.

GMO Genetically modified organism; any living organism whose genetic material has been manipulated or altered using genetic engineering techniques

GPA Game Production Area; South Dakota Game, Fish and Parks property owned and held for wildlife purposes

IBA Important Bird Area

JV Joint Ventures; subunits of NAWMP that work to create, conserve, and sustain waterbird habitats, depending on a network of private and public partnerships, nongovernmental organizations (NGOs), and state and federal agencies

LCRA Lower Colorado River Authority; a conservation and reclamation district formed by the Texas legislature in 1934. Among other duties, the LCRA manages the water supply for the Lower Colorado River Basin.

MBCA Migratory Bird Conservation Act

MBCC Migratory Bird Conservation

Commission (responsible for awarding NAWCA grants)

MBCF Migratory Bird Conservation Fund; collects the funds from Duck Stamp sales and import taxes on firearms and ammunition

MBTA Migratory Bird Treaty Act

NAWCA North American Wetlands Conservation Act, signed into law in December 1989. Provides funding to support NAWMP and has expanded to support all wetland habitat conservation.

NAWMP North American Waterfowl Management Plan; an international agreement between the United States, Canada, and Mexico that spells out a continent-wide conservation plan.

NGO Nongovernmental organization; this includes nonprofit organizations such as Ducks Unlimited and the National Audubon Society

NRCS Natural Resources Conservation Service; part of the US Department of Agriculture

NWF National Wildlife Federation; one of the nation's oldest conservation organizations

NWR National Wildlife Refuge

PPR Prairie Pothole Region

PR Pittman-Robertson Federal Aid in Wildlife Restoration Act; refers to funding for conservation derived from a tax on arms and ammunition

Ramsar The Convention on Wetlands, known as the Ramsar Convention, is an intergovernmental environmental treaty established in 1971 by UNESCO, which came into force in 1975. It provides for national action and international cooperation regarding the conservation of wetlands and wise, sustainable use of their resources. A Ramsar site is a wetland site designated to be of international importance under the Ramsar Convention.

TNC The Nature Conservancy

TPWD Texas Parks and Wildlife Department

TPWP Texas Prairie Wetlands Project; a collaboration between DU, TPWD, NRCS, USFWS, and private landowners to create wetlands and emergent wetland-mimicking moist soil units in the coastal prairie

USDA United States Department of Agriculture

USFWS United States Fish and Wildlife Service

WHSRN Western Hemisphere Shorebird Reserve Network

WMA Wildlife Management Area; area set aside by the Crown and the government of Manitoba for wildlife. WMAs also exist in Texas.

WMD Wetland Management District; complexes of Waterfowl Production Areas, managed by USFWS

WPA Waterfowl Production Area; small natural wetlands and grasslands, and interests in wetlands and grasslands, acquired under the authority of the Duck Stamp Act, paid for through the Migratory Bird Conservation Fund, and managed by the USFWS for waterfowl and other migratory birds. WPAs are located primarily in the Prairie Pothole Region of the upper Midwest of the United States.

PART I
Revelation

1

Conservation Contretemps

We were desirous of obtaining some of the Herons as specimens for stuffing, and the ladies were anxious to procure many of their primary feathers for the purpose of making fans. . . . We brought home with us forty-six of the large White Herons. Many more might have been killed, but we became tired of shooting them.
   —Great American Egret, *Ornithological Biography*, vol. 4

In 1905, the National Audubon Society was founded, with the protection of gulls, terns, egrets, herons, and other waterbirds high on its conservation priority list. In 1953, Audubon adopted a flying Great Egret, one of the chief victims of turn-of-the-century plume hunters, as its symbol.
   —Audubon Society, History of Audubon and Science-Based Bird
      Conservation

I stand at the edge of a flooded rice field with a group of birdwatchers. Thousands of birds are wading, feeding, and roosting in the shallow water. Coots, avocets, willets, egrets, herons, black-necked stilts, dowitchers, and other shorebirds mingle with the ducks and geese. My heart rate slows and my neck muscles relax. Our voices rise and fall in counterpoint to the trilling, quacking, honking, whistling cacophony of birds, frogs, and insects around us. We are in the heart of the rice prairie, just outside the town of Eagle Lake, not far from where the Texas Colorado River meanders southeast toward Matagorda Bay and the Gulf of Mexico.

As I scan through the dowitchers and sandpipers with my binoculars, I hear a woman say, "It is such a *shame* that all this is just to lure in poor ducks so some macho hunter can blast them out of the sky." I look over, wondering who'd spoken. Several of the women look primly sad, pursed lips expressing what seems like disgust at the idea that anyone would shoot ducks.

Something about the statement and the expressions needles me. There is an undercurrent of smug certainty, a breath of self-righteousness that creeps up my neck like nettles brushing bare skin. I look again at their calm expressions. Maybe I'd imagined their disdain. What I couldn't ignore, I suddenly realize, is my own.

Of course, being a birdwatcher is better for the birds than being a bird hunter, I say to myself. After all, I am not trying to *kill* birds. Duh. I brush away the unpleasant feeling. As a member of conservation organizations like the National Audubon Society and the Cornell Lab of Ornithology I am firmly on the side of birds—and the moral high ground. It is ridiculous to think of bird hunters as conservationists. Of course not—they kill birds.

I scratch my neck.

I look past the birdwatchers at the flooded rice field and the extraordinary avian display created by a rice farmer, ostensibly for waterfowl hunters. Even though the Audubon Society was founded with the protection of waterbirds as a priority, I couldn't think of a single birdwatcher who created wetland habitat on this scale, especially not for this number of birds.

What if I'm wrong?

I had spent the day stuffed in a luxury tour bus full of cheerful and chatty people. My happy-to-be-out-of-the-office bus mates are state and local politicians, water supply managers, engineers, hydrologists, employees of the Lower Colorado River Authority, and a few environmentalists.

We were assembled to discuss the future of the Texas Colorado River and its valuable water in a casual and relaxed setting. By bringing decision-makers together from both sides of the aisle and both ends of the water supply chain, the nonprofit Colorado River Alliance hoped to encourage conversation and collaboration. As the writer and illustrator of a book on the river, I'd been invited along to give a talk about my work. Our itinerary followed the Texas Colorado River downstream from Austin, through the Blackland Prairies, into the rice prairies and freshwater wetlands of the coastal plain all the way down to the salt marshes where the river empties into Matagorda Bay. Talks, slide shows, tours, a happy hour, and a shrimp boil had been planned to encourage us to converse, mingle, and learn.

Within the first hour of our trip, one unrelentingly bleak fact has threaded its way throughout the programs. There isn't enough water. Not enough for the state's booming population—much less for farmers, irrigation, birds, wildlife, and bays. Not the way we use water now. We stand on high sand banks looking down at the river, wander around the massive pumps of an irrigation plant, teeter wind-whipped on the concrete shore of the South Texas Project Electric Generating Station's nuclear power plant reservoir, and try to absorb the gloomy news. With each talk my mood sinks lower. I already knew these facts from researching my book, but today they wear me down. More river water has been allocated by permits than would flow down the river in even a moderate drought. If all the permit holders used the water assigned to them, the river would dry up long before reaching Matagorda Bay on the Gulf Coast. Future droughts and climate change are hot topics with grim prospects for everyone. Happy hour can't arrive soon enough. The experts offer professional optimism and examples of small successes, but the solution is summed up at a lunchtime panel. As we eat barbecue, reasonable men and women, knowledgeable and concerned, discuss the ways to provide water to farmers, cities, power plants, and industry without jettisoning the needs of the environment and wildlife. There is enough water, we are assured; we just have to change the way Texans view water and then change people's behavior.

Good grief, I think, snorting tea out of my nose, *ALL we have to do is change people's behavior?* I cough and choke. Talk about daunting. As long as water flows from the faucet, most of us don't think about where our water comes from, much less how much is left. The City of Austin has resorted to keeping water usage at drought-level restrictions year-round to encourage conservation—yet new residents flood into the city every day. Austin, like Houston and other Texas cities, is growing at a stunning rate. The cities fling roads into the surrounding countryside, spraying housing developments and big-box stores like sparks from a pinwheel. Everyone needs water.

The miles roll past and time drags. We tour the LCRA's Matagorda Bay Natural Science Center perched at the junction of an old Colorado River channel, Matagorda Peninsula, and the Gulf of Mexico. (The main river channel is diverted upstream so that it feeds into Matagorda Bay.) I stand and look out over the Gulf, the horizon a flat line of gray sky against gray water, a sticky sea wind covering my glasses with a film of salt. I turn, back to the wind, to look over the salt marshes nestled behind the barrier of dunes and sand between Gulf and bay.

Every December birdwatchers assemble to count birds for the National Audubon Society's Christmas Bird Counts (CBCs). For one day, in fifteen-mile-diameter circles scattered across the Americas, birders do their best to note every single bird they can find, from owls calling in the predawn hours to song-birds, sparrows, and shorebirds. The CBC that regularly counts the highest num-ber of species in the continental United States is centered just a few miles up the road. The Mad Island Marsh / Matagorda Bay CBC is a birding bonanza with its rich and multiple habitats. Everything from sandhill cranes in cornfields to water-fowl roosting in flooded rice fields, ibis prowling freshwater marshes, shorebirds skittering along the Gulf beach, egrets and herons striking poses in salt marshes along the bay, songbirds in the woods along the river, owls, falcons, and hawks; there is habitat for nearly everyone. And that habitat is virtually all dependent on the freshwater supplied by the Colorado River and her tributaries—water that nourishes marshes from fresh to salt; water that irrigates rice fields and floods the same fields for wintering waterfowl and migratory shorebirds; water that mixes sweet into salt, creating an estuary essential to life in and on Matagorda Bay.

Back on the bus, I listen to a brilliant hydrogeologist cheerfully stumble through a list of dull-as-dirt facts and a wastewater engineer joke that recent environmental industry awards mean that the city of Austin is "Number 1 in Number 2!" I pick at my soggy sandwich and watch the fields ripple past.

Kirby Brown, outreach biologist for Ducks Unlimited, sways at the front of the bus, talking into a microphone as we jolt down a rough road. I can't see him and his voice ebbs and flows with the motion of the bus. "Wetlands . . . flood-waters . . . water quality . . . sixty thousand . . . acres lost." *More bad news*, I think. The bus slows and I hear with sudden clarity, "Fifteen million wintering waterfowl."

That is a lot of birds, I think to myself. He talks about something called the Prairie Pothole Region. Then the Texas Mid-Coast Rice Prairie Wetlands Com-plex. The bus speeds up and I hear only fragments, but two stick: two hundred species of wildlife and twelve million shorebirds.

Our bus turns off the county road and down a gravel driveway. A flock of greater white-fronted geese stands in the stubble of a harvested rice field and watches us drive past. As the bus groans to a stop in front of a broad sheet of water, mixed flocks of birds spook, lifting off to circle over us and relight in nearly the same place.

Black-necked stilt

Like a wren exploding from a nest I bolt out of the bus and its claustrophobic intimacy. I plunge into a rich cacophony of sounds: quacks, gabbles, honks, squawks, trills, whistles, and splashes, plus the groans of leopard frogs, the deep foghorns of bullfrogs, and the background percussion of insects clicking, singing, and buzzing. The ringing calls of distant sandhill cranes hang in the air like so many revelries. Humid air and the aroma of water-saturated soil, freshly mown grass, and the tang of bird guano settle around me like a warm cape, a relief after the miles of canned air. I exhale. If I had feathers, I would fluff, shake, and then smooth my ruffled plumes into neat order.

I tromp over to a cabin with a group and walk up to a covered porch and deck overlooking hundreds of acres of flooded fields. Thousands of birds are wading, feeding, and roosting in the shallow water. A group of about eight people, mostly women, is clustered near the shore peering intently at the birds and passing binoculars around. I turn and at the end of the porch is another group, mostly men, who are surveying the flooded field and birds with nearly the same intensity. I sidle along the deck and listen as they point to the flooded field and note specks, snows, sprigs, green-wings, bluebills, and spoonies. I don't have a clue what birds they are talking about. I don't see any roseate spoonbills in the mix. They speak of birds folding and dropping; limits filled in minutes as birds flood into decoy spreads. The jargon clicks and I realize they are talking about hunting.

Ick, I think, *hunting*. And cruise over to the birdwatchers.

That was when someone made the comment about luring ducks in for macho hunters. The statement that reveals my own ugly, smug self-righteousness. A jagged shard of contempt lodges in my throat. Not for the hunters or the bird-watchers, but for myself. Yes, keep deer and feral hog populations in control, but I realize with a start that I have considered bird hunting the antithesis of conservation. I wonder, am I, as a birdwatcher, really inherently virtuous? On the side of the birds? Am I intrinsically a better person and conservationist than a duck hunter? Could duck hunters even be considered conservationists?

What if there is another side of the conservation issue that I've ignored because I was sure I already had all the answers? Or, God forbid, what if I am just flat-out wrong about hunting and conservation? I know that Duck Stamps fund national wildlife refuges (not that I have ever bothered to buy a stamp), but that is really all I know about duck hunters and conservation.

A thought rises and hovers at the edge of consciousness before coming into focus. *If I was truly interested in wetlands conservation for bird habitat*, I think, *I'd be a duck hunter.*

The idea sparks and burns. I feel like I've just grabbed the hot wire on an electric fence. I look over at the group of hunters, then at the birdwatchers. We are all looking at the same group of birds, yet it isn't clear whether we see the same thing at all.

We load back onto the bus and I huddle in my seat, my brain popping and sizzling as the radical idea scorches all other thoughts. *Stupid*, I think, *no way killing birds could protect them.* It is completely illogical. Besides, I abhor guns— their power and potential for violence frightens me. Days go by when I don't eat meat of any kind—and don't miss it at all. But above all, could killing birds really make a difference?

Preserving or creating habitat is the gold standard for saving species, so any-thing that helps habitat also helps save birds as well as the butterflies, moths, amphibians, reptiles, mammals, and plants that rely on the same environment. But shooting birds? That glimpse of my own smugness and prejudice that birdwatchers are better conservationists (and people) than any real or imagined hunter crawls over my skin, a stinging recognition of an ugly, unquestioned arrogance. I think of John James Audubon, who shot birds to create his famous *Birds of America* portfolio of hand-colored prints. And author John Graves. When I'd read his seminal river book, *Goodbye to a River*, I'd reveled in his descriptions of the Brazos River's wildlife but skimmed over the sections about the ducks and squirrels he shot and ate. Aldo Leopold's *Sand County Almanac*, now that I think about it, illuminated goose hunting along with the seasons on his property.

When I arrive home, I dump my bags on the floor and corner my husband, Bill. "Do you realize," I say, "that rice farmers and duck hunters could be doing more to preserve and create wetland habitats than birdwatchers?"

"Yep," he replies.

"And that those wetland habitats are incredibly important for all sorts of birds—not just egrets and herons but migratory shorebirds and songbirds too."

He nods.

I take a deep breath, "John James Audubon hunted birds for his art. John Graves shot ducks on the Brazos. And Aldo Leopold was both a hunter and a conservationist." Bill, a lifelong (although infrequent) hunter, narrows his eyes as I continue. "If I'm serious about habitat conservation for birds, I think . . ."

He waits.

"I think I need to be a duck hunter."

"What?" he asks. "But you hate guns."

I nod. Shrug. Nod again.

"It's crazy, but yes."

"Hallelujah," he replies, "let's go shoot the twenty gauge."

🦆 2 🦆

Legacy

Bill takes out a shotgun from the gun safe. "This," he says, "is an Ithaca twenty gauge pump-action shotgun. My father gave it to me on my fourteenth birthday." He does something and the gun makes a loud kerchunk sound. "What year was that?" I ask, too distracted to do the math. "Nineteen sixty-seven," he replies and hands the gun to me while he bends over to pull out another gun. I hold the gun upright awkwardly, away from my body. Bill's voice seems to echo from a distance as my vision narrows and the room darkens around me. I take a deep breath and lift my chin. I can do this. If I can discipline myself to do our taxes, clean up dog barf, and butcher feral hogs—I can do this. If I'm serious about duck hunting as conservation, I have to learn to handle and shoot a shotgun.

"Now this," Bill says, voice muffled behind the steel door, "is a Ruger twenty gauge over-and-under." He thumbs a lever and the gun breaks open. "It's easy to see whether an over-and-under is loaded," he says as he angles the gun so I can see there are no shells in the barrels.

As we walk down to Bill's make-do shooting range at the back of our property, I carry the empty 20 gauge pump. He carries the over-and-under like landed gentry, with the gun open and resting on his forearm as he strides through the woods. The scent of oil and metal reacting with my sweaty palms wafts up as we crunch through leaves, brushing past red berry–covered yaupons and dusty cedars. I don't know how to hold the heavy gun and it feels dangerously slippery. I keep wanting to wrap my fingers around the trigger and trigger guard, but Bill has emphatically told me to keep my fingers off the trigger until I'm ready to shoot. "Treat every gun as if it is loaded. No exceptions," he said. "Watch the barrel and *never* point it at another person." He locked eyes with me and I had to suppress a nervous giggle. It was the same concentrated look I'd seen him give my nephews when teaching them to shoot cans with the .22 rifle.

This is the first time I've held a shotgun, though not the first time I've held a gun. Twenty-five years before, I held a .38 Smith & Wesson revolver long enough to fire a couple of rounds. Long enough to know I wanted no part of it.

It was for my protection, Bill said. We'd just moved out to the country and he worried about me being home alone.

We walked to the back pond, where I fired a couple of rounds into the dam. I hated it. It was too loud, it wrenched my wrist, and above all, I knew I could never see a handgun as a protective or defensive tool. With my family history, a handgun would always represent violence. Carefully handing the revolver to Bill, I thanked him for wanting to protect me. "But I don't want to have anything to do with guns," I told him. I loathed guns so much I'd make Bill retrieve any valuables stored in our safe. Just smelling the heavy oily steel of the firearms made me queasy.

Bill sticks empty cans on a splintered yaupon and we both stuff earplugs into our ears. He loads a single shell into the over-and-under and hands the loaded shotgun to me.

The gun feels even heavier with the single shell, awkward and, in a word, alien. My breath, quick and shallow, rattles in my ears. Acid rises in the back of my throat. I clamp my trembling hands around the stock and barrel, afraid that it will slide out of my sweat-slicked palms. I think, *What the hell am I doing?* This isn't revulsion or dislike—this is fear. I've never questioned my antipathy before; I've always just embraced it. Now I hear a fearful voice whisper, *Guns are bad.* A monochromatic statement that paints all gun owners and users with the same unyielding judgment. With a jolt I realize I'd easily condemned my husband, brother-in-law, father-in-law, and all hunters without examination or consideration. *But guns kill people,* my fear insists. *Enough!* I think, *I'll listen to you later.*

"Okay," Bill says, "shoot."

"How?" I ask, in a dangerously reasonable voice.

"Point the shotgun and pull the trigger," he says.

I stare at him.

"Could you at least show me how I'm supposed to hold the gun?" I ask. He lowers the pump shotgun, nestles it into his shoulder, and sights down the barrel. "Just look down the barrel, line up the beads, and pull the trigger when you are ready."

I put the gun to my shoulder. Bill made it look easy, but it feels like my neck

Mourning dove

is too long and I can't figure out how to get my face down to the gun. My heart is pounding. I finally hunch up my shoulders and manage to look down the barrel. My right elbow rises up like a chicken wing and the longer I hold the gun up, the higher my elbow rises. I slip my finger onto the trigger, hold my breath, and pull. BOOM. I stagger backward, the barrel of the gun pointing skyward. The cans dangle from their twigs, pristine. Bill hands me another shell. I manage to break the gun open and put in the shell. I put the gun on my shoulder again, squinch my head down to peer along the barrel, and fire again. As the roar echoes down the gully, Bill says, "Uh, you really might want to keep your eyes open when you pull the trigger." I give him a stink eye, reload, and shoulder the gun again. This time I focus on my breathing, but I tense up until the shotgun nearly vibrates as my muscles tremble under the strain. I exhale and pull the trigger.

I wing a bean can.

"Just a fluke," I say as I grin.

Bill fires two shots in succession with the pump. Cans fly through the air.

He hands me the pump. I aim and pull the trigger. Nothing. I didn't remember to load a shell. "That's okay," says Bill, "better to forget to put a shell in than to forget you've chambered a shell." I focus on the cans.

After three more shots I've dinged another can and I feel tender lumps rising on my jaw and shoulder. I call it quits. I'm in the middle of working on a massive drawing, and with deadlines looming, I can't risk hurting my shoulder.

"You did fine," he says.

"I sucked," I cheerfully reply. He shakes his head. "It was the first time you've ever fired a shotgun. You did great."

We crunch back through the leaves to the house. I can smell the gunpowder on the guns and our clothes. My hands buzz, a faint current running through my body, but the nausea has receded.

"The first time my dad took me dove hunting," Bill starts, "I was six years old. He propped up his twelve gauge and I aimed and shot a mourning dove sitting on a mesquite branch. I'd never shoot a bird in a tree now, but I guess he wanted me to succeed.

"Every year, no matter what, Daddy, Seth, and I would go to the Marlin farm on the first day of dove season. We never missed a year dove hunting."

He is quiet for a moment. "I was never sure my dad really liked to hunt and fish. I sometimes wonder if he just thought it was important that Seth and I learn.

"And it was about the only time we spent together without my mother," he adds as we walk into the house.

A sudden vivid memory of my mother seizes me. She is standing at a kitchen sink wearing cat-eye glasses and weeping over a pile of limp birds—quail or doves—as she tries to pluck them. Feathers float around her and drift across the linoleum. My father's German shorthaired pointer scratches at the screen door. I shake my head; I haven't thought of that dog for decades. It's been fifty-odd years since the lieutenant colonel deserted us for a new wife and family, and I'd never realized that my father was a bird hunter.

We sit on the upstairs deck and clean the guns. Leaves rattle as they fall from the post oaks. Bill instructs me in the traditions of Hoppe's No. 9 cleaner, cleaning rods, mops, patches, and brushes. As we work, I quiz Bill on types of guns. What is a sawed-off shotgun? Why is an over-and-under with the barrels on top of each other better than a side-by-side, the archetypal double-barreled Jed Clampett shotgun? What about 20 gauge versus 12 gauge? He tells me I need a 12 gauge for duck hunting and that I should go to the skeet range for lessons. As we finish, lightly oiling all the pieces and reassembling the guns, I notice my hands have stopped shaking. I'm still awkward carrying the shotguns back to the gun safe, but my palms are no longer slicked with nervous sweat.

3

Teal Dreams

> On land, the Green-wing moves with more ease and grace than any other species with which I am acquainted. . . . On the wing it has no rivals among Ducks.
>
> —Green-winged Teal, *Ornithological Biography*, vol. 3

A week later I meet Renée Blaine, a licensed firearms instructor, at Capital City Clays just east of Austin. Tall and striking, Renée sports diamond studs in her ears, a shooter's vest, jeans, and black alligator-skin cowboy boots. "I started shooting 'cause I wanted to impress a guy," she tells me and goes on to say that she was out with a group that went to a skeet range. "I was just hanging around," she grins, "keeping my eye on one guy in particular, and his friends teased me into taking a turn." When she talks, she waves her manicured hands. With ear-plugs in, I have trouble hearing her and I keep getting distracted by the flashes of hot pink painted on her nails. She laughs, her blue eyes gleaming. "I don't know who was surprised more—them or me—that I hit a bunch of clays." She smiles conspiratorially at me with her blinding white smile.

We load Bill's Ruger 20 gauge over-and-under and boxes of shells into her golf cart and park at one of the sporting clay stands. She starts me with the basics: The butt of the shotgun should land on my bra strap. Chin forward, cheek firmly up against the stock, feet solid with belt buckle facing the direction of the target. Lean into the gun with weight forward on the left foot so any recoil just flexes the upper body backward. It sounds easy enough, but I struggle to get the shotgun into position. I'm focused on Renée, my emotions safely shuttered while I listen to her instructions.

With my second shot of the day I shatter the clay pigeon. My hands vibrate, not from recoil but from the adrenaline that surges through my blood. I laugh out loud and call "pull" again. And miss. After another dozen or so misses, I finally manage to chip the edge of a clay. Someday, I think, I'll be able to lift the gun without thinking, to see past the gun the way I look through binoculars, my focus flying across the sky.

Tired and with my arms shaking from holding up seven pounds of shotgun, I'm guzzling water in an unladylike fashion when Renée says, "Look at that duck! Is it injured?"

I turn. In the shadow cast by the golf cart, a tiny green-winged teal hen looks out at us. We watch each other, her dark eyes bright as she tracks my movements. I walk slowly over to look at her. She is so tiny—smaller than a Cornish game hen and not much bigger than the squab I've eaten in France. I get too close; she darts under the cart and flies, winging easily toward the distant glimmering silver of Decker Lake. I could see no sign of injury. By that time my arm muscles refuse to hold up the shotgun any longer and my shoulder is throbbing, destined to turn purple.

Renée ends the lesson with a warning: "Always carry your shotgun with the barrel pointed up," she says. "Girls with guns make men nervous. It is better to, you know, exaggerate how safe you are being." I thank her for her help, pack up my gear, and start the drive home, wondering why a duck was sitting less than five feet away from me as I blasted a shotgun over and over.

Growing up, I was fed a diet of spiritual beliefs, religious rituals, and superstitions appropriated from cultures around the world. At various times during the late 1960s and 1970s, my mother had primal screamers reliving the trauma of their birth in our living room, scientologists bull baiting each other in the kitchen, a schizophrenic artist living in our basement, Sufis quoting mystic poets, Buddhists camping in the dining room, and gray-skinned macrobiotics teaching cooking classes. Seven days a week there were seekers, friends, and strangers who gathered in our house, looking for spiritual answers in the clouds of pot and the psychedelics that simmered and flowed through the group. They talked, and talked, and talked some more, always against a relentless background of rock and roll. My brother, sister, and I absorbed fragments of Buddhism, Jungian psychology, American Indian beliefs and legends, ghost stories, and pop psychology—a stew of ideas more superstition than faith. While I've long since abandoned the crystals, dream catchers, sage smudging, tarot reading, coin toss-ing, and yearnings of my upbringing, the teal hen's appearance hatched a sprig of scrawny mysticism unseen for decades.

"Maybe the spirit of the great duck came to check me out?" I tell Bill, laughing.

"Why would a teal be at the range?" he wonders. "That is just weird."

"To judge me?" I reply. "To remind me of what I'm planning to do?"

I laugh at myself and tell Bill about Renée and her statement about men and girls with guns. Yet the memory of the hen lingers, a sheen of sadness muting the day's memory. Supernatural or not, she brought breath, blood, bone, and feath-ers into my abstract plan to become a hunter.

If I love birds, as I profess to, then why am I so determined to kill them? Why do I believe that by learning to hunt, I am, in a twisted way, becoming more of a conservationist than I ever was toting my binoculars, sporting T-shirts emblazoned with birds, and sending my dollars to The Nature Conservancy and the National Audubon Society?

4

Gearing Up

Me thinks I now see the charming creature gliding sylphlike over the leaves
that cover the lake, with the aid of her lengthened toes.
—Purple Gallinule, *Ornithological Biography*, vol. 4

Before I can go hunting, there are a few things I need. First and foremost is a
hunting license. Chest waders are also a must-have along with a basic camouflage raincoat and hat. And Bill is convinced I need a 12 gauge shotgun.

I order a coat online. It is made for a tall, slender woman with no hips and
an ample bosom. I am neither tall nor slender, and my proportions are reversed
from the designer's ideal size ten. But I can make it work and it fits better than
Bill's oversized gear.

At the local general store, I tell the friendly young man at the register I need
a hunting license. He asks whether I want a combo or a supercombo. I stare at
him. A deep voice drawls, "Wat're you gonna hunt?" Leaning against the counter
is a fellow about my age, arms crossed, head tilted back, with a ball cap pulled
low. He is not smiling.

"Ducks," I say.

"Weeellllll . . ." He draws the word out into a tense silence. I can hear the
young cashier tap, tap, tapping a pen against the counter as the silence stretches
on. "You're gonna need a federal Duck Stamp as well as the state Migratory Bird
Stamp. Come on, we'll get you set up." He pushes off the counter and spends the
next few minutes helping the cashier plug my information into the computer and
print out my new license.

"My mom always shoots more birds than me or my dad when we go hunting," the cashier tells me as he rings up the license. He smiles. "Makes my dad mad as heck too."

"Yeah," chimes in the older fellow, "women are generally better shots than men—when they bother to pick up a shotgun. Most men don't want women competing with them, though." He laughs.

I wave goodbye and sit in my car for a minute, genuinely befuddled. It is a first to be compared to someone's mother. Plus, I'm still not sure whether the last statement was a compliment, a warning, or both.

Bill is convinced I need the power of a 12 gauge shotgun for duck hunting. I want a gun that fits—I am tired of a bruised shoulder. The day after Christmas, we head to a giant retail hunting store with a list: one 12 gauge shotgun and one pair of women's waders.

The mega-hunting-fishing store is brimming with holiday shoppers. We wade through the thickets of clothes, trees of camouflage coffee mugs, mountains of sugary snacks, and displays of mysterious hunting gear to the gun department. We tear off a numbered tab as if we are at a meat counter and wait for our number to be called. I stroll along the glass display cases, looking at the rifles and shotguns lining the back wall. A trio of tiny hot pink camouflage rifles stops me in my tracks. *Princess rifles? Really?*

A young man calls out our number. Bill steps up. "We're looking for a 12 gauge shotgun for my wife." The salesman cuts his eyes at me, then turns back to Bill. They confer. A gun is brought out, the chamber checked, and then it is presented to Bill. I almost expect the salesman to bow slightly, as if Bill is royalty (Bill's beard has that effect on many). In turn, Bill inspects the gun and presents it to me.

"Not my gun," I say. I move to hand the gun to the salesman, but he looks only at Bill. I hand the gun to Bill, who in turn hands it back to the young man.

Another gun is presented to Bill. Again, he inspects it and then gives it to me.

"Not my gun," I say. And hand it back to Bill.

In an absurd waltz, we plod through a dozen shotguns: compact and youth models, massive semiautos built for mighty hunters, and camouflage-patterned guns specific for waterfowl hunting. I am not only invisible, but inaudible as well. If I have a question, I must ask Bill, who turns to the salesman.

"Not my gun," I say.

The salesman, starting to despair of making a sale, brings forth his final offer:

Purple gallinule

a Benelli Montefeltro 12 gauge semiautomatic with walnut stock. Bill shoulders it, swings it high as if following a bird across the sky. It passes inspection and he hands it to me.

I shoulder the gun, lean into it to see whether we balance together. I prop the butt on my hip, open and close the action. Bill and the salesman are mirroring each other with both hands on the display case, their heads nearly touching as they look down at a pistol Bill is inspecting.

"This is my gun," I say.

They look up. Surprise flashes across the salesman's face as he glances at me before turning away again.

"Are you sure?" Bill asks. We go over the gun's attributes one by one until he is nearly convinced. But the gun has a twenty-eight-inch barrel and Bill believes I need a twenty-six-inch barrel.

It is not my gun after all.

The salesman wishes Bill good luck, cuts his eyes at me for a split second, and then whispers to Bill that there will soon be a big sale on handguns. They nod, shake hands. We walk away.

We ford the streams of shoppers and stumble into the quiet of the shoe department. Right away I find a pair of women's sock-footed waders that fit surprisingly well. I walk around in the waders, looking for wading boots. A salesman from the fishing department pitches in as we circle the shelves and racks. "They must be here somewhere," he says. He pulls up inventory on the computer. Nothing. "This doesn't make sense," he murmurs as he plugs another search query into the computer. He calls headquarters and then apologetically delivers his report: women's wading boots are available only online. Bill and I crowd around the computer monitor while he shows us the available models. Except there is not a pair of size eight in stock anywhere in the country. He brightens. Maybe a youth size! We search but the youth sizes go up to six and the men's start at eight. I, troublesome woman, need a man's seven to fit my wide feet. The kind and thoroughly flustered salesman apologizes and flees.

I end up in camouflage waders with heavy lug-soled boots a size too large. The waders are huge on me and must have been designed for a busty woman closer to six feet tall rather than my five foot three. I could almost use the waders as a blind. I pull the bib up over my head and tuck in my arms and stomp around the shoe department. Bill shakes his head and pretends not to know me.

I catch a glimpse of myself in a mirror and laugh out loud. I look like a short, squat, moldy haystack. Accordion pleats of camo fabric ruck up and down both legs and crackle in folds around my waist. The only consolation is that with all that extra fabric, I can easily sit down, touch my toes, lunge, and even squat. Figuring out how to take a pee while wearing waders, I realize, will take some work. There'll be no discreet watering out of the side of a blind for me.

I wander through the racks of camouflage hunting clothes feeling naive and foolish. I thought that finding hunting gear was a matter of going to the right store. I find a saleslady and ask where I can find the women's hunting clothing. She looks at me, pity in her eyes. "I only have what's in the corner—and it's not much." Alas, the section for women's hunting gear is tiny. I circle the few displays and racks, darting in to check a size before returning to the prowl, hoping that the next go-around will reveal something I missed on the previous circuit. I advance into the men's department with blind hope.

Instead I confirm that the average duck and goose hunter—the target market for the manufacturers of waterfowl hunting gear—is male, Anglo, over fifty years old, and remarkably wide and tall. The first three characteristics I knew from US Fish and Wildlife Service statistics; the fourth I discover while pawing through the racks for hunting gear, hoping to find anything that even comes close to fitting. I leave defeated.

Bill and I break out of the megastore and plunge into traffic streaming into Austin. We drive to McBride's Gun Shop in the heart of the city. The salesman recognizes Bill and says hello.

"We're looking for a twelve gauge for my wife," Bill says.

The salesman turns to me, looks me in the eye, and asks me whether there is a particular gun I am interested in.

I freeze. I stammer but get out that I want to see a 12 gauge Benelli Montefeltro with a twenty-six-inch barrel. He nods and reappears moments later with a box. He assembles the gun, pointing out the best way to align the barrel, and cautions me that the choke should be checked regularly. And hands the gun to me.

I hold the gun in my hands, the metal cool and the wood smooth against my palm. I aim it at the wall, sight down along the barrel, and practice putting it up to my shoulder. I run my fingertips over the engraving and the carved checkering on the stock. "This," I whisper, "is my gun." When I look up, the salesman is watching me. He raises an eyebrow in question. I nod in return and hand him the shotgun. He takes it apart and stows it in its box, then walks me through the paperwork for purchasing a firearm. Bill wanders the store. While we wait for the background check, I whisper to Bill, "What if I don't pass?"

He frowns at me. "Why wouldn't you pass the background check?" I can see from the tension at the corners of his eyes that he's a little nervous. Is his wife of twenty-six years about to reveal a hidden felonious past?

I shrug. "No reason," I say. "Just a touch of paranoia. I mean, what if they find out I'm a birdwatching environmentalist?"

"Don't worry," he says, "they'll sell you a gun anyway."

⸎ 5 ⸎

The Painted Bird

The worse my drawings were, the more beautiful did I see the originals.
—Introduction, *Ornithological Biography*, vol. 1

Maybe it was Boris, the myna bird. Maybe it was the crows that lived in Audubon Park with their pranks and wily eyes. All I know is that when I started making art, birds showed up. Blackbirds hatched from the velvety black of an aquatint to sing out of a crusty pie. Atmospheric smudges of color and light behind a nude model transformed into ghostly doves whirling out of the background. Ravens perched, bold and glossy eyed on a fence post, growling and laughing under the long skies and terre verte landscape of West Texas. I finally gave in, looked directly at the birds, and asked, "What do you want? Why are you here?"

I got no answer. To this day when strangers ask me, "What kind of art do you make?" or "What do you paint?," honestly, I'm stumped. Because if I say landscapes, well, that's not quite true since my landscapes are invariably upstaged by a prowling heron or a sprawling spiny agave. But am I a bird painter? How boring that sounds, like painting a face at high noon when the brassy light washes out the detail and shadows submerge the rest.

When I was still in art school, struggling to create an artistic identity for myself (believing that I was destined to paint large canvases covered with luscious swirls of oil paint), I ran across a quote. I no longer remember who was quoted or where I found it. "Style," this wry sage pronounced, "is an inability to do anything else."[1]

I paint and draw birds because I don't know how to do anything else. I stand and stare at a blank sheet of creamy white paper and a roadrunner materializes in front of me, gazes at me with a knowing eye, raises her crest, rattles, then disappears. I spend weeks coaxing her into reappearing on the paper using pencil, watercolor, and a stubborn determination. In my studio, a pair of belted kingfishers laugh at me from within gilded arches on two pure-white panels. Someday I'll capture them and force them to sit still—though I hope they'll retain a whisper of their giddy defiance.

Gaily colored songbirds, woodpeckers, beetles, and occasional flowers emerge from battleship linoleum as I release them using just a few sharp cuts to define wings and attitude. While I've painted specklebelly geese and a solo black-bellied whistling-duck (those feet!), ducks don't often appear in my studio. Honestly, they've always seemed just a bit ridiculous. Even Audubon's attempts to create a watchful and regal air falter when a duck stands flat footed on land. Most of his ducks are stretched out, darting after an insect; a few paddle or bob in water. With a duck, there is no leggy curve, elegant neck, or long, tapered wing to fill the page. No, there is something a bit comical but inherently lovable about ducks.

Nowadays, time spent in duck blinds is training my eye to see in new ways. While birding, I would count ducks floating singly or in rafts on ponds or in coastal bays. Rarely would I stop to watch them in flight. Yet now I close my eyes and see a group of six blue-winged teal cupping their wings, feet outstretched, as they glide down to join a flock bobbing on the water. I see the silhouette of a pintail drake as he flares away from our decoys. I doubt I'll ever be a crack shot; too often I'm simply mesmerized by the surprising grace and beauty of a duck on the wing.

I also doubt I'll ever be a real duck painter. There is a legion of artists who specialize in skilled renditions of an idealized world that is designed to evoke the traditions, camaraderie, and memories of waterfowl hunting: a flock of ducks wing their way over marsh or pond, the perspective often from an imaginary blind; a majestic retriever splashes through decoys with a bloodless duck held in its mouth; still-life compositions of decoys, shotgun, and calls are reminders of the next season's potential. This is art that you can hang over a mantelpiece or next to your shotgun.

And then there are the Duck Stamps. And the intensely competitive national contest to select the painting for the next year's Migratory Bird Hunting and Conservation Stamp. It is the only juried art competition sponsored by the federal government.

The world of Duck Stamp art is a different place altogether. Today it is made up of images of ducks and geese that are pushed beyond life to a hyperrealistic intimacy, all rendered in impossibly sharp focus with details, colors, and theatrical lighting. Some of this is necessitated by the art's final reproduction as a 1¾" × 1½" stamp, but much of it is the style that has developed specifically around the Duck Stamp.

I'm not a wildlife artist. Yes, I paint birds, but the idealistic photo-realism portrayed by many wildlife artists does not appeal to me. I paint both invasive species and common birds, hoping to bring attention to both. I'm married to a man who renders every scale on the rattlesnakes he paints, but he doesn't put them in pristine wild landscapes. Instead he paints the collision between humans, our detritus, and wildlife. Personally, I enjoy painting the details of feathers and color that give birds such personality, but to create a painting for the Duck Stamp competition? I don't think I have the desire or the self-discipline. The paintings are beautiful, exquisitely detailed, and as close to perfection as can be imagined. From what I can tell, there is no room for error, no space for improvisation, and certainly no place for the stray intuitive line that gives life to a two-dimensional creature. Honestly, I doubt that Audubon's original watercolors would win in today's competitions.

Some deride the paintings as mere illustrations, images created for someone else's story, because of the contest's regulations on size and subject matter. The artist must include, in the 7" × 10" painting, a "live portrayal" of one or more of the annually designated eligible species as the dominant part of the entry. For the 2020 stamp and the 2021 stamp, artists were also required to include a "hunting-related accessory or scene" that illustrated the theme "celebrating our waterfowl hunting heritage." Ducks Stamp paintings were littered with spent shotgun shells, lost duck calls, decoys, retrievers, blinds, and distant figures of hunters. It wasn't a popular requirement, and many of the comments listed in the *Federal Register*'s published rule were against the additional creative restrictions; others worried about the effect the rule could have on the birdwatchers and other conservation supporters who buy one out of every three stamps sold. One commenter noted that celebrating the contributions of hunters—who are legally required to buy the stamp—is a bit odd. How many duck hunters, he or she wondered, would buy Duck Stamps if it wasn't mandatory?

The Duck Stamp is part of an extraordinary conservation success story. It started in 1929 when Congress passed the Migratory Bird Conservation Act. This landmark legislation authorized the federal government to acquire and permanently protect refuge lands to be managed as "inviolate sanctuaries" for migratory birds.

While the law is the foundation of our system of national wildlife refuges, there was, alas, no funding to procure the land. No way to protect the large tracts of habitat needed. A few tentative proposals faltered and died before becoming law. It wasn't until Franklin D. Roosevelt was president of the United States that ducks and other migratory birds had a chance.

And ducks needed all the help they could get. The Lacey Act (1900), and then the 1918 signing of the Migratory Bird Treaty Act (which regulated the hunting of waterfowl and other migratory birds), helped initially. But the continued destruction of wetland habitats for farmlands and growing cities was taking its toll. A series of droughts rolled across the Great Plains, and duck and crane populations plummeted. It was a devastating time for both people and birds.

In 1934, in the midst of the Depression and the Dust Bowl, FDR shrewdly appointed three unlikely men to create his President's Committee on Wild Life Restoration: Aldo Leopold, a midwestern academic; Jay Norwood "Ding" Darling, a renowned Hoover Republican and Pulitzer Prize–winning political cartoonist; and Thomas Beck, a wealthy magazine publisher. While Beck was a personal friend of FDR, "Ding" was no fan of the president. What the four men had in common was an unswerving commitment to conservation and a belief that a New Deal program was needed to save the dwindling wildlife of North America.

The committee worked fast. Within two months, despite considerable internal strife and antagonism, Leopold, "Ding," and Beck had worked up a comprehensive plan. The twenty-seven-page "National Plan for Wild Life Restoration" proposed that the government immediately start purchasing land critical to wild animals: four million acres for migratory waterfowl and shorebird nesting grounds, plus eight million acres for the restoration of mammals, nongame birds, and upland game. Even after FDR knocked the original $50 million budget down to $8.5 million, the plan was not feasible in the midst of a depression. Human needs were paramount. But the men worked their charms, made their promises, and devised a way to fund the Migratory Bird Conservation Act to secure nesting grounds and other critical habitat.

Somehow (and I'm sure there is more than one story on how it came to pass), in 1934, Congress passed the Migratory Bird Hunting Stamp Act. The act requires all waterfowl hunters sixteen years of age or older to purchase and carry a federal Duck Stamp. It also decrees that ninety-eight cents of every dollar collected has to be used to permanently secure habitat (but not for maintenance or operations).[2] "Ding," whom FDR appointed as head of the Bureau of Biological Survey (predecessor of today's USFWS), drew the first stamp: a pair of mallards landing in a marsh. His brush-and-ink drawing was transferred to a metal plate, engraved, and then printed in blue ink.

Duck Stamp dollars started flooding into the Migratory Bird Conservation Fund. Within five years, the annual total was above $1 million a year. Before Duck Stamps, there were fewer than 100 refuges; at the end of the 1930s, with help from Duck Stamp dollars, there were 266 national wildlife refuges protecting 13.5 million acres of land. Were duck hunters enthused about supporting conservation and preserving habitat? Or did they grumble and swear about the government taking their hard-earned dollars?

When you read about Duck Stamps, the current bragging states, "Since 1934, the Federal Duck Stamp Program and Migratory Bird Conservation Fund have provided more than $1.1 billion for habitat conservation in the National Wildlife Refuge System." That equals more than 6 million acres of the refuge system's current total of 95 million land acres (plus an additional 760 million acres of submerged land and waters). But the Duck Stamp total is a little misleading because it doesn't include the $500 million spent on Waterfowl Production Areas (WPAs) in the Prairie Pothole Region or the permanent conservation easements on private land in the same region.

The Duck Stamp press releases also omit that stamp sales account for only about half the income; the rest comes from import duties on arms and ammunition. In fiscal year 2018 federal Duck Stamp sales deposited nearly $38 million into the fund (1.5 million stamps sold), while the import duties added another $33 million. Yes, guns funding conservation. Maybe that is why artists were required to include a hunting motif in the Duck Stamp paintings. Not solely because the history is important (it is), but perhaps because firearm manufacturers successfully lobbied to remind the public of their contributions.

Today's Duck Stamp is, visually, a long way from J. N. "Ding" Darling's first drawing of mallards in flight, but the stamps were works of art from the beginning. At first, they were designed in-house or artists were invited to participate. Then, in 1949, the selection was opened as a contest. Today's tournament-style public judging came nearly two decades later. Up to 1958, the engraved images were printed in one color of ink; Maynard Reece's 1959 Labrador retriever carrying a mallard was the first multicolor image, with black, blue, and yellow inks. His design also includes the phrase "Retrievers save game." The full-color lithographic reproduction I associate with the Duck Stamp didn't start until 1990. James Hautman won that year with a painting of black-bellied whistling-ducks in flight. The painting combines the extraordinary detail and ethereal light that now dominate the contest's aesthetics.

I don't know whether I'll ever enter the Duck Stamp contest. If I'm honest, I would bridle against the regulations on size and subject matter. I follow inspiration when it arrives, wherever it leads me. On this day, the compact bodies

American coots

and silly faces of coots with white beaks, and moorhens with bright yellow and red beaks, rise and congregate in my sketchbook. They are legal to hunt but will never be on a Duck Stamp. Their mewling calls seeming to pipe through the chamber music on my stereo. "Oboe!" "Clarinet!" I scrawl in my sketchbook. "Coot and Moorhen Orchestra!!!" And I find myself sketching black birds, once again.

6

All In

The *tsh, tship* is uttered with a strong aspiration. While thus engaged, his head and tail are alternately depressed and elevated, as if the little odd performer were fixed on a pivot.
    —Nuttall's Lesser Marsh Wren, *Ornithological Biography*, vol. 2

I wake suddenly, listening for the sound—a footstep, a turning lock, an opening window—that wrenched me out of sleep. The house is still, yet I am at the edge of the bed, the covers thrown off and my feet on the floor ready to run. Over the thumping of my heart, I can hear a breeze rustling the dry leaves on the post oaks. Our three rescue mutts snuffle and dream-twitch in their kennels. The warm bulk of my husband rumbles lightly in deep sleep. I can hear the ticking of my watch on the bedside table; the refrigerator compressor kicks on in the quiet.

Only then do I notice the heaviness that fills my chest. I get up and fill a glass with water, drink it at the sink, and still listen. Nothing. I slip back into bed, arrange myself, and wait for sleep, but the darkness seems to pin me to the bed; I can feel a murky weight centered under my rib cage shifting and coiling slowly through my limbs: a combination of ambivalence, shame, and a gnawing sense of something deeply wrong. I pull words out of the night, looking to define the dark shape. Dread? Regret? Remorse? Guilt?

Each word clicks and slips into place. In just a few hours I am going on my first hunt. For the first time I will slip on the identity of hunter, shoulder my shotgun (my shotgun!), and shoot at ducks to kill. Am I out of my mind? How can I believe that shooting, killing, and eating wild ducks is in any way going to protect habitat or save future ducks? Hunting as an act of conservation? Shooting a shotgun?

Who am I kidding?

"It's not like I could actually hit a duck," I mutter out loud before sliding back into sleep.

Two hours later, I wake at 4:00 a.m., but this time I take up my gun, my notebook, and my pencils, and I go forth to the river.

Actually, John James Audubon was the one who said, "I took up my gun, my notebook, and my pencils, and went forth to the woods as gaily as if nothing had happened." He wrote those words in the introduction to volume 1 of his *Ornithological Biography*, written to accompany the monumental *Birds of America*. And while I am, like Audubon, both an artist and a writer, I wasn't traveling as lightly. In addition to my gun, notebook, and pencils, I had a kayak, kayak paddle, coffee thermos, granola bars, camouflage netting, decoys, canteens, life vest, waders, shotgun, earplugs, binoculars, and ammunition. Bill and I had loaded our kayaks and gear into the pickup the night before. We stumble to the truck with coffee and shotguns, leaving behind three very confused dogs.

We arrive at Little Webberville Park on the Colorado River, about nineteen river miles downstream of downtown Austin, Texas. A truck and boat trailer indicate that another hunter or two are already out. Working in the narrow beams of our headlamps, we unload the boats and stomp and wriggle our way into our waders. At the river's edge I step out and sit down in my kayak with a loud "woof"—without a hint of grace—and drag my oversized wader boots in after me. We push away from the boat ramp. I'm pleased to discover that I can paddle the kayak while wearing waders, thermal underwear, and fleece leggings, plus a Polar Tech shirt, down vest, and camouflage jacket. Move over, Michelin Man, Duck Girl is heading downstream.

Ribbons of mist float just above the surface of the river, obscuring the line between water and sky. The stars fade as dawn approaches and the sky brightens, but the surface of the river collects and holds light. I feel oddly weightless, suspended. The dip of my paddle sends ripples through the silver mirror of the river but does not shatter the illusion. I turn a twisted tree into a hunter's silhouette standing at the river's edge, but the distant purr of an outboard motor places the other hunters far downriver. The pinks and oranges of dawn creep across the sky while the riverscape remains somber, gray with white mist and black tree limbs. By the time we reach our site it is full light, although the sun will not crest the horizon for another twenty minutes.

We'd scouted the river the day before, looking for the perfect spot to set up decoys and hunt. It was, I thought, a rational reason for a slow paddle in our kayaks on a temperate New Year's Day. Floods, coupled with a blowout in an upstream gravel mine, had drastically changed the river. The floods had scoured the vegetation out of the river channel and stripped the banks as well. There are scattered clumps of wild rice growing in the water along sandy shores, and cattails anchored in sheltered backwaters. But few aquatic plants wave beneath the surface of the water, and the usually abundant species that I can recognize, like duckweed (in backwaters), hyacinths, elephant ears, smartweed, pickerelweed, and water willow, are scant or missing entirely. Our friend Neal Cook, proprietor of Cook's Canoes in Webberville, had warned us that there were not many ducks on the river. We discover that he was right about the ducks, but there are piscivores galore: ospreys, belted kingfishers, a zone-tailed hawk, a juvenile bald eagle, and a few white pelicans snacking on fish.

Bill spots a little backwater along Cook's Island. It is small but has ample room for the decoys. Plus, we can hide the kayaks upstream and easily walk down to a bank with tall grasses to use as a blind. And all on public land since we are on the island.

Bill hunted for years on the Colorado River downstream of the Montopolis Bridge in Austin, just a few miles as the river flows from downtown. A small island in the river created a quiet pool that was, he tells me, perfect for ducks. Bill, his brother Seth, and friends would meet under the concrete ramparts of the highway and launch small johnboats to paddle down to the island in the dark. They'd set their decoys and wait for first light, nearly always returning with their limits. He remembers it as a happy, carefree time spent with friends.

But islands in the Colorado River are few and far between. Texas law states that the river itself is public—as are any islands—but the banks and shorelines are private. The laws are not easily interpreted since they are full of designations and terminology that mean much to hydrologists and geomorphologists but little to the majority of casual river paddlers, fishermen and fisherwomen, and landowners. Duck hunters can hunt from a boat, stand in the river, or, like us, luck into a spot on an island.

We unpack the kayaks and Bill puts out the decoys while I trudge back and forth with gear. By the time we settle behind a stand of tall dried grass and rattlebush overlooking the decoys, the light is gold around us and Carolina wrens are singing in the brush. A sedge wren works clumps of grass across the water. Dark-eyed juncos and chipping sparrows peer at us from a yard away, then keep foraging for seeds along the sand bank around us. Cardinals flash back and forth over us while red-bellied woodpeckers bang overhead. An osprey perched just downstream stretches his wings, his back to the sun, and then launches himself to glide upriver and bank over us in a long, slow turn.

We hear the hollow booms of shotguns echoing down the river corridor and then four scaup fly over, too high and too fast for a sane shot. It isn't long until we hear the sputtering of an outboard on the far side of the island. Another half-dozen scaup fly over, but Bill's pleading quacks cannot tempt them to join our flock of decoys.

We wait, enjoying the warmth of thermos coffee while the pale January sun slowly warms the air. After another hour with no sight or sound of ducks, I reluctantly agree it is time to pack up.

We paddle and walk back upstream to the boat ramp. As I pull my kayak through a gravel riffle next to a stand of wild rice, a great blue heron flies past, skimming just above the water's surface. For a moment we lock eyes and he turns his head to watch me as he wings upstream. Is he just curious? Or maybe my jacket and waders, patterned with blades of grass and shadows, confuse him for a moment. The cool river water pushes against my legs, whispering through the rice and cattails as the winter sun sparkles off the river.

No ducks, but no regrets for either of us. And not a single shot fired.

If this is duck hunting, I think, I'm all in.

Carolina wren

PART II
Pulling the Trigger

7

An Act of Conservation

Persons unacquainted with these birds might naturally conclude that such dreadful havock [*sic*] would soon put an end to the species. But I have satisfied myself, by long observation, that nothing but the gradual diminution of our forests can accomplish their decrease, as they not unfrequently quadruple their numbers yearly, and always at least double it.
—Passenger Pigeon, *Ornithological Biography*, vol. 1

One day at the skeet range, I am surprised by a surge of affection for Bill's old Ruger 20 gauge over-and-under. I'd just taken my turn at sporting clays, smashing the bouncing rabbit, and completely missing the high bird that flew into the sun. *Not bad*, I think. Wisps of gun smoke trail from the barrel. I thumb the lever to break open the breech; the barrel smoothly pivots and the shells pop out with a dramatic flair. It is immensely satisfying, using this beautifully crafted and well-designed tool. The shotgun is no longer alien; instead I feel the sort of affection I've held for my favorite cars. I rest the open gun across my arm as we walk to the next station. When it is my turn, I load shells and click the breech closed. I call and miss the first bird but clip the second. I nearly pat the gun's stock and tell it, "What a good gun."

I don't, however, feel the same affection for my 12 gauge semiautomatic shotgun. It is new and seems somehow more lethal with its gleaming metal receiver. Firing it feels different too, with the judder of a shell cycling into the chamber and the empty round ejecting half a dozen feet away. I remind myself that I'm just getting to know it.

Even as I admire my shotgun, I have to admit I am still a little frightened of its potential. My growing confidence hasn't entirely erased my long-held fear and dislike of guns. If Bill reminds me to watch my barrel because I've let the gun drift in his direction, I feel a stab of fear. *What if*, I think, *what if I screw up and hurt someone?* I shudder and take a deep breath and touch the safety. Yet as soon as I load the gun and swing onto the clay targets, the fear falls away. For that second, there is nothing but the target flying across the sky.

It has been six weeks since the idea of hunting as conservation first sparked and burned. In that time, I've voluntarily picked up a shotgun. I've gone hunting—even though I haven't actually fired a shot—and I am ready to try again.

But unknowingly, I'd already committed an act of conservation. Two, in fact. I bought a gun. And I bought a Duck Stamp.

Most nights, after work, Bill and I sit on the porch before dinner. He drinks a glass of bright gold India pale ale while I sip bourbon. It is usually a quiet time where we talk about our day, our successes and failures making art, current projects, and future plans. But on this day, I'm about to pop. He's just sitting down when I turn to him.

"Did you know about the tax on guns and ammunition?" I ask. Bill sips his beer and shakes his head. "What tax?"

"Starting in 1939," I tell him, "with every new gun or box of ammunition sold, an eleven percent tax is collected from the manufacturers. That money goes into the Wildlife Restoration Fund, which distributes it to state wildlife agencies."

Bill nods and crunches a pretzel. Clearly, I haven't impressed him with the importance.

"Every year *hundreds* of millions of dollars are collected. At first it was just on rifles, shotguns, and ammunition; then they added handguns and bows and arrows. In 2021 it was nearly seven hundred million dollars. Texas's share alone was over thirty-one million. Money that is used for habitat restoration, buying land, funding research, and restoring wildlife."[3]

"Seven hundred million dollars," I repeat. I watch his eyes as the number finally sinks in.

"I had no idea!" Bill says, wiping foam off his mustache. "How did I not know about this?"

It is a silent tax, I explain. The tax is built into the sales price—not added on at the time of sale. It's painless and easy to overlook, yet the Wildlife Restoration Act has to be one of the most successful wildlife programs in our nation's history.

Mallard drake

It all started when our country was young. I'd always taken it for granted that wildlife belonged to everyone—and no one. But in Europe, wildlife doesn't belong to the people. Sport fishing and hunting are reserved for the monarchy and the wealthy, elite members of society (and the poachers and scofflaws). In America, we declared our wildlife a public trust: game belonged to the people of the United States. As a young nation with a frontier mythology of unbounded wilderness and seemingly unlimited wildlife, we both celebrated the abundance of animals and took it as an unchangeable fact.

There were no seasons, no limits, no restrictions on when, where, or how hunters shot or trapped wildlife. Market hunters, the commercial hunters who made a living off supplying vendors and shops, went to extremes to provide whatever kind of birds, feathers, rabbits, deer, or other game they could kill. Audubon's first stop in a new city was often the market to look for new species among the heaps of songbirds, shorebirds, owls, ducks, quail, egrets, and cranes for sale. Pothunters used their guns and traps to feed their growing families with feathered, furred, finned, and shelled wildlife. Sportsmen and sportswomen who hunted and fished for pleasure rather than commerce or necessity could be wasteful as well since there were no set limits or hunting seasons. Farmers slaughtered flocks of birds that threatened their harvests. In time, improved fire-arms and ammunition made the killing all that much easier while railways, motor vehicles, and improved roads brought hunters into formerly remote areas. The number of wild animals plummeted, especially around cities and settlements. A few hunters, noting the decline, began to speak out against the nation's tradition of unrestrained killing. The public resisted, hearing any mention of game laws as an attempt by the wealthy few to impose an old-world order of aristocratic privilege and shut out the common man from his livelihood.

As early as the 1870s, citizens formed local and state associations that forced legislatures to pass laws limiting the take of wildlife by commercial hunters, including plume hunters, as well as by sportsmen and pothunters. But with no money to pay game wardens, those early state laws were nearly impossible to enforce. Across the country, the income from state hunting and fishing licenses, money earmarked for game protection, was regularly raided by state legislatures for other projects.

The 1900 Lacey Act was the first federal law protecting wildlife. While most often associated with the plume trade, the law made it illegal to transport poached wild animals, birds, or feathers across state lines.

But in-state local markets across the United States—such as Houston, New York, Chicago, and San Francisco—still demanded extraordinary numbers of birds and other game for their customers. The Migratory Bird Treaty Act of 1918 (MBTA) set a national standard for migratory species and defined hunting seasons for waterfowl and other migratory game birds (nonmigratory species such as quail, prairie-chickens, and wild turkeys were declared under state jurisdiction). With little or no funding for wardens, enforcement was spotty and difficult. Myriad and sometimes contradictory state game laws complicated the issue even more. Wildlife continued to disappear, despite the national protections of the Lacey Act and the MBTA.

By the 1930s America's wildlife was in a sorry state. The multitudes of creatures that gave rise to our national self-image as a land of infinite resources and superabundance were diminished or long gone. The herds of bison that had roamed the plains vanished before the turn of the century. The passenger pigeon, whose extraordinary numbers seem implausible now, had been hunted into memory. Waterfowl populations, already in trouble after years of year-round hunting, declined further with the continued loss of nesting and breeding grounds as wetlands were drained and prairies converted to cropland. The drought of the 1930s precipitated a catastrophic drop in the numbers of ducks, geese, and other wetland birds.

Not that the decline hadn't been foreseen by many. Audubon described a migratory scene with thousands of birds falling "as the drops of a hail shower" into riverside marshes to rest overnight. He predicted that in years to come his description would seem improbable:

When the Reedbirds, the Redwings, and Soras, shall have become so scarce as to be searched for with the same interest as our little Partridges [quail] already are; when the margins of our rivers shall have been drained and ploughed to the very tide mark; when the Grouse shall have to be protected by game-laws; when Turkeys shall no longer be met with in the wild state;—how strange will the tale which I now tell sound in the ears of those who may walk along the banks of these rivers, and over the fields which have occupied the place of these marshes!" (Audubon, *Ornithological Biography*, 1:496)

In 1930 Aldo Leopold and a group of other wildlife conservationists got together and drafted a plan. Conservation was a relatively new concept and their American Game Policy laid out a broad vision that recommended a wide-ranging restoration program implemented by scientifically trained wildlife specialists. While a number of lawmakers, sportsmen, and sportswomen thought it was a dandy idea, there was no money to pay for an ambitious nationwide plan that would take years, millions of dollars, and untold hours to implement.

But as luck would have it, a group of hunters and other conservationists recognized a fix. At the time, Congress was in the process of abolishing excise taxes, but there remained on the books an 11 percent tax on sporting guns and ammunition.[4] What if, they thought, we diverted the proceeds from the existing tax into a fund for the states to use for wildlife restoration projects? Surprisingly, the firearm and ammunition manufacturers supported the proposal.

Senator Key Pittman of Nevada agreed to sponsor the bill. Congressman Absalom W. Robertson of Virginia also agreed, but only after he had amended the document to include a brilliant clause: twenty-nine words that forbade the diversion of state license fees for any purpose other than administration of state game, fish, and wildlife departments. If a state wanted that federal money, it had to guarantee that every dime from the sale of hunting and fishing licenses would go to support its fish and game department. The Pittman-Robertson Federal Aid in Wildlife Restoration Act sailed through Congress with widespread support by hunters, the very group that would be most affected by the tax.

That very first year, $890,000 trickled into the Wildlife Restoration Fund. Nearly a million dollars of what most call Pittman-Robertson Funds (or PR Funds) were distributed to state wildlife agencies. In the decades since, gun sales have steadily risen until the annual sums collected for wildlife are breathtaking, resulting in over $14.6 billion to date. The program was so successful that another law, the Sport Fish Restoration Act (a.k.a. Dingell-Johnson), was passed to collect funds from the sale of fishing equipment.[5] The total grants from both programs for fiscal year 2022 amounted to over $1.5 billion.[6] The grants are critically important to most state and territory wildlife agencies, which depend on license sales and Pittman-Robertson and Dingell-Johnson Funds for a significant percentage of their annual budgets. PR Funds are allocated for multiple purposes, using different formulas for different programs, but states typically provide an investment of one dollar, usually from license fees, for every three dollars they receive in federal grant funding.

It stuns me that I knew nothing about one of the most successful and important conservation programs in history until I became a hunter and gun owner. At this time there is no other source of funding that comes close. Birdwatchers don't pay a tax on binoculars, hikers don't pay a tax on boots or backpacks, and the sales of mountain bikes and ATVs don't fund restoration or conservation.

Ducks, deer, bears, turkeys, quail, and nongame species have benefited for nearly a century as hunters, sportsmen, and gun buyers have supported the greatest conservation effort ever undertaken in our country. Nevertheless, I can't help but wonder: just how long can gun and ammunition sales continue to fund conservation?

I'm looking over a spreadsheet of Wildlife Restoration Act apportionments from 1939 to 2021 and gloating over the dollars for conservation when I notice that in 2008 there was a huge spike in revenue. Between fiscal year 2000 and 2007, apportionments to the states hovered at around $200 million a year, inching up incrementally. But in 2008, gun and ammunition sales went through the roof. By 2018, the annual total of money in the fund more than tripled.

With a queasy feeling I follow the money. Gun and ammunition sales spiked during and after each of the last five presidential elections, especially the 2020 election. I dig a little more and discover that after each mass shooting, especially ones where the shooter used so-called assault-style firearms (military style), gun sales spiked again. Some of the buying was by enthusiasts who snapped up guns like AR-15s or those with high-capacity magazines in fear of restrictions that could limit future sales. Others were buying handguns or home defense weapons for personal protection. An upward jag in the value of gun manufacturers' stock after another horrifying school shooting leaves me disgusted and repelled. And with the increased demand for guns, especially handguns, retail prices have skyrocketed. All of which leads to increased revenue for the Wildlife Restoration program.

Since 1986 US companies have manufactured more than 180 million firearms, with a quarter of the total (over 45 million guns) produced within the last five years. In this greatest of ironies, gun sales are pouring money into federal coffers and thence to states for wildlife restoration.

Guns and ammunition are saving wildlife and wildlife habitat. Not just game species like deer and ducks, but all the native creatures that depend on wild spaces, as well as professional biologists, habitat restoration, and the research that is the foundation of modern game management. But for how long? Even though the US population has skyrocketed, the number of hunting licenses sold has hovered around 15 million a year since the 1970s. Because the distribution of PR Funds is linked to those license revenues, the future looks uncertain.

In 2016 there were 2.4 million migratory bird hunters. Add in the wild turkey and quail hunters for a total of 4.4 million bird hunters. However, 45 million Americans—more than ten times the number of bird hunters—were birdwatchers. Some watched birds at backyard feeders. Others traveled to parks, national wildlife refuges, or other spots to watch birds. Another 41 million people watched other wildlife (mammals, reptiles, amphibians, insects, spiders, and fish), for a grand total of 86 million wildlife watchers. In one year, the watchers spent nearly $5 billion on birdseed, feeders, birdbaths, and nest boxes, and another $5.5 billion on binoculars, spotting scopes, cameras, and related gear. That isn't chicken scratch.

Some birdwatchers do buy Duck Stamps, and a number buy fishing and hunting licenses as well. Yet there are no federal or state stamps, no licenses, and no taxes that birdwatchers and wildlife watchers pay. Without a direct funding mechanism, wildlife watchers, their purchases, and their activities may support local economies but only indirectly support conservation.

Meanwhile, the Recovering America's Wildlife Act (RAWA), first introduced in 2016, has been introduced again in both the House of Representatives and the Senate. RAWA would invest $1.4 billion annually into the Pittman-Robertson Wildlife Restoration Act accounts (in addition to the funds collected from gun and ammunition sales), dollars that would go to the states and territories for conservation, research, and education. No new taxes would be required. Instead the money would come from either (1) fines and sanctions for violations of environmental and natural resource laws and regulations, or (2) revenues from mineral development (mining, oil and gas drilling leases) on federal lands and offshore energy development. While linking conservation to either environmental fines or fossil fuel development makes me pause, states and territories (and tribal nations) would be able to implement their existing state wildlife action plans that identify species of greatest conservation need. RAWA is a national strategy for local action and research to protect game and nongame species—birds, butterflies, insects, plants, fish, and more—before they are considered endangered. Although the legislation has broad bipartisan and public support, the bill has yet to pass.

I wonder whether we will find a new way to support wildlife conservation. Will birdwatchers ever band together to voluntarily tax themselves to support the birds they enjoy, or will they join forces with hunters, optics makers, manu-facturers of bird feeders and birdbaths, and sellers of birdseed to push for leg-islation that funds conservation? I fantasize about a collaboration of people and groups from across the nation, ignoring partisan boundaries and joining together, as we've done before, to fund conservation.

A gal can dream.

8

Redheads on Redfish Bay

The flesh of this bird is generally esteemed, insomuch that many persons know no difference between it and that of the Canvass-back Duck, for which it is not unfrequently sold; but I look upon it as far inferior to that of many other ducks.
　—Red Headed Duck, *Ornithological Biography*, vol. 4

In the predawn darkness of a January morning, Bill and I turn in to Jamie Spears's place on Highway 361 on the road to Port Aransas. We pull on our waders and join the hunters checking their gear for this late-season hunt. We load guns and blind bags into an airboat and take off into Redfish Bay with a roar. Periodically the boat slows, the pilot shining a powerful light onto oyster flats and marshes to check location. Then we are off into the darkness. With a headset on I feel the pulse of the engine and propeller as a low roar that thrums through my spine while we speed through darkness along the Texas coast. I would be happy to ride around all morning, but we are the first dropped off. In my headlamp's puny beam, I feel my way into the blind, lugging shotgun and ammunition. The high tide sloshes around our feet, washing in through gaps in the plank floor. Looking up from the darkness of the blind, I see the bay water glowing silver with light reflected from the cloudy sky. The full moon is a bright smear under clouds opaque as quilt batting. Marshes rise from the water, flat black shapes that make it impossible to tell whether the grasses are tall or whether the marsh stretches far into the distance. Pintail, redhead, and green-winged teal decoys bob on all sides of the blind. I strip down to a T-shirt, put my camouflage coat back on, and swat mosquitoes. The high tide laps around our feet and the smells of saltwater, mud, and bird guano drift around us as we wait. Chortles, quacks, and whistles from birds ebb and flow across the water under the brightening sky.

Long before the sun rises above the horizon, the ducks begin flying. They fly swiftly and silently. A solo bird drops from the darker sky down into the quick-silver water and our flock of decoys. Half an hour before sunrise the repeated pops of shotguns announce the start of hunting hours. The hollow booms follow a flock of ducks as they circle the bay. We crouch behind the mangrove branches and plywood walls of the blind, waiting. Ducks wing past us, just out of range, to join a nearby congregation of whistling and chortling ducks.

Then a pair of redheads circles around us and slows to land. I aim and fire but miss, the recoil from the high-base hunting shells nearly knocking me down.[7] Bill hits the drake just as it cups its wings to land in the decoys. The bird somersaults to the water, the mahogany red of its head and neck spinning around its gray and black body. Bill wades out through the shallow bay waters and picks up his duck, slogging back with the bird securely tucked under his arm as if it could escape. He drops the bird onto the floor of the blind, where water rocks its body.

I pick up the redhead, its warm body limp and the feathers miraculously dry. There is a single pink smudge of blood on its bright white belly. I run my hands over its springy feathers, probing beneath the breast and back feathers for the flesh beneath. Unfolding the wings, I admire the layers of flight feathers and the tensile strength of the interlocking barbed filaments that lift and carry a bird through air. With my fingernail I zip over the serrations on the sides of the bill as if it is a miniature xylophone, and I spread the webbing between the toes, testing the sharpness of each toenail and the peculiar stubby hind toe.

I've held the bodies of songbirds, both alive and dead, that have smashed into windows; picked up bird skulls in the woods cleaned by fire ants to brilliant white; collected the orange keratin curls of cardinal beaks. In my studio I pin the wings of dead chipping sparrows open on a board so I can draw and photograph the feathers. I open and close the beaks, learning how the jaw hinges with the skull, flex legs, and spread wings.

I've had the chance to look over drawers full of museum specimens. The skins retain all the brilliant feathers but are stiff and foreign, their empty eyes bulging cotton fluff in white sightless stares, feet with toes pointed down, while the smell of mothballs (naphthalene) wafts from their plumage.

When I first read John J. Audubon's rather overwrought assertion that as a young man he wished to possess "all the productions of nature," I understood his urge. I admit to feeling the same way. But I have no desire to possess stuffed and mounted birds or animals, regardless of how lifelike or graceful the taxidermy. Yet I held the redhead drake, stroking its plumage as the bird cooled and stiffened.

A pair of redheads flies past, checking out the decoys. I shoot wildly, and Bill brings down another drake. The heavy recoil from the high-base shells is shocking, and I stagger every time I pull the trigger. The stock of the gun drags across my camouflage coat, and it feels like my arms aren't long enough to get the gun up and seated on my shoulder. After the first shot, I start flinching when I pull the trigger. With every decoy-shy bird that wings past, I try to get my gun up and into position. Every shot I take recoils against my throbbing shoulder and jaw. Any affinity I have for my gun dissipates as I stubbornly shoulder it, hold my breath, and persist. I am not having fun. I finally unload my gun and sit in the blind, gingerly probing what will become a bouquet of black and purple bruises blooming from my bicep to collarbone.

A dozen white ibis fly straight into the sun, which has broken through the clouds. It is beautiful and hallucinatory—the flare of sunlight casts dark shadows beneath each bird. With each upward wingbeat the birds reappear with the shadow sculpting the underside of each wing. On the downstroke, the white birds disappear into the light. Roseate spoonbills cruise over and coots paddle past. Cormorants flap by in pairs and trios, and a flock of more than twenty little blue herons, the color of storm clouds, wings past with one white great egret schoolmarm lagging behind. Honeybees buzz in the mangrove branches tied to the blind, and a few slow mosquitoes feast on my neck before I smash them into black and red smears. At 10:00, when the airboat returns for us, we have four redheads. Since the limit for each hunter is two, technically I have two. But I know better. The ride back is gorgeous with the sun sparkling off the bay and blue skies as the clouds disperse.

As we clamber off the airboat, another hunter offers us some of his ducks. "Don't you want them?" I ask. "No," he says, "my wife won't eat duck, so it's too much for me." He hands me a pair of pintails and a trio of bluebills (scaup).

Bill and I sit on the tailgate of the truck plucking ducks while the other hunters wait for the guides to clean their birds. One large group, which seems to be a family, laughs and poses for a picture with their dead ducks staged in front of them. Bill and I yank breast feathers, then back, leg, and wing until a cloud of feathers swirls around us. I pick up a bluebill and photograph the ridges on the sides of its bill, the astonishingly bright yellow eye, and the green and purple iridescence on the sides of the head. Scaup feet, redhead feet, and pintail feet. Close-ups of the ridges on their bills, the adaptations for different foods and habitats.

Northern pintail drake

The sun is warm as we look out over Redfish Bay, a salt tang in the wind. Occasionally a funk of dead fish and putrefying flesh drifts over us. The smell of dead fish drying in the sun is standard for the Texas coast. I bend to my task.

We look up and realize that everyone is gone. At the gutting table, we work quickly; the ground around it is saturated with blood and bits of flesh and smells of death. I cut off feet and wing tips (leaving a single fully feathered wing on each bird for identification). Bill guts the birds. In the process, he pulls out the quacker, the syrinx or vocal organ, attached to the windpipe of one drake. It is a beautiful translucent ivory, spiraling in shell-like whorls. I want to keep it, but Bill assures me I will find others.

In search of the trash can, I step past a line of bushes. I slam into a wall of stink so solid I recoil. Before me, hundreds of duck carcasses rot in the sun. Most are breasted, the duck equivalent of taking only a deer's backstrap. A trio of mergansers (not breasted) catches my eye. Why would anyone shoot a merganser? Filleted redfish carcasses curl in macabre replications of swimming motions. Surrounding the refuse pile is a ring of older bills and white bones already cleaned by vultures and coyotes. White feathers stir next to red gashes where breast fillets have been sliced away.

We load into the truck to start the drive home. The smell stays with me. I sniff my hands; a distinctly fishy smell emanates from my skin. What pisses me off, I tell Bill, is the waste. The wanton disrespect for the birds and the way they are treated as trash. He nods but reminds me that there are lots of hunters who don't care a bit about conservation. For them, duck hunting is a sport with no more consequences than knocking clay pigeons out of the sky. I fume most of the way home.

For dinner that first night we decide to eat the big pintail drake. I rub scented lotion into my hands in an attempt to dispel the lingering fishy smell. I cut up the pintail and marinate the pieces in a sweet and spicy soy and garlic mixture for an hour. Then I grill the duck hot and fast and serve it with the marinade cooked down into a sauce. The caramelized sugars and garlic form a crust that complements the rich dark meat.

And mostly neutralizes the fishy flavor. By this time, I am convinced that I am having olfactory hallucinations or flashbacks related to the pile of dead ducks and fish guts. The next night I roast one of the redhead drakes and it fills the house with a pungent smell reminiscent of a fish store dumpster. The duck looks succulent, with a crispy skin surrounded by roasted potatoes and onions—but I can't get near it. Bill, meanwhile, happily eats the entire bird while I run around opening windows and lighting candles and perusing online discussion threads about fishy ducks. I learn, too late, that many hunters are cautious about bay ducks—especially diving ducks that feed on shellfish or mollusks in addition to vegetation. You are what you eat, and in ducks it comes through loud and clear.

9

Epicure's Scaup Gumbo

They are not worth shooting, however, unless for sport or examination,
for their flesh is generally tough and rather fishy in flavour. Indeed I know
none, excepting what is called an Epicure, who could relish a Scaup Duck.
—Scaup Duck, *Ornithological Biography*, vol. 3

I like to eat duck. A lot. Duck gumbo. Crispy roasted whole duck. The snap of
the seared skin on a grilled duck breast as my teeth tear into the fat cap and tender dark red meat. Duck simmered in wine. Duck legs stewed in their own fat
until the meat becomes heart-achingly tender. Rillettes, that same meat shredded and spiced so it spreads like butter but tastes like heaven. How can I, with
honesty, enjoy eating duck (and goose, guinea fowl, quail, dove, chicken, and
squab) as much as I do, and look down on bird hunters?

I have no aversion to killing and eating animals. Early on I determined that
if I was going to eat other animals, I needed to accept my place in the food cycle.
My stepfather, Dr. Richard E. Tracy, a research pathologist at Louisiana State
University School of Medicine in New Orleans (my mom's second husband),
regularly brought home "four-legged chickens" from his lab. After the rabbits
had fulfilled their purpose in arterial plaque studies (they were really fat bun-
nies), they arrived headless, skinned, and dressed and were quickly turned into
stew or fricassee that we happily ate. As teenagers living in a Texas hippie commune, my brother and I harvested rabbits kept for the dual and contradictory
purposes of meat and pets. It was, honestly, a gruesome experience, but it was
the first time I felt the intimate link between prey and predator: what I call the

truth of the plate. Since then I've never been able to fool myself into ignoring that the grilled chicken breast was once a live bird or that the pork chop once squealed and stamped in the mud. It is easier to see the binding thread when cutting up deer for our freezer or helping Bill gut feral hogs for turning into sausage. Mild mannered I may be, but I am a predator, and, then as now, I must take responsibility for the lives of my prey, be they feathered, finned, or furred. And part of that responsibility is not wasting our harvest.

I am determined to eat the ducks we brought home from the coast, fishy or not. I look through cookbooks and search for recipes and information about cooking scaup, or bluebills, on the internet. The consensus seems to be that the ducks' diet of shellfish makes their flesh too fishy to eat. Yet I know that herbs and spices can mask flavors; otherwise, no one would ever eat crawfish, a.k.a. mudbugs.

Surprisingly, it is John James Audubon who comes to my rescue. In his notes on the American coot, he writes: "They are extremely abundant in the New Orleans' markets during the latter part of autumn and in winter, when the poorer classes purchase them to make 'gombo.' In preparing them for cooking, they skin them like rabbits instead of plucking them."

Aha! I think, skin the birds and make gumbo. So as tradition dictates, first I make a roux. I stand at my stove, stirring flour and oil in an ancient black iron skillet while my mind wanders and the roux slowly browns to the color of dark chocolate. I put on nitrile gloves and skin the three scaup, removing the rich yellow fat with its pungent fish smell. I laugh, thinking of all the work plucking those birds as I break them down into parts. The dogs, eternally optimistic, watch and hope in vain.

I sauté the trinity of onions, green peppers, and celery, then add the roux, chicken stock, bay leaves, thyme, Worcestershire sauce, allspice, cayenne, and paprika. I pour several big glugs of dry white wine into the pot (and a couple into the cook), add coarsely chopped garlic, and a fistful of fresh parsley. I slip the duck pieces in, put a lid on the pot, and leave it to simmer. After a couple of hours, when the meat is falling-off-the-bone tender, I fish out the duck and dice the meat. I add links of andouille sausage, sliced and fried, to the pot along with a couple of pounds of peeled Gulf shrimp.

With friends we ladle gumbo over mounds of fluffy Texmati rice and pass bottles of homemade vinegary pepper sauce and filé gumbo. The herbs and spices mellow the birds' musky bay flavor and the sweet shrimp masks any residual fishiness. Conversation ceases, and later, over emptied bowls, we raise a glass to the ducks, the rice farmers, the shrimpers, and the hunter who made our meal possible.

🦆 10 🦆

Feather Heads

Twenty or thirty seen at once along the margins of a marsh or a river, form
a most agreeable sight. . . . When in good condition, its flesh is excellent
eating, especially in early autumn, when it is generally very fat.
   —Snowy Heron, *Ornithological Biography*, vol. 3

"BOOM BOOM!" The guide swings his imaginary shotgun across the sky, his camo-painted 12 gauge ignored at his side.

"Those wood ducks just folded and SPLASH SPLASH! They hit the water!"
The imaginary shotgun swings down.

"And then," he says, "believe it or not, another pair of woodies comes gliding
in right behind and—BOOM BOOM!"

He grins at me, twenty-something years of bravado, reeking of testosterone
and body spray. He starts another story about derring-do and hunting high jinks.

We are on a late-season hunt, and it seems that ducks have no interest in
joining the decoys surrounding our blind. A few birds silently drop into the
spread in the half-light before dawn, but they are gone by shooting time. The
outfitter's website lured us in with talk of the Texas Prairie Wetlands Project, DU
Canada, and birdwatching tours. What we have is a guide who won't shut up and
who impetuously takes the first shot on the few birds that wing into range. I can
feel a slow burn of irritation radiating from Bill; this kid is getting under his skin.
Usually I'm the one who gets vexed.

Our blind is a mostly buried concrete septic tank on a small saltgrass-covered mound in a stretch of shallow open water near Bolivar Peninsula. Spartina marshes surround us on all sides. In the distance, push boats and barges seem to float through the salt marsh as they work their way up and down the Gulf Intracoastal Waterway. A breeze blows a sticky salt tang from the Gulf of Mexico.

"If it flies, it dies," the guide announces and then starts a tale about goose-hunting exploits. A cluster of dowitchers flash white rumps as they settle into the shallow water around our island to probe the mud like a battalion of sewing machines stitching the mud and water together. A flock of terns swirl around us, diving for small silvery fish between the decoys. They circle close enough that no binoculars are needed to distinguish bill color. Forster's terns with black smudges behind their eyes mingle with common terns. A stately royal tern glides through, its partial black crest looking like a monk's tonsure above its orange bill. Great blue herons, great egrets, and delicate snowy egrets stalk the edges of the spartina marsh. Six green-winged teal rocket toward us. The guide grabs his gun and takes a wild shot. The flock curves around us to settle, females quacking and males whistling, into a growing congregation of ducks out of range but not out of sight.

In the brilliant morning light, a trio of roseate spoonbills fly overhead, their hot-pink toes pointed like gangly ballerinas. A swamp sparrow hops around the blind, rufous wings glowing against the dark green spartina.

"Two thousand birds from this blind alone this year." A common tern swoops low and seems to look right at me, its pale plumage illuminated in the slanting light. A black-and-white image arises in my mind: a woman in a hat with a pair of tern's wings arrowing off each side like Mercury's winged helmet.

"BOOM!" says our guide, and the sparrow flutters off.

The old photo reminds me of the National Audubon Society's origin story. Like a classic Victorian melodrama, the story line has evil villains and virtuous heroines. The champions of the waterbirds, a duo of Boston society matrons, stood for the preservation of nature and feminine modesty, fighting against vain women who thoughtlessly adorned themselves with dead birds and their parts. The plume-wearing women were cast as oblivious to the winding trail of dead birds, rapacious hunters, wealthy merchants, and colluding milliners that ful-filled their feathered fancies. The two society women held tea parties in 1896 to convince their friends to boycott the wearing of feathers. That same year, they would organize the Massachusetts Audubon Society, one of the state groups that would eventually join to form the National Audubon Society. And, the story goes, the two ladies were almost single-handedly responsible for the passing of the Lacey Act, the first federal law protecting wildlife.

Royal tern

But when I start looking into the history, I realize that they were just two players in a wide-ranging and complex tale. First, I discover that the Lacey Act wasn't just about plume hunters. Or even limited to birds. And then I learn that the first Audubon Society was started by a hunter.

Just wait until I tell Bill, I think. And then I wonder, *What will my bird-watching friends say?*

That hunter was George Bird Grinnell, and he was deeply concerned about the loss of America's rapidly diminishing wildlife. As a sportsman, hunter, angler, author, naturalist, and editor in chief of the weekly national newspaper *Forest and Stream* (published from 1873 to 1911), he wrote editorials vividly lambasting the actions of market, pot, and plume hunters and pleading for women to stop wearing feathered hats. In 1886 Grinnell published a front-page editorial that was a call for action: he proposed the formation of "an association for the protection of wild birds and their eggs, which shall be called the Audubon Society."

Women rallied to the cause and joined this first Audubon Society in droves, and within two years the organization had nearly fifty thousand members nationwide. But it fizzled financially, lasting just three years. Although Grinnell's

Audubon Magazine had loudly decried the use of ornamental plumage, there is little evidence that the organization's antiplumage campaign made a substantial impact. It did, however, demonstrate the public's fascination with bird life.

But, I discover, it isn't just Grinnell who has been sidelined by the Audubon Society's sanitized history. Frank M. Chapman, who famously counted dead birds on hats on a New York walk as if birdwatching in a park, is also credited with starting the Audubon Society's annual Christmas Bird Count. But his career as an ornithologist for the American Museum of Natural History is rarely, if ever, mentioned. As a scientist and a bird lover, he saw no contradiction between being a collector of birds (whole, skins, skeletons, eggs) for the museum and a conservationist. He stalked, shot, and skeletonized the only ivory-billed woodpecker he ever saw for the museum. On the same trip, he collected thirteen now-extinct Carolina parakeets, later lamenting that he would have secured more if he had been able to predict their future. Yet the same man founded, edited, and published *Bird-Lore* (1899), a magazine for the general public devoted to the study and protection of birds, which later became *Audubon Magazine*. As a man of science, Chapman collected specimens for study as part of his job; as a conservationist, he was a vocal advocate and encouraged the public's fascination with birds through *Bird-Lore*, his many books, and museum education.

It seems something vital has been lost by the Audubon Society's minimizing of the role of these conservationists. And defining the Lacey Act as concerned only with plume hunters and feathered hats diminishes its importance and impact. This was a law designed to protect all of America's rapidly disappearing wildlife—feathered, furred, and scaled.

What some historians have called the age of extermination was about more than women's hats. By the late nineteenth century, it was as if we were in the midst of a war against wildlife. Plume hunters were just one of the many types of commercial, or market, hunters that were devastating wildlife across the continent. Mammals of all kinds were also succumbing to market hunters, trappers, pothunters, and settlers as well as the growing numbers of sportsman-hunters. Any furred animals that could bring a few coins for meat, hide, or bounty were killed without restraint.

Plume hunters, feeding the global feather trade, systematically destroyed breeding colonies of egrets from Florida to Brazil, as well as in India and Africa, so they could pluck unbloodied decorative aigrette feathers from the dead and dying bodies of herons and egrets (leaving behind nests full of eggs and young to die). Seabirds were shot for their white feathers, and breeding colonies were destroyed by "eggers." The United States imported and exported tons of feathers and pelts. In 1896 alone, it exported more than one million pounds of feathers, a weight that represents a staggering number of dead birds when you consider that the breeding plumes from four egrets weigh about an ounce.

At the same time, market hunters shot and shipped birds of all kinds as table fare. Shorebirds like plovers, sandpipers, tattlers, curlews, and rails were considered delectable treats. Songbirds were killed to decorate hats and to bake into hearty pies. Farmers slaughtered flocks of birds they considered agricultural pests. Amateur ornithologists collected specimens and eggs without regard for season or rarity.

Improved firearms made spectacular kills possible. While muzzle-loaded flintlocks continued to be used by some until the turn of the twentieth century, percussion caps and then center-fire preloaded cartridges were faster and more reliable. By the mid-1870s choke-bored, hammerless, double-barreled breech-loading shotguns were sold commercially for bird hunting. Anyone could fire a couple of barrels' worth of shot into a feeding or sleeping flock and kill dozens of birds—if not more. Less than twenty years later, a repeating shotgun was available, followed by Browning's 1898 design of the first mass-produced semi-automatic shotgun. By then, ready-made shotgun cartridges were commercially available. The days of ramming gunpowder, paper wadding, and lead pellets for each shot were long gone.

Waterfowl were a mainstay of the market hunters. "Outlaw gunners" slaughtered scores of sleeping and feeding ducks using outsized guns, some of which were twelve feet long, had two-inch bores, and could hold half a pound of lead pellets per shot. Live duck decoys—Judas birds—lured wild birds into range, and baiting with grain was a common practice. With no regard for season, commercial hunters packed railcars, wagons, and, later, trucks full of birds and game to ship to market. Across the country, hunters systematically depleted wildlife for food, feathers, and furs.

In 1887, Grinnell, along with Theodore Roosevelt, Gifford Pinchot, and other early conservationists, founded the Boone and Crockett Club. Named after Daniel Boone and Davy Crockett, then, and now, it is a national alliance of hunters who recognize a need for responsible management, ethical hunting standards, and laws to protect wildlife for future generations. The Boone and Crockett Club joined the American Ornithologists' Union, the National Association of Audubon Societies, and a slew of state and local sportsmen's clubs and associations to push the federal government to curtail the relentless harvests. Together they threw their considerable weight behind the legislation drafted and pushed through Congress by conservation-minded Representative John Lacey of Iowa.

In 1900, President William McKinley signed the Lacey Act into law over the objections of commercial hunters, plume merchants, and milliners. At first glance, the act seems almost arbitrary. What does interstate commerce have to do with protecting wild birds and game? And prohibiting the introduction of nonnative plants and animals is important, but what did that have to do with feathered hats?

Like so much in our government, the avenue to reducing the wholesale slaughter of birds and game was not a straight road. It was believed that if hunters couldn't legally ship poached Texas feathers and skins to New York buyers, the plumage industry would slowly strangle. If loads of illegally killed birds and other wildlife couldn't be sent across state lines to the big metropolitan markets, maybe the hunters would put down their guns. As the first national law protecting wildlife, it did give federal teeth to existing state game laws. Unfortunately, it was nearly impossible to enforce the myriad state laws.

The Lacey Act honestly didn't have a dramatic effect on the buying and selling of feathers. The plume trade was an international affair, with millions of dollars changing hands every year, and the act did nothing to curtail imports to the United States, or exports of plumes and birds harvested and shipped from in-state ports. US imports of processed plumage and finished birds grew from $6 million in 1891–1900 to over $10 million in 1901–1910.

While the coalition of hunters, ornithologists, naturalists, and conservationists celebrated the signing of the Lacey Act, they continued to push for more protections. Attempts to regulate wildlife harvests at the state level were largely ineffective, especially for migratory birds. Market hunting and shooting during vulnerable periods—nesting and molting—continued to devastate populations.

It would take time to convince the public that migratory birds were more than game to be harvested at the shooter's convenience. Or that birds were essential to agriculture, not destructive pests determined to make the farmer's life harder. Before Roundup Ready crops and industrial spraying with insecticides, birds protected crops from pests, gleaned weed seeds, and cleaned up waste grain. Audubon wrote about the red-winged blackbird, saying, "That it destroys an astonishing quantity of corn, rice, and other kinds of grain, cannot be denied; but that before it commences its ravages, it has proved highly serviceable to the crops, is equally certain." Unfortunately, a flock of blackbirds gorging themselves on ripe corn was far more memorable than the quiet industry of insectivorous sparrows, wrens, flycatchers, and swallows.

Migratory birds, the conservationists declared, were an international public resource to be protected for the benefit of all North Americans. States chafed and rebelled at the idea of more federal controls, but after a decade of intense lobbying by waterfowl hunters, birdwatchers, naturalists, and conservationists, the Migratory Bird Act passed Congress. President Howard Taft signed the act, also known as the Weeks-McLean Act, into law in 1913.

The Weeks-McLean Act declared that migratory birds were not the property of any one state and envisioned the creation of a federal migratory bird committee to begin the process of setting harvest regulations.

Skirmishes over the Weeks-McLean Act's constitutionality encouraged conservation leaders to push for an international treaty to protect birds across the continent. Disagreements over harvest regulations nearly derailed the process, but in 1916, the United States and England (acting on behalf of Canada) signed the Migratory Bird Treaty.

While the international treaty was a significant accomplishment, it was not yet law. Both Canada and the United States needed new legislation to establish clear authority over the management of migratory birds. Canada quickly passed the Migratory Birds Convention Act in 1917. The following year, Congress passed the Migratory Bird Treaty Act (MBTA). At long last, market hunting, spring shooting, and the use of shotguns larger than 10 gauge were banned. Treaties with Mexico (1936), Japan (1972), and Russia (1976) followed.

The MBTA isn't a perfect law. It has been amended, updated, and tweaked over the years, but, along with its Canadian and Mexican counterparts, it clearly establishes federal authority over the management of migratory birds. The birds belong to the people of North America, and they are a resource to be protected and managed. The law lists protected species and makes it illegal to pursue, hunt, take, capture, kill, possess, sell, purchase, barter, import, export, or transport any migratory bird, or any part, nest, or egg of any such bird, without a valid permit issued by the secretary of the interior. Committees set federal hunting seasons and bag limits for waterfowl and other migratory birds as well as a permit system for scientific collections.

According to many popular stories, the MBTA ended the plume trade for good. While regulations on hunting and trade had an effect—as did dwindling supplies and rising prices—ultimately it was societal changes that ended the plume trade. Attitudes and fashions were evolving along with the rapidly changing world. Rumbles of war in Europe did put a damper on the plume trade, but the simple truth is that extravagant hats decorated with feathers and birds just went out of style.

The Lacey Act didn't end the plume industry or market hunting, but it was the first federal wildlife protection law and is still in use today. Amended over the years, the Lacey Act is now the foundation against global trafficking of wildlife and plants. It was also the first law prohibiting the introduction of nonnative, or exotic, species of birds and animals to native ecosystems. After decades of importing plants and animals from around the world, the United States realized, belatedly, that importing tallow trees, salt cedar, Johnson grass, water hyacinths, and other exotic plants wasn't such a good idea. Nor were the starlings and house sparrows that displaced native songbirds. Introduced nutria (and the imported water hyacinths they were supposed to control) wreaked havoc on marshes and wetlands—and continue to do so.

The century-old MBTA continues to protect migratory birds. But in today's contentious world there are always those who argue that it does too much, or not enough. As lawyers argue back and forth over the definition of the word "take" in the law, and who should be liable for incidental bird deaths, settlement money from the BP Deepwater Horizon violation of the MBTA is preserving wetlands and essential nesting areas both on the Gulf Coast and in the Prairie Pothole Region, restoring Gulf coastlines, rebuilding rookery islands, and helping to protect our migratory birds.

At the blind, we pack up our gear (including the two ducks the guide shot) and load into the ATV. As we churn across the marsh, a flock of tree swallows surges around us. The birds dive and soar, catching insects flushed by our slow muddy progress. Their high chirping is just audible over the grinding of the ATV, and we watch as they spin through the air, flashing snow white and dark indigo with flares of iridescent cerulean. Would I dress in a gown trimmed with the iridescent feathers of tree swallows? The answer is no, but I still collect found feathers (even though it is illegal for most species), keeping them for reference or tucking them into the edges of picture frames as feathered talismans.

It is still early in the day. We decide a detour to Anahuac National Wildlife Refuge is the antidote we need after the morning with our garrulous hunting guide.

It feels a little strange to walk into the visitors' center clad in muddy camo. I'm ready to pull out my hunting license with the federal Duck Stamp, but here, as at most NWRs, there is no admission fee. The volunteers greet us with kindness and enthusiasm. We buy books and gifts for nieces and nephews and then head out to the marsh.

It is, I tell Bill, the day of the wren. Sedge wrens flit in the grasses, hopping out to glean insects on the woodland trail in front of us. Carolina wrens trill from the woods. Dancing among the reeds, busy marsh wrens buzz and pluck spiders from webs. Alligators and ibis prowl the edges of Shoveler Pond. A raft of the pond's namesake dozes and suns with a gang of green-winged teal, gadwalls, scaup, and mottled ducks. Coots nibble grass along the roadside. The silhouette of a rail darts in and out of the rippling shadows under cattails.

An hour before, I would have pulled a trigger on the ducks. Yet I feel no contradiction in the enjoyment I get from watching the same birds that I would have tried to kill from a blind. I ask Bill whether he feels any conflict. The answer is a decided "no." We are both birdwatchers and bird hunters. But above all, I see myself as a naturalist and conservationist. On our way out, we stop at the visitors' center and stuff cash into the donation box in honor of the Lacey Act and the Migratory Bird Treaty Act. Two laws that continue to protect wildlife and birds in the face of climate change, power lines, wind turbines, petroleum exploration, invasive species, and other threats. The same laws that George Bird Grinnell, Frank M. Chapman, Theodore Roosevelt, and the other hunter-naturalists and birdwatchers rallied to support. Laws I've taken for granted too long.

♪11♪

A Feathered Prize

The food of this bird being thus more select than that of most other Ducks, its flesh is delicious, probably the best of any of its tribe. . . . On the wing it has no rivals among Ducks. They rise from the water at a single spring, and so swiftly too, that none but an expert marksman need attempt to shoot them.
  —Green-winged Teal, *Ornithological Biography*, vol. 3

There, I'd done it. Pulled the trigger and watched a shower of steel pellets shatter the water around a sitting duck. My host and mentor, Dr. Ken Sherman, had pointed and whispered, "Shoot that bird!" I stared at him. He shouldered his gun, pointed it at the drake, and, lowering it, mouthed again, "Shoot that bird!" I mounted my shotgun, lined up the barrel with the green-winged teal drake floating on the far side of the pond, and pulled the trigger. The recoil of the high-base shell knocked me backward onto my stool. The stool promptly dumped me onto the ground. I heard Ken say, "Good shooting. When a bird goes belly-up like that, you know it is a clean kill."

I roll over and struggle to my feet. I feel like a camo-clad snowman in my waders and multiple layers of long underwear. Piecing together enough dignity to reseat myself, I look up to see the drake's belly bobbing pale in the dark green water as the north wind pushes it toward the far shore. Twenty-five feet away, a pied-billed grebe pops to the water's surface before diving again. A belted kingfisher hen rattles from a mesquite limb and swoops low over the water looking for fish.

I sit back and wait. The drake is the first bird that I know, unequivocally, I killed with intent. Exactly one year after I went on my first hunt, I shot a duck. I am now a hunter. I take a deep breath and wait, expecting a surge of emotion—sadness, guilt, or even pride. Instead I feel only the cold January wind and a mild confusion over my lack of feeling. Maybe, I think, I'm in shock and it will come later. I settle back onto my stool, keeping my head down and watching for birds.

Ken and I sit for two more cold hours tucked behind the mesquite trees, but no other ducks come in to the pond. We haul our gear back to his ATV and I return to look for my teal. Ducking under mesquite limbs and dodging prickly pear, I squelch along the shore until I find my drake. I pull off my glove and reach into the cold water. The drake is stiff and yet he glows with patches of luminous green in the gray light. I hold the bird, the springy feathers shedding water and a tiny smudge of pink blood on the breast feathers. With clear intent and a single shot I killed this beautiful wild creature: this death cannot be excused as an accident or a mistake. The drake is stunning, the delicate black-and-white striations of the back feathers, the gold and brown of the breast, the iridescent green swoop surrounding each eye, and the vivid patch of color on each wing. A warm feeling unexpectedly fills my chest. But not sadness. No tears; not even a catch in my throat. I'd expected a sense of loss, but this is not grief. I study myself. Gratitude. A sense of thankfulness burns through me. The air around me fractures into shards of light as I feel the ground beneath my feet and the wind swirling around me. The smell of the black Bastrop County mud, the bitter notes of rotting wood and anaerobic muck, the sharp tang of cedar and the gunpowder on my hands hit me. I bring the drake up and smell its breast, the metallic tang of blood, the smell of pond water and mud, and the dusty smell of feathers. An appreciation so deep that I want to call it love makes me close my eyes and I stand silently at the edge of the water. This feeling isn't what I'd expected—at all. I gently smooth the drake's feathers and tenderly tuck it under my arm to head back to the ranch house.

As we drive, I remember Audubon writing that "my rambles invariably commenced at the break of day; and to return wet with dew, and bearing a feathered prize, was, and ever will be, the highest enjoyment for which I have been fitted."[8] I am not feeling pleasure, but what I am experiencing is different from anything I've felt before.

Back at his house, Ken and I stand on his porch, still dressed in our waders, looking out over what he calls the roost pond. There are easily forty ducks bobbing on the waves—scaup, wigeon, teal, and spoonies, many with their heads tucked beneath wings while others paddle on sentry duty. Egrets and herons prowl the pond margins and a flotilla of coots mews and feeds in the shallows. A trio of pied-billed grebes disappears and reappears like tiny magicians. Meadow-

Green-winged teal drake

larks and sparrows pop up and down out of the long grass like an arcade game. "We used to hunt this pond," he tells me. "Now we leave it for the birds." My arms and legs are heavy with exhaustion. I've been intensely cold for hours and I want to strip off my waders, take a hot shower, and pile on the couch with dogs and blankets until I can feel all my fingers and toes again. He apologizes for the lack of ducks coming in to the little pond we hunted. "I really thought that they'd be flying this morning," he says. He pauses and we look out at the birds. "I don't usually allow people to shoot ducks on the water, but I wanted you to get one." In spite of the lack of ducks, the gray cold, and the bitter north wind, the sense of gratitude lingers. "It was an amazing experience," I tell him. And thank him for sharing his duck and bird sanctuary with me on this nippy New Year's Day. I drive home with the teal on the passenger seat, reaching over to smooth its feathers again and again.

A dozen years before, I had noticed Dr. Sherman's ponds when Bill and I lived down the road from his property. On those long-ago morning walks I'd stop to watch the birds that packed the flooded creek bottom. Owls called out of the woods and woodpeckers whacked the dead trees until they thrummed like wooden drums. In the spring, warblers flitted from the trees to the surrounding brush, and in the winter, sparrows clustered in the vine-clad barbed wire and thick bunchgrasses.

When I'd started this journey, I heard that Dr. Sherman was a duck hunter. I wrote a letter to his office, explained my project, and wrangled an invitation to visit.

On a May morning I drove into his property and, as instructed, parked next to the ranch house and walked through the garage to knock. Dr. Sherman answered the door wearing a faded Obama/Biden T-shirt and a camouflage Ducks Unlimited ball cap. He shook my hand and explained, "There is a phoebe nesting on the front porch so we don't use the front door. You know there would be no ducks without Ducks Unlimited and duck hunters?" "That's what I understand," I replied. Sherman, now retired, was a general practitioner in Elgin for decades. As we got into his ATV to tour the property, we reminisced about mutual acquaintances in our small town. Remembering one infamously irascible old coot, Sherman told me that he enjoyed working with grumpy old codgers and the challenge of making them laugh.

We drove through a cattle pasture with scattered mesquites and into a field full of vibrant green knee-tall native sunflowers highlighted with splashes of purple Dakota vervain and lavender bee balm. "We leave the sunflowers for the doves," he told me. "And the other birds." Mockingbirds and mourning doves perched in the upper branches while gaudy male painted buntings and cardinals flitted through the surrounding mesquites. White-eyed vireos called and a chorus of titmice, chickadees, and wrens rose and fell as we crossed the field. He explained that the number of days he and his partner hunt and the bird limits they set on doves and ducks are lower than those set by USFWS and TPWD. I asked whether they had ever gotten any help from DU, state, or federal programs. "No," he said, "we just add more ponds when we have the money." Five ponds dot the property. The big roost pond, over three acres, is mostly shallow and full of chara, or muskgrass. We skirted the edges of the pond looking for the plant he calls "duck caviar," but the small floating plant was not to be found. Other aquatic plants have arrived (likely via duck foot or egret leg) to provide a banquet for the birds. "We've stocked some of the deeper ponds with bluegill and bass," he told me. Pointing to mosquito fish swimming at the pond's edge, he continued, "But those fish just magically appear." While not keen on cormorants, he's happy to supply fish to the diving ducks, kingfishers, herons, and egrets. Occasionally a bald eagle visits and steals Dr. Sherman's harvested ducks before he can collect them. He showed me photos of the birds, their breasts sliced open and the meat neatly stripped away, cached under mesquites in the pasture. For over a decade he has kept records of the ducks harvested and made notes about what species show up and when they pair up and leave for their summer nesting grounds. When I asked, he told me he fries doves whole but breasts out most ducks, grilling the lean fillets. He will pluck out gadwalls for gumbo. Looking out over the pond, he mused, "I just like birds."

On New Year's Day I arrive home from the hunt, cold and tired, to show Bill the teal, my first duck. When I describe shooting it on the water, he narrows his eyes. "I'm not sure that is legal," he says. "But since Ken told you to, and it was on a private pond, it was probably okay." I am stunned. My first bird and I shot it illegally? I drape the drake over the counter and fire up the computer. In short order I learn (as does Bill) that while some hunters consider it to be unsporting, it isn't illegal to shoot a sitting duck (on the water). It is, however, against the law to shoot a setting duck—a bird on a nest. I muse that the terms have been conflated, resulting in the confusion. Bill wonders out loud when I am going to clean the teal. I ignore him.

When Bill leaves the house, I take my bird and camera out to the deck. In the pale January light, the drake is beautiful and perfect. I examine individual feathers and the delicate coloring, details that I've never been able to see through binoculars. I photograph it, posed with its wings spread, head thrown back. Then with wings tucked, looking behind its shoulder. I don't have Audubon's soft pine board and sharpened wires to run through neck, legs, and wings to set the pose, so my photos are graceless. I focus on the details of black beak and gray feet. Green feathers and half-closed black eyes. Before I begin to pluck the feathers from its breast, I hold it between my palms and close my eyes. I suddenly feel as though there are threads that extend through me, not only connecting with this drake but looping into the cardinals that toss seed out of feeders behind me, into the red-shouldered hawk and crows arguing in the woods, and into the snakes, frogs, turtles, and insects that crowd this land. My eyes pop open and I take a deep breath. How peculiar that shooting a duck could give me such a strong sense of belonging. After a lifetime of feeling like an observer, it is a profound and intimate sense of connection.

I'd feared that shooting a duck would emotionally wreck me, that a debilitating sense of guilt and loss would paralyze me. Yet, honestly, I have never felt as vitally connected as I did holding that teal. I'm not sure I know myself anymore.

As I pull out the breast and belly feathers, the wind picks up and the feathers swirl around me. As much as I love birds, I know that I'm not particularly sentimental. Too many years of living in the country and hanging out with biologists have taught me over and over that everything eats. And some creatures eat other creatures.

I know that some people, including members of our own families, would condemn the loss of a single bird's life (or rat or mouse), staunch in their belief that all life is precious and demands equal protection—especially from sportsmen and hunters. Yet others I admire would say it is *only* a duck and not worth getting worked up over—it was going to die someday anyway. Suddenly I no longer have the luxury of contemplating such choices from a safe distance.

I knew that in following in the footsteps of conservation heroes like George Bird Grinnell, Aldo Leopold, and "Ding" Darling, I would have to confront my own emotions around hunting and killing. Yet these men, like Audubon, were not only hunters but skilled and knowledgeable naturalists as well. They saw no contradiction in preserving wildlife and habitat for hunting, science, and recreation. Because hunting was central to his studies, Audubon never made much of a distinction between sport and science. Indeed, his writings reveal a deep affection for the birds he shot, ate, and painted. But does killing a bird make me more of a conservationist? Maybe it does, because now I'm straddling the divide between modern birdwatchers and bird hunters. I've realized that they are two sides of the same conservation coin. Sides that don't always see eye to eye, even when their objectives are nearly identical: preserve, protect, and build habitat. I've met a few birdwatchers who don't see duck hunters as the opposition, and a few duck hunters who believe birdwatchers are friend, not foe. But generally, few recognize how essential they are to each other. Clearly, we need more hunter-conservationists along the lines of Dr. Sherman. A man who identifies first as a duck hunter but in the process of developing a private hunting refuge has created habitat and sanctuary for birds and creatures of all kinds.

I finish plucking the teal. Naked, it is tiny and plump. I tuck a pile of wing and tail feathers into an envelope for future reference; cut off the head, feet, wing tips, and tail; and then, holding my breath, pull the guts out. I am glad that the cold afternoon air suppresses the smell of viscera. I freeze the bird, saving it until we have enough for a meal. I carry the glossy copper and green head and strangely pliable beak, the feet, and the entrails to a clearing in the woods where I lay out a small feast for a winged or four-footed scavenger.

🦆 12 🦆

The Birds of America

None but aerial companions suited my fancy.
—Introduction, *Ornithological Biography*, vol. 1

My first hunting season has ended. My deadlines for paintings have been met and passed. I turn to the man long considered a conservation icon, John James Audubon. I know that as an artist, he shot birds to pose them for his paintings. How, I wonder, did he balance his passion for birds with killing them for art? In my quest to find some sort of balance between my own identities as artist, bird-watcher, and now bird hunter, I hope to find answers in his work and life.

My ideas about Audubon are bound up in childhood memories. I grew up with his name as part of my daily life: Audubon was the park I roamed; the public grammar school where my brother was a pale flash in a sea of dark faces. Audubon was the street where my grandfather and step-grandmother resided in a tall house with hand-colored engravings and lithographs of birds and flowers lining the walls, where uniformed maids silently served fried chicken on petal-thin china. I was certain I'd shatter something: the plates, the glasses, the quiet. In my memories, even the birdsong and traffic noises are muted, quelled by propriety; tension dancing like dust motes in the light pouring in from the gardens. Audubon was, and is, inextricably linked to my cool, elegant step-grandmother and her passion for birds and gardens.

Beyond my neighborhood, his iconic images were everywhere: mass-produced cards, posters, and books displayed his handiwork. Audubon's images were so abundant that I learned to dismiss them as common, as ordinary. When I finally got around to college and art school, Audubon barely rated a mention. His work made no modern statement; it challenged no beliefs. It was the barely tolerated status quo. In the print-making department at the University of Texas at Austin, we reviewed his work, along with that of other masters of natural history, by nose-to-glass analysis of the techniques of the engravers, etchers, and lithographers who produced the plates and stones for publication. As a naturalist, I considered his luscious images an extravagant, albeit questionable, resource. He often painted his birds in unlikely and torturous poses to show multiple identifying features. A chickadee is twisted to show the belly, the underside of the tail, and, improbably, the top of the head at the same time. When I started painting birds myself, I used reproductions of his Birds of America the way I used Peterson's Field Guides: as a reference for the details of feathers, colors, plants, and other animals. As an artist, he was passé. As a naturalist, well, that rattlesnake with the extravagantly recurved fangs and other mistakes made his work seem quaint and out of date.

Over the years I had gleaned ideas and impressions about Audubon and his work from who knows where—public school, articles, websites, or conversations with friends. The result is that I started this project believing that he shot birds only to create art, that shooting birds was repugnant to the great man, and he lamented the unrestrained killing and collecting of birds and animals by others. Quotes selected from his writings convinced me that he loved birds so much that he could never take pleasure in killing the creatures portrayed in his paintings. One of the oddest notions was that, in order to avoid starvation in the wilds, he was forced to pluck and eat his subjects after he'd finished painting and drawing their carcasses.

A gun was essential equipment for Audubon and other early ornithologists. There were no field binoculars for observation, and no cameras to snap photos of birds and habitat. Hence, the only way to closely examine subjects was to trap or shoot them. While other collectors skinned birds and preserved the skins for future study and illustration, Audubon was unique in believing that a freshly killed bird in the hand was the only way to achieve the verisimilitude he demanded of his art (although he did preserve the skins after finishing his sketches). But surely, this conservation icon, this hero of birdwatchers, the immigrant who is considered the pinnacle of conservation and avian art, didn't enjoy shooting and killing?

The articles and biographies I read contradicted each other. By some authors' measure, he was saintlike in his love for nature; other authors described a man so bland and tedious that I wondered how he accomplished anything. So,

I went to the source, Audubon's surviving (unedited) journals, and his comprehensive five-volume Ornithological Biography, written to accompany his Birds of
America portfolios of prints.

My first dip into Audubon's writings left me aghast. Contrary to modern lore,
Audubon didn't find shooting birds repugnant—he actually reveled in killing and
eating birds. And nothing made him happier than a plump fledgling roasting on
the fire.

A quick scan through the first volume of his Ornithological Biography
revealed that his oft-quoted statement "The moment a bird was dead, however
beautiful it had been when in life, the pleasure arising from the possession of it
became blunted" actually continues with a lament that taxidermy didn't give him
the lifelike results he wanted: "and although the greatest care was bestowed on
endeavors to preserve the appearance of nature, . . . it could no longer be said to
be fresh from the hands of its Maker."

Audubon stuffed birds? I thought. I soldiered on through his florid text.
The species descriptions and anecdotes are filled with information about the
palatability of nearly every bird—grackles "dry and ill-flavored"; bobolinks
"extremely tender and juicy"—along with instructions on the best way to shoot
the creatures: "The Sanderling affords good eating, especially the young, and

the sportsman may occasionally kill six or seven at a shot, provided he fires the moment the flock has alighted." He wrote overwrought and sentimental prose such as this gem about the Carolina Turtle Dove (our mourning dove): "The Dove announces the approach of spring . . . . Her heart is already so warmed and so swelled by the ardour of her passion, that it feels as ready to expand as the buds on the trees are, under the genial influence of returning heat." Yikes. Then a few paragraphs later he notes that "the flesh of these birds is remarkably fine." In short order I learned that he collected, prepared, and sold bird skins, eggs, and furs to collectors to fund his work. He regularly shot many more birds than he could use and was an insufferable braggart about his skills as a marksman. There is no doubt that he was a considerable shot and, by necessity, lived off whatever animals he could shoot. Or that he could steal from a nest; he recounts that immature night-herons were "quite as good for eating as those of the Common Pigeon, being tender, juicy, and fat . . ." The idea that he'd pluck or skin and then roast a bird after it had been pinned to a board for a day or three suddenly seemed improbable. True, in the day, game birds were often aged before eating, but if Audubon regularly killed multiple birds in an outing—indeed, he bragged about shooting dozens of birds (even hundreds) a day—why would he bother eating a bird that had been dead for days?

As a modern birdwatcher I was appalled. As a hunter I was offended by his excesses. Audubon was overtly racist, a snob, and unbelievably arrogant. Where had my virtuous conservation hero gone?

In his day, Audubon despaired of being taken seriously as an ornithologist by the fledgling American scientific community. In hope and desperation, he fled America and traveled to England. There he found fame, not only for his life-size paintings of American birds, but for his buckskins, flowing locks of hair, and tales of the American frontier. He cast himself as the "American Woodsman" (pitting himself against Daniel Boone in the public imagination), and he rented halls where he pinned up his paintings in what must have been a stunning display: an immersive panorama of vibrantly colored New World birds and plants. He made a spectacle of himself and his art, and in the process, he found subscribers to his Birds of America portfolios of prints.

In his Ornithological Biography, he continued as both entertainer and ornithologist. His descriptions of wildlife and the frontier were clearly written to entertain an old-world audience, specifically the upper-class English and European subscribers to his Birds of America portfolios. He consistently emphasized the idea of the American frontier, underscored the limitless bounty that the continent originally possessed, and extolled the freedom with which anyone could shoot and kill game of any type or number. His sixty-plus sketches of American life and culture include outlandish concoctions of facts, exaggerations, and outright lies. Many of the vignettes are ugly reflections of our early society and of his racism and snobbery. A few of the sketches casually describe acts against wildlife of jaw-dropping brutality. Audubon was a talented man and a dedicated self-promoter; he reworked his stories—as well as his own history—to please and engage his audience. With that in mind, I plow through his writing. After peeling away the bombast, the pandering, and the preening, (and skipping his sketches of Americana), what remains is a trove of natural history, extraordinary observations, and revealing anecdotes about birdlife, hunting, and the skills necessary to survive on the frontier. I find it impossible to look up the description of one bird without getting drawn away, slipping from one account to the next, lured on by the extraordinary details and observations that are the foundation of the Biography.

As I read the Biography, I look at reproductions of his prints. Details I'd overlooked reveal these contradictions and complexities. His birds of prey are rapacious, nearly everyone with freshly killed prey. One of his Esquimaux Curlews appears dead, what looks to be a pellet hole disrupting the even chevrons on its belly. The Goldeneye drake falls through the sky, wing-shot, with bone protruding from the torn wing. His Great Black-backed Gull has plummeted to earth with a shattered wing, its head thrown back as it cries out. In the essay, Audubon begins by describing the gull as a destroyer, a tyrant, and a coward. Yet if you read on, you find his descriptions of the pair that sailors kept as pets on his Labrador trip; he reprints a letter about a gull as a pet; and he notes that they are so wary that they are nearly impossible to kill except in a gale. Was the only adult he was able to procure wing-shot? Or is there a moral I'm missing?

The John James Audubon I've found is not the conservation icon we have unthinkingly promoted over the last century. Our hero's feet of clay—never hidden, just ignored—are in the spotlight now. His private journals and letters, along with his published work, make it clear he was an unrepentant racist. He was a slaveholder. He was an extravagant liar who, despite his protestations of innocence, appropriated other's work. He was not what anyone would call a conservationist. He killed many more birds than he could use for his art, lived off the money he made selling bird skins to collectors, and stole fledglings and eggs from nests. He harshly criticized the men collecting seabird eggs in his essay "Eggers of Labrador, "[9] yet on that same trip he amassed crates of seabird skins and eggs to sell to collectors.

Yet this deeply flawed man created a work of extraordinary artistic and ornithological achievement; a record of American birdlife, in word and image, that is still vibrant and, I believe, valuable. Early on he predicted that our country would someday be tamed and plowed to the edge of every creek, with the flocks of birds and herds of wild animals diminished or gone.

While we grapple with the hard evidence of Audubon's moral turpitude, especially his racism and slaveholding, the Audubon name is being dropped by groups around the country as conservation organizations reckon with their namesake's legacy. As I look at Audubon's art and read his natural history, I wonder if we can separate the man and his failings from his life's work. Yes, he was a man of his time but we want our heroes to be more: virtuous and enlightened. Does Audubon's racist and slaveholding legacy taint everything associated with him? Should both the man and his work be relegated to a cultural dumpster?

Clearly the best of Audubon survives in his Birds of America paintings, prints, and in his natural history writing. Maybe it is because I am an artist and writer, but I choose to appreciate Audubon's birds while consciously and adamantly rejecting the man and his considerable failings.

And examining my own.

13

I'll Fly Away

In 1947, the Fish and Wildlife Service adopts the 4 flyways concept to regulate waterfowl hunting.
—Historical timeline, US Fish and Wildlife Service

As winter turns to spring, our woods fill with migrant songbirds and the winter ducks leave for their nesting grounds somewhere up north. I pull out an old *National Geographic* map, *Bird Migration in the Americas*, and pin it to my office wall. I've carried it with me from home to home since I discovered it in a stack of old magazines. It may be out of date, but I've always loved the graceful swooping arrows tracing the migratory pathways of different birds up and down the continents. I trace the rusty brown arrow for canvasbacks, then the longer line for blue-winged teal from Peru all the way to Canada. The arrow for whooping cranes starts on the Texas Gulf Coast and swerves across the center of the country in a wide arc before landing in northern Canada. It is a glorious mess of aerial trails that twist and curve over the continents, skimming along mountain ranges and coastlines, and forging across oceans and the Gulf of Mexico. I imagine flocks of birds buffeted by fronts sweeping above the Great Plains, swerving to circle thunderstorms, and flying for hours over open water to land for a day's rest and feeding before taking to the air again. This map isn't the tidy graphic that neatly divides the country into four major flyways: Pacific, Central, Mississippi, and Eastern. That concept was adopted in 1947 by the US Fish and

Wildlife Service as a way to simplify the management and regulation of water-fowl hunting.

I put away my pencils, paints, and brushes and turn to research. My bookshelves fill with used books about waterfowl and wetlands. I download scientific papers, old and new; pore over articles about ducks and hunting; and read John James Audubon's journals and *Ornithological Biography*. As questions come up, I send emails, write letters, and leave voicemail messages for duck and waterfowl experts at the Texas Parks and Wildlife Department and for conservation biologists at Ducks Unlimited (DU) in Texas.

No one, it seems, takes my requests for information seriously. Perhaps they think it is a joke—a birdwatcher, a woman no less, turned duck hunter? Or, as Bill suggests, my inquiries could be viewed with suspicion. What if I am an animal rights advocate hoping to infiltrate their ranks in order to write an exposé revealing the horrors of waterfowl hunting?

I wait, with a stranglehold on hope, while emails go unanswered and promises evaporate.

I flee to the Gulf Coast and High Island with fellow artist and writer Carol Dawson to spend days in the Houston Audubon Society sanctuaries watching spring migrants fill the hackberry and oak mottes of Boy Scout Woods with bright feathers and to witness the twig wars at the Smith Oaks Rookery. Carol and I join lines of other birdwatchers along the boardwalks to watch roseate spoonbills, great egrets, and snowy egrets steal twigs from each other's nests to add to their own ramshackle constructions. While we relax in easy camaraderie, standing shoulder to shoulder with strangers, alligators float in the water below or rest their chins on the shore of the rookery island. Purple gallinules poke around under the trees, resplendent in iridescent purple and green plumage, with pale blue shields on their red bills and long candy-yellow legs. Common gallinules look like their plainer siblings with duller black plumage, shorter legs, and red shields and bill. A black-crowned night-heron stalks around the base of the trees below the nests in a solemn promenade, looking vaguely malevolent, red eyes glowing in the evening light, with hunched shoulders under a funereal black hat and cape.

Sentiment doesn't belong in a rookery; nevertheless I take the side of a puny egret nestling as its larger nestmates stab and slap it with their bills. I know it won't be long until it is pushed from the nest to feed a gator or a night-heron. Young roseate spoonbills walk around and I hold my breath as one walks toward a sunning alligator, stopping just out of range. I exhale and briefly wonder what

Black-crowned night-heron

kind of person I am that, honestly, I am a little disappointed that the gator didn't grab a pink snack. A snowy egret picks up a small tree branch twice its height and tries to walk through the brush while holding it sideways. After catching the branch on the surrounding tree trunks several times, it drops the stick, walks to the larger end, and pulls it backward quickly and easily through the brush.

I return to my desk rejuvenated from my birdwatching interlude and ready to tackle the reluctant duck experts. A scheduled call with a particular DU biologist has me hovering like a lovelorn teenager for a full day, mooning around my office, staring at my phone, and willing it to ring. Lunch is peanut butter on a spoon at my desk; I am not going to miss this call. The afternoon slouches toward evening. As my stomach grumbles, I steam. I have been stood up. Again. I release my grip on the last shred of hope and it flops to the floor like a dead duck.

In the fading evening light, I leave my studio and stomp through the post oak woods. Cattle take one look at me and whirl around. Songbirds flee before me. Zeke heels at my side, seventy pounds of shepherd mix nervously eyeing my every move. As I walk, I think (not for the first time), *To hell with Texas*. I wonder if being twenty years younger or having bigger boobs would make any difference. I decide not, since most of my communications are electronic or voice only. I stop short in the middle of a yaupon thicket. Zeke plows into the back of my knees as I think: *Follow the ducks*.

If no one will talk to me about winter ducks in Texas, then by gad, Duck Girl will head north up the Central Flyway to the land of summer ducks—nesting ducks—in the famed Prairie Pothole Region of the northern Great Plains.

The next morning, I download a list of DU biologists in the Central Flyway and, gritting my teeth, pick up the phone to make cold calls. I assume I will be leaving messages and waiting, as usual, for someone to return my call (or not). I dial the number for Steve Donovan, conservation biologist for South Dakota. He answers, his voice cheerful and friendly. Stunned to be speaking to a person, especially someone who sounds like a cast member of the movie *Fargo*, I stumble through my elevator speech. "What a neat idea," he says. "Come on up. We've got a number of restoration projects you can visit." I thank him, make plans to contact him when I reach South Dakota, and hang up the phone. I sit in stunned silence, then start laughing and the dogs crowd around, wagging. "I'm going to the land of ducks!" I tell them.

Within a matter of days, the trip falls into place. My friend Martha calls her duck-hunting cousin in Watertown, South Dakota, and wrangles an invitation that gives me one migration stopover in the heart of the Prairie Pothole Region. DU biologists in Kansas, the Dakotas, and Canada offer help and suggestions on where to go and what to look for. A Canadian visitor to Austin sees my art in the Austin airport and contacts me about buying several pieces. I agree to sell her prints at a price that includes only a sliver of profit, but the sale will free up enough cash to pay for some of my travel expenses. I'll save us both money by mailing the art once I arrive in Manitoba.

Bill eyes my itinerary with both envy and disbelief. "All the way to Canada?" he wonders, out loud. I plan the first week of the trip, hopscotching from Texas to national wildlife refuges and wetland sites in Oklahoma, Kansas, and Nebraska up to Watertown, South Dakota. Then I will head to Canada, circling back to meet Bill in either Minnesota or North Dakota.

More than one friend wonders out loud why I am going to North Dakota (or Canada, Oklahoma, Kansas, etc.). "Aren't there enough birds around here for you?" one persistent friend queries. Bill vetoes my cheapskate plans to camp out along the way. "No way," he says, "you'll end up staying out too late looking at birds and won't find a campsite. I don't want to worry about whether you're sleeping on the side of the road somewhere." I agree, reluctantly, to stay in motels along the way—even though it means I will end every day in a town instead of out with the birds.

On May 18, I wake early, kiss my husband goodbye, and drive north, merging into the streams of traffic on Interstate 35 and heading up the open expanses of the Great Plains.

PART III
River of Ducks

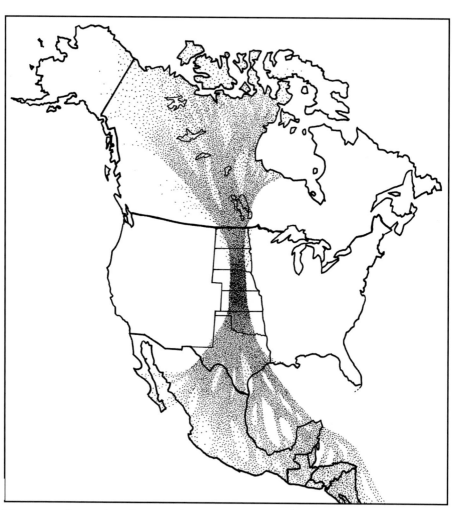

Migratory pathways along the Central Flyway.

14

The Waist of the Hourglass

Oklahoma
Salt Plains and Troubled Skies

> They move with great swiftness at times, at others balance themselves like
> hawks over their prey, then dart with the velocity of thought to procure the
> tiny fry beneath the surface of the waters.
>
> —Lesser Tern, *Ornithological Biography*, vol. 4

I've noticed that something peculiar happens to Texans when they start a long
trip. It manifests as an overwhelming urge to *get somewhere*. In other words,
OUT OF TEXAS. Depending on which of the cardinal directions I take, the Texas
state lines are a minimum of six or as many as twelve hours of driving.

I cross the Red River into Oklahoma and breathe a sigh of relief. I've made
it out of Texas. Yet I know that crossing the state line is ultimately arbitrary to
my journey. Rivers may define political boundaries, but flowing water doesn't
abide by those rules. Birds may nest in Canada and winter in Texas, but they
have no notion of borders, national identity, or political allegiance. Migratory
birds generally follow north–south routes as they fly between nesting and wintering areas.[10] The exact boundaries of the flyways are rather fluid depending on
the biologist or map you reference. I'm heading up the Central Flyway, which I
am defining as running from the Texas Gulf Coast (and Mexico) up the stately

progression of the Great Plains, through the continental United States into Canada, and up to the boreal forests and into the Arctic.

As the traffic on Interstate 35 plows across Oklahoma, I imagine the flocks of birds that stream north in the spring and south in the fall. Songbirds, shorebirds, and waterfowl need different foods, but they all need water. My itinerary focuses on the surviving wetland habitats known for attracting migratory waterfowl and shorebirds.[11]

In Cherokee, Oklahoma, I collapse in a whimsically decorated house surrounded by grand old trees. The owner of the Airbnb shows me around and points out the entrance to the basement. She assures me that she'll text or call if there is a tornado warning.

"Tornado warning?" I repeat, rather stupidly.

"Oh, yes," she says with calm assurance and tells me that just a few nights ago they had 100-mile-per-hour winds and the town's tornado sirens went off. I think of the open landscape and what little I know about tornadoes. Images from *The Wizard of Oz* jostle in my mind with news clips of leveled towns. At bedtime I stuff wallet, binoculars, camera, and laptop into my daypack and heave it onto the bed. Curled next to my pack, I crash into sleep long before I can worry.

During the night, thunderstorms pile up and rush the small town, but I'm oblivious to the lightning and rain. I wake early and slip out of town, arriving at Salt Plains National Wildlife Refuge before dawn. Heavy clouds whirl overhead as I thread my way along the Sandpiper Trail into a small wetland on the edge of the salt flats. Shorebirds work the edges of algal mats rumpled like discarded carpet. Wilson's phalaropes spin in deeper water, stirring up the muck. Snowy plovers, dapper with striking black accents on their heads, tilt up and down next to black-necked stilts and American avocets. Dowitchers and spotted sandpipers bob like jerky metronomes. A squadron of eight mallards zooms past. My trail takes me along the northern edge of the salt flats, the remnant of a prehistoric sea. I read on a sign that the refuge's 11,200 acres of salt flats, used by the military as a bombing and strafing range in the mid-1940s, are a major nesting site for the least tern (which was just removed from the Federal List of Endangered Wildlife), threatened western snowy plover, and American avocet. In the spring, summer, and fall, the flats and the refuge's wetlands along the Salt Fork of the Arkansas River and other creeks are a regional rest stop for hundreds of thousands of shorebirds, geese, ducks, sandhill cranes, and whooping cranes. A board lists the refuge's designations: Important Bird Area and a Regional Stopover Area in the Western Hemisphere Shorebird Reserve Network.

The wintering birds are long gone, and I've arrived at the tail end of spring migration. There are abundant birds, just not the cacophonous masses that I might have seen a few weeks earlier. I imagine the uproar of bugling sandhill cranes, honking geese, and quacking and whistling ducks, with the peeps and shrill calls of shorebirds and songbirds. I'm disappointed, but I console myself that I'm looking for nesting ducks—this is just a stopover on the way.

As it is, I'm waylaid by birdsong again and again as I drive and walk around the 32,197-acre refuge. I see fledgling indigo buntings, pairs of painted buntings, coveys of bobwhite quail, and dozens of Mississippi kites spinning in the sky along the creeks and wetlands. I see a pair of elegant wood ducks that spook and fly from their pool in the Little Marsh, and a trio of blue-winged teal paddling around a roadside pond. Flowering dogwood laces the woods along the creeks, milkweeds with round fleshy leaves and hot pink buds stand roadside, while some sort of spiderwort blooms side by side with purple-flowered silver night-shade. Groves and windbreaks of massive cottonwood trees toss in the wind. Feathery salt cedar thickets encroach on water wherever it flows. I pass a field of silvery wheat that shushes and rustles against blue-gray storm clouds. It is one of many fields planted in the refuge to lure birds away from neighboring crop-lands. American goldfinches and indigo buntings splash color as they fly around the yellow heart of a shattered cottonwood tree whose trunk is the width of my SUV. I think of the 100-mile-per-hour winds the landlady mentioned, and I'm surprised that I haven't seen more downed trees. I tiptoe into the blind at Sand Creek Bay. It looks out onto hundreds of acres of open shallow water. A blue-winged teal hen dabbles while a trio of Wilson's phalaropes follow her and spin like satellites. There are dozens of northern shovelers, both hens and drakes. I have no idea whether they are late migrators or residents. I realize that without the irrefutable evidence of a nest with eggs—or ducklings—I will have no idea which birds are indeed breeding, nesting, or just passing through. Casey Tower Overlook and Blind is perched at the edge of stubble-filled fields surrounded by dikes. It is dry now, but it is easy to imagine it flooded and filled to the brim with sandhill cranes, waterfowl, and a few elusive whooping cranes.

The salt flats are sandy barrens with white mineral crusts that form as the saltwater seeps to the surface and evaporates. Heat waves ripple above the flats on this unseasonably warm day, making my binoculars useless for spotting nest-ing or feeding birds.

For thousands of years—or longer—the flats drew native peoples who gath-ered the salt. Bison, pronghorn, and deer gathered to nibble and lick the mineral crusts. Nowadays the only people who mine the salt flats are in search of selenite crystals with hourglass inclusions. No one hauls wagonloads of salt off to cure meat or to sell. But the birds still come. I suspect that by virtue of their saline nature, the salt flats and wetlands of the Salt Plains National Wildlife Refuge were deemed unsuitable for cultivation and, except for the four years the mil-itary used them as a bombing range, have miraculously been left for the birds.

Least tern

Salt Plains National Wildlife Refuge was established in 1930, after the stock market crash that signaled the beginning of the Great Depression, and just as the drought of the Dirty Thirties descended and pulverized the land and the lives of farmers and their families. The refuge is barely outside the boundary of the Dust Bowl, the epicenter of drought and devastation brought about by weather and a rush to convert grassland to farmland. Before plows ripped into the native sod, the central Great Plains, what Francisco Vásquez de Coronado in 1541 called "an immensity of grass," covered 21 percent of the United States and Canada in a rolling swath of grasslands. It was the largest single ecosystem on the continent outside Canada's boreal forest. Swept by nearly constant winds, rippling with grasses, and often rich with wildlife, the prairies inspired awe and stoked ambition—and greed—in the newcomers who explored the seemingly limitless plains.

By the turn of the twentieth century, land developers and promoters were embellishing, exaggerating, and resorting to outright fraud to sell parcels of the plains from Texas to the Dakotas. Hyperbole was the norm as developers got rich selling lots and farmland sight unseen to eager buyers. The developers and boosters conjured a landscape of gentle climate, towns with artesian wells, and graceful tree-lined streets. The new settlers arrived and, if they stayed (after realizing they'd been duped), tried farming the land as if rain were abundant and breezes gentle—as if they were not on an often arid, treeless expanse buffeted by wind on all sides. Repeat a lie often enough and it starts to sound true: rain, they repeated, follows the plow. As the sodbusters converted grasslands into wheat fields, the theory was that "the commotion created by the act of plowing itself would bring additional rain, causing atmospheric disturbances." The hoped-for rain was in addition to the existing climatic variables including blizzards, hailstorms, tornadoes, flash floods, droughts, and prairie fires.

Nevertheless, the Homestead Act of 1862 allowed nearly 1.5 million people to acquire nearly two hundred million acres of land in the Great Plains region. Settlers plowed up the prairies, planted wheat, and prayed for rain.

As I drive away from Salt Plains through the miles of silvery wheat fields rippling in the wind under blue-black clouds, every small town I pass has grain elevators. Creeks are plowed nearly to their banks. If there were once other wetlands in these prairies, they were drained and converted to cropland long ago. I realize with a start that I'm driving through the heart of the Dust Bowl, looking for water and birds.

Kansas
Up to the Bottoms

> I was truly sorry to rob them of their eggs, although impelled to do so by
> the love of science, which affords a convenient excuse for even worse acts.
>   —Little Sandpiper [white-rumped sandpiper], *Ornithological*
>   *Biography*, vol. 4

Crossing into Kansas, I drive due north to the Great Bend of the Arkansas River. Beware, naive traveler, of the river's name. Whatever you do, don't call it the "Ar-ken-saw," as you would the state. Oh no, the disdain on the faces of Kansans will make your heart falter. The Arkansas (Ark-an-sas) River, familiarly known as the "Ark," drains the eastern slopes of the Colorado Rocky Mountains, then slides across the Colorado plains and through westernmost Kansas. Just east of Dodge City, the Ark swerves northeast, toward the heart of the state, then arcs southeast in a perfect bell curve to Wichita, where it drops due south to Oklahoma. At the great bend of the Ark reside two of the nation's prime wetlands: Cheyenne Bottoms Wildlife Area and Quivira National Wildlife Refuge.

In search of water and nesting ducks, I spend a morning under the tutelage of Joe Kramer, former chief of the Wildlife and Fisheries Division of the Kansas Department of Wildlife, Parks and Tourism. After retiring from the state, he went to work managing projects for Ducks Unlimited. "They seem to think that I've got some value still," he tells me over a platter of eggs and hash browns. He has a warm, deep voice that is easy to listen to, even when the news is dismaying. Knowing that I'm in search of nesting ducks, he is quick to tell me that Kansas is considered a migratory state and that, statewide, nesting ducks are insignificant to the overall population. My disappointment must show. "What is important," he continues, "is that the Central Flyway pinches in over central Kansas, so we are in the waist of the hourglass along with Quivira NWR, Kirwin NWR, and the Rainwater Basin in Nebraska." He tells me that shorebird people recognize Cheyenne Bottoms as a Western Hemisphere Shorebird Reserve and as a Globally Important Bird Area. I can nearly see the capital letters as he speaks. I jot down the figures he rattles off: 45 percent of the North American shorebird population stops at Cheyenne Bottoms during migration; about 90 percent of the entire population of white-rumped sandpipers, Baird's sandpipers, long-billed dowitchers, and Wilson's phalaropes stop during migration. Whooping cranes visit the bottoms but spend more time at Quivira's salt marshes. The bottoms, he tells me, is the largest marsh in the interior United States and is listed as a Ramsar Wetland of International Importance.[12]

As we drive out to the bottoms, he points out the 1957 diversion canal that runs from the Ark to the wetlands. Then he nods toward a campground, sheltered by a line of towering cottonwoods, that he says will fill with waterfowl hunters in the fall. He quietly remarks that he helped plant the windbreak a few decades ago. A fallow wheat field ringed with deep ditches is a recent DU purchase that will be restored to native prairie and then added to The Nature Conservancy's preserve. He tells me that DU buys land and helps restore it to wetland or prairie, then hands it off to The Nature Conservancy or the state to hold and manage.

Small bluffs ring three sides of Cheyenne Bottoms' gentle basin, and the fourth side merges with the surrounding prairies. From the top of a bluff, I look across the 41,000-acre (64-square-mile) bowl. Natural pools and ephemeral wetlands sparkle in the sun, surrounding the glittering hard-edged pools in the heart of the basin. Prairies shimmer green and gold amid the dark squares of cropland. Joe points out scribbled lines of tree-bordered creeks that feed into the bottoms. The far side of the basin merges with the horizon, which stretches uninterrupted into the distance. The state of Kansas owns the lion's share of the basin, nearly 20,000 acres that were purchased with PR Funds in 1949. "You do know about

Pittman-Robertson Funds, don't you? The excise tax on guns and ammo?" he asks. I nod yes, my pen skittering across my notebook. The Nature Conservancy has about 7,700 acres, he tells me, but I've stopped listening. Cheyenne Bottoms is a geological and biological wonder, a giant water-filled dish in the sky-wide plains of central Kansas. It hits me then, the facts that Joe had reeled off. Every other shorebird in North America flies across thousands of miles to reach the bottoms. Plus the ducks and geese and cranes and other waterbirds. How many hundreds of thousands of birds depend on this wetland aberration in the arid plains? It isn't just the water. The marshes produce bumper crops of the protein- and calcium-rich invertebrates that the birds need to fuel their migration and nesting. If the bottoms dried up, where would the birds go to get a drink or find food to fuel their flights up and down the continents?

We tip down over the edge and drive into the basin. We circle Pond One, a lake-like expanse of rough, muddy water ringed and divided with riprap-clad dikes. "Not levees," Joe gently corrects me. White pelicans huddle together, feathers askew as the group bobs unevenly on the waves. A massive amphibious backhoe sits in a ditch next to the road. Pointing to the machine, he explains that it is a full-time job clearing ditches and managing silt. We stop next to a pair of hulking propane-powered pumps that are used to move water between

Muskrat

the five main pools. Water is pumped from one pool to another to create a variety of levels: deep water for storage, a foot or so for dabbling ducks, deeper for diving ducks, sheet water for shorebirds, moist soil units for invertebrates, and completely drained to knock back the overabundant cattails. A mournful drone pitches up and down as the wind blows over an open pipe. The sound is both eerie and irritating. Joe either can't hear it or ignores it. "Duck lovers don't care about shorebirds, but shorebirds set the table for shooting ducks," he tells me and goes on to describe the techniques used to farm the essential bloodworms (midge fly larvae) and other invertebrates that shorebirds and ducks thrive on. Black terns in elegant breeding plumage fly over the brown waves, dipping down to snatch fish. A few scruffy juveniles stand out with glaring white patches in a sleek gray and black pattern. Cliff and barn swallows skim near the ground for insects and are torn up and away by gusts of wind. A muskrat sits placidly on a pile of dead cattails in a sheltered channel, munching away on a green stalk.

Cheyenne Bottoms' design—impounded pools held by dikes and canals—is from a time when we thought that we could build our way out of future droughts. Engineers designed the intensively managed wetlands certain that the right infrastructure could protect the bottoms from another catastrophic environmental disaster like the Dust Bowl. It wasn't the first time that someone tried to manage the bottoms. In the 1890s, an ambitious developer diverted water from the Arkansas River and built a dam to turn the wetlands into a 20,000-acre lake. It worked for a time—until a flood flushed the dam away. Plans to drain the entire basin for farming were put on hold when the state assumed responsibility for the development of the bottoms in 1925. The US Department of the Interior recommended that the basin become the first site in the developing network of national wildlife refuges, even as market hunters filled refrigerated boxcars with waterfowl, shorebirds, and songbirds harvested from the bottoms to sell in Kansas City and beyond. The legislation passed, but the funding dried up and the bottoms was never designated a national wildlife refuge.

And then the Dirty Thirties hit. The excesses, exploitation, and mismanagement of natural resources came home to roost. Waterfowl and crane populations cratered. The few ducks that had managed to survive the unrestrained hunting, draining of wetlands, and plowing up of nesting prairies on the plains during the last century struggled to find safe harbor. The stock market crashed and the Great Depression stripped away dignity and basic sustenance as the sun and wind pummeled the former grasslands.

The Dust Bowl, the epicenter of the drought, covered western Kansas, the southeastern corner of Colorado, and the Oklahoma and Texas Panhandles. Where the prairies had been plowed, the sun stripped moisture away from the broken soil. The earth turned to dust, and wind whipped the dust up into vast clouds that crossed the country. At its peak, the Dust Bowl covered one hundred million scorched acres. Author Timothy Egan says in *The Worst Hard Time* that this is the story of the southern Great Plains, "how the greatest grassland in the world was turned inside out, how the crust blew away, raged up in the sky and showered down a suffocating blackness off and on for most of a decade."

As the Depression and the drought ravaged lives and land, a few men rallied, determined to save America's ducks and the wetlands the ducks called home.

A few weeks earlier, I had been surprised to hear an esteemed friend refer to Franklin D. Roosevelt as our greatest conservation president during a discussion about ducks, hunting, and birdwatching. I knew FDR had started the tree-planting crews of the Civilian Conservation Corps but beyond that, I had no concept of him as a conservationist. His cousin is the one I think of as the Conservation President. After all, Theodore Roosevelt created the first national wildlife refuge, Pelican Island in Florida, to protect nesting egrets from plume hunters. By the end of his second term in office, he had established national parks, national forests, national monuments, and a total of fifty-three refuges. His conservation legacy is indisputable.

But FDR, I discovered, saved our ducks.

I knew he created the Civilian Conservation Corps (which carried out reforestation as well as built infrastructure on public lands), and that he appointed knowledgeable men and women to develop strategies for soil conservation. With two-thirds of the nation's farmland depleted and the Great Plains blowing away into massive dust storms, he was determined to develop methods to keep soil in place, healthy and rich for farmers. He initiated the Shelterbelt Project, which planted rows of trees as windbreaks all the way from Texas to Canada. He made sure that the federal agencies building dams and other engineered water structures set land and water aside for wildlife, all of which were helpful to migratory birds and waterfowl.

But he saved our ducks by signing into law the two acts that are the financial foundation supporting waterfowl and wildlife conservation to this day: the Duck Stamp and the Pittman-Robertson (Wildlife Restoration Act).

In Kansas, the state wildlife department used Pittman-Robertson Funds to develop the bottoms as a public wildlife area. With the same heavy equipment used to drain and destroy natural wetlands, they built the canals, dikes, control structures, roads, and blinds that are still in use today. Three years later, the bottoms opened for hunting.

But with rainfall a measly average of twenty-four inches a year, there wasn't and isn't enough rain to keep the basin full. Visionaries, Joe tells me, wanted a reliable water source. In 1957 diversion dams on the Arkansas River, Walnut Creek, and Dry Walnut Creek directed water from the river though twenty-three miles of canals to the bottoms.

Today those dusty and dry dams and canals wait for a flood. Wait for enough water to flow down the Ark and the creeks so the bottoms can claim its permitted share. Joe tells me in that calm voice that it doesn't matter that the bottoms has senior water rights if there isn't any water—the river is overappropriated and overpumped, and pivot irrigation has drained the alluvial aquifer as well. He delivers a devastating litany of facts: the evaporation rate is sixty inches a year, higher in drought from heat and the unrelenting wind; the High Plains aquifer (which includes the Ogallala aquifer) is overpumped and water levels are drawing down faster than they can be replenished; local farmers know water is a finite resource but they have to make a living; and finally, when there are floods, the bottoms provides a safety net for the farmers, towns, and people who live downstream of the Ark and the creeks that drain the property. "If the property owners only understood the benefits Cheyenne Bottoms provides, they'd all be supporting our work," he states, a faint burr of irritation in his voice. "We save them millions of dollars in land and property damage."

I'm trying to keep up with the flood of wrenching news and scribble semi-legible notes as Joe talks. He smoothly changes gear.

When there is water, Cheyenne Bottoms can host up to eight hundred hunters in one day, with both morning and evening hunts. He describes tens of thousands of birds and lots of satisfied hunters. Hunters whose licenses and fees support the bottoms as they bring money into the local economy.

"Unfortunately, hunters are on the decline in Kansas—and the rest of the country," he adds.

We've reached the 7,700 acres of The Nature Conservancy's Cheyenne Bottoms Preserve. Joe points out patches of salt sacaton grass and tells me that blue-winged teal hens nest in the preserve and spend their days feeding at the pools.

The Nature Conservancy manages for grassland birds and leases its land for cattle grazing. Joe waves his hand at the prairie and tells me that cows and birds are fine together. "They get sandhill cranes, ducks, geese, and seventy percent of all the semipalmated plovers. And whooping cranes. The peregrine falcons like it out here but the bald eagles stay closer to the pools."

Joe and I stand looking out over the restored prairie. It is lush with flowers and bunchgrasses that ripple in the air that rushes in a constant exhalation across the plains. I push hair out of my eyes. I'm about to ask him how he stays optimistic about the future when he says, "The thing is, the passion that hunters and birdwatchers feel about the bottoms is actually very similar. If you can get people to make the connection over their passion—and then let the individuals work it out—it can be really successful."

"Better habitat for shorebirds brings in waterfowl. And hunting waterfowl brings in Pittman-Robertson Funds that help support the entire area."

"You can't have one without the other," he says genially. I sigh, relieved to end on a positive note.

"And you can't have either without water," he says. I groan and he chuckles.

"How do you stay positive in the face of all this soul-crushing information?" I ask.

He looks out at the prairie, gravely considering my question. "Surround yourself with optimistic people, with visionary people who challenge old ideas," he answers. "Just because we've always done something one way, doesn't mean we should do it that way." He smiles at me and confides, "And I just love to see birds—of all kinds—in their habitats. Not just in hunting season, but all year long."

Salt Marsh and Sand Prairie

> The young are considerably more numerous than the old white birds; and this circumstance has probably led to the belief among naturalists that the former constitute a distinct species.
> —Whooping Crane, *Ornithological Biography*, vol. 3

I leave Joe Kramer in Great Bend and drive off to see the third wetland in the waist of the hourglass. The wheat fields are ripening to gold. Corn is two to three feet tall, with glossy dark green leaves that rasp in the wind. I'm on my way to Quivira National Wildlife Refuge, 22,135 acres that carry a list of accolades and acronyms: National Audubon Society Important Bird Area (IBA); Western Hemisphere Shorebird Reserve Network (WHSRN) Wetlands of Hemispheric Importance; Ramsar site of International Importance; and American Bird Conservancy Important Bird Area (IBA). It is another one of the essential stopovers for migrating waterfowl and cranes, as well as shorebirds, white pelicans, gulls, and other migrants that stop for food, water, and rest.

Amid endless center-pivot irrigation circles and cattle pastures, I find salt marshes surrounded by saltgrass and sand prairie. Forty white pelicans float regally like schooners under full sail across Big Salt Marsh. Columns of midges dance along the gravel roads. Ornate box turtles trundle across sandy tracks and I stop to photograph a rare massasauga rattlesnake. Showy milkweed blooms along the roadside, heavy with butterflies. Flocks of white-faced ibis and shorebirds work the mudflats of Little Salt Marsh. In a gravel parking lot killdeers keen and bow, as if welcoming me but really trying to lure me away from their gravel nests and spotted eggs. Battalions of dragonflies work the air over the marshes, and big softshell turtles push off the sandy shoreline when I approach.

I jump out to look at a snake in the road. A juvenile racer, it is freshly dead. I am winding the soft limp body between my fingers, looking at pattern and scales, when I'm suddenly surrounded by an extended family curious to see what I've found. I hand off the racer to one of the five or six boys and girls (I never get a definitive count), who hand it around and then give it back to me. I follow the boys down into a water control structure where water spills out of the Little Salt Marsh and flows into a small canal. The few inches of water are full of wriggling water snakes (northern and diamondback) and slippery frogs. While mom and grandmom lean over the rail cheering us on, each snake and frog is admired and then released. It is fifteen minutes of glorious muddy fun that ends when mom rallies her brood to head home.

I walk down the canal until its even, straight lines relax into natural contours. I realize that I have been walking down Rattlesnake Creek.

Rattlesnake Creek winds through Quivira, its freshwater feeding the salt marshes and wetlands. A narrow, slow stream, most of its water comes from a

Ruddy duck drake

local aquifer that seeps into the channel. Unfortunately, irrigation wells upstream are lowering the water table and diminishing the creek's flow. There is no longer enough water in the creek to fulfill the national wildlife refuge's senior surface water right[13]—water that is essential to fill the marshes and ponds when the scant and inconsistent rains aren't sufficient.

In the 1980s the refuge started reporting that it wasn't getting all the water it was entitled to, water necessary to provide habitat for migratory birds including endangered whooping cranes. Voluntary efforts to reduce groundwater pumping were unsuccessful, so the refuge filed a formal complaint in 2013. A two-year investigation confirmed that the refuge's water right was (and still is) being impaired. There are no simple solutions. Farmers say cutting their pumping limits would be unfair—they have to live off the money from their crops. Without irrigation, high-yield cash crops are difficult to grow in the arid plains. If the farmers suffer, so do the schools, businesses, and communities. The refuge knows that without the creek's water the future of the wetlands is at best uncertain. At this time, negotiations are ongoing, with all parties hoping for water allocation solutions that aren't too painful. With the uncertainty of climate change demanding creative and sudden adaptations by land managers and farmers up and down the Great Plains, it is unclear how long traditional irrigated farming can continue. I'm hopeful that some innovative and visionary person or group can devise a solution to return water to Quivira without depriving farmers of crucial water.

As I drive the roads and walk the trails of the refuge, one of three large natural marshes left in the state, I wonder how it survived. I suspect the natural brine water that percolates up from dissolving mineral beds is the reason the salt marshes have not been drained and converted to farmland. Because ducks, geese, and cranes don't mind salty or brackish water—and it is the preferred habitat of many shorebirds—the land was valued for its game birds. The first hunters were the indigenous people, then settlers, and then the tourists who came to hunt the Quivira marshes, as well as Cheyenne Bottoms. When the area was designated a refuge in 1955, much of the land was purchased from private hunting clubs. Hunting, including duck hunting, is permitted on one-third of the refuge.

As I watch mixed flocks of black-necked stilts, American avocets, long-billed dowitchers, and assorted small brown peeps foraging along the edge of Big Salt Marsh, I think of J. J. Audubon and his descriptions of succulent sanderlings. The idea of eating a killdeer, plover, or sanderling seems absurd. But are they so different from a mourning dove? Would I shoot a snipe? Or a woodcock? Both are still considered game birds. Would I shoot a sandhill crane? "Ribeye in the sky," I've heard them called. More than one hunter has told me they are delicious and require enormous skill to successfully hunt. Audubon mistook sandhill cranes for immature whooping cranes and thought the "young" birds quite tasty: "Its flesh was tender and juicy, of a color resembling that of young venison, and afforded excellent eating."

When Audubon confused America's two crane species, he noted that "the young [likely sandhill cranes] are considerably more numerous than the old white birds." It seems that there may never have been as many whooping cranes in the early days as we were led to believe. In his writing, Audubon details the different cranes he shot, including one instance when he only wounded the bird and it chased him, both of them running flat out, until Audubon was neck deep in the Mississippi River with an angry crane belly-deep and striking at him with its bill. He was rescued by his delighted boatmen, who quickly dispatched the bird with an oar. The whooping crane used for the original painting in *Birds of America* was a one-winged amputee, shot in Florida and given to Audubon as a subadult. He writes that he kept it in a pen with a snow goose and fed the tame crane on corn and scraps from the kitchen along with bread, cheese, and apples.

Regardless of the number of whooping cranes in the 1800s, by 1937 fewer than forty birds were left in the world. There was one flock, which did not survive, that wintered near White Lake in Louisiana, and another flock on the coast of Texas. On the last day of 1937, Franklin D. Roosevelt signed an executive order creating the nearly 48,000-acre Aransas Migratory Waterfowl Refuge. In the last seventy years the whooping crane population has slowly climbed. But if you follow the endangered birds' migration path, it is a narrow track from the Texas coast, up the Central Flyway through the waist of the hourglass, and then up and across Saskatchewan, Canada, to Wood Buffalo National Park. Salt Plains NWR, Cheyenne Bottoms, and Quivira NWR all host the endangered birds on their way between their wintering and breeding grounds.

I'm walking a trail called Migrant's Mile that winds through a small wood and across a wetland. The wind has died down and the mosquitoes are large and fierce, as are the ticks. I slap at mosquitoes and flick ticks off my pants, nearly running the last part of the trail to get away from the pests. Red-winged blackbird males squabble deep in the cattails, their thrashing sounding like a massive animal stomping through the marsh. A flash of cerulean blue catches my eye, but I see nothing but rippling water reflecting sky and cattail green. Then a male ruddy duck pops to the surface. He is resplendent. Bright blue beak, high-contrast flaring black crown and nape, with snowy white cheeks and chin over a glossy mahogany-red body. He erects his long black tail, spreading the feathers into a spiky fan. Feathers on his head rise into twin horns as he tucks his bill to his chest and murmurs. It sounds like someone is squeezing a leopard frog. It is one of the most absurd and charming things I've ever seen. He bill-pops and chuckles, swimming in tight circles with his tail held high. If there is a hen, I'm not seeing her. I laugh at the ruddy drake as he pops his bill and spins and spins.

Nebraska
O Willa Cather!

> But hark! the song of the Shore Lark fills the air, as the warbler mounts on high.
> —Shore Lark [horned lark], *Ornithological Biography*, vol. 2

I point my car north toward Nebraska. Under the wide-open skies, the land seems limitless, a geometric pattern of section squares that stretches away from me like a perspective grid. Streams and rills have gently carved the land into low rolling hills so gradual and gentle that I hardly realize they are there until I cross a lightly wooded creek bottom. As a reminder of how treeless these former prairies were, lines of stone fence posts string barbed wire along the road frontage. Windbreaks rise up, ranks of uniform dense trees around homes and farms. Rotund grain bins squat at the edges of farmyards. The next town down the road appears on the horizon, announced by the vertical thrust of its grain elevator.

As I approach the Nebraska state line, the rolling swales crest into hills, and cattle dot the green fields. Pivot irrigation circles are few and far between. I turn in to visit The Nature Conservancy's Willa Cather Memorial Prairie. This tract, 624 acres of virgin prairie, has never been broken by a plow, but it isn't covered with the tall, lush grasses Cather wrote about in her luminous prose. The green skin of mixed-grass prairie covering the hills is cropped short. Big square-bodied black cattle graze while crushed-velvet brown calves peer timidly at me. As I park, the cattle gather at the hilltop gate, mooing and looking at me with great expectations. I call out, telling them I have no corn or range cubes. But they stare in disbelief and bellow, waiting for me to produce an afternoon treat. They follow me to the lee side of the hill, where I sit in the blazing sun and they return to the business of grazing. The calves, suddenly, brazenly, romp into the open before dashing back to hide in their mothers' shadow. I put down my camera and notebook, dig my fingers into the dirt. I feel a thrumming. It could be the residual vibration of engine and tires against asphalt, or could it be the prairie itself, buzzing with life? Flowers are just throwing their foliage up and out to the sun and rain. A few have unfurled petals, but if I'm honest, this prairie looks—and smells—a lot like a plain old cow pasture. A few tentative blooms and unopened buds are rising above the grasses: purple locoweed, yarrow, prairie iris, a few prairie spiderworts, and the delicately scented scarlet gaura. Silvery thistle and mullein just spreading their leaves are glamorous invaders. Flies and bees buzz, the cattle swish their tails. Bobolinks and meadowlarks trill and call, their voices rising and falling in counterpoint to the wind. The wooded ravines and riverbanks of the Republican River lie dark and shady to the north. I'm surprised by the number of trees. Clusters of trees rim farmsteads and homes, forming windbreaks around barns and the edges of fields. It is still a broad country, but it doesn't hold the fierceness I'd expected. When the settlers first came, were there any trees? Or was it a land stripped by wind to its most essential form: prairie?

I spend the night in the Willa Cather Foundation's host-free bed-and-breakfast. It is beautifully restored and immaculate with thick carpets and glossy alabaster woodwork, but I can't get comfortable, certain (even after a shower) that I'm going to trail prairie dust, grass seeds, and dried Kansas mud wherever I go. I roam the house after I eat my dinner sandwich, looking for a

Horned lark

place to sit and write up my notes. There isn't a single desk in the entire place, and I fall asleep nestled into the billowing upholstery of an overstuffed couch.

In the morning, bleary eyed, I stop to buy ice for my cooler and gas for the car. I ask the clerk for a bag of gas. Hilarity ensues among the regular customers who cluster around the coffeepot. I'm too dull to even understand what is funny. The clerk points out the coffee and gently suggests a cup might be better than a bag of gas. *At least I'm entertaining*, I think as I sip coffee and point the car out of town.

The Rainwater Basin

> With ease and elegance of flight, the Marsh Hawk ranges over the wide extent of the prairie. The diligence and industry which they exhibit remind you of the search of a well-trained pointer.
> —Marsh Hawk [northern harrier], *Ornithological Biography*, vol. 4

I follow the tree-lined Republican River west and then cut north into the western portion of the Rainwater Basin. According to my map, I'm in the midst of the last major wetland area in the Central Flyway's tight waist. I turn off the highway and scan the fields. I see . . . cropland. Grid-like section roads, grain elevators, and windbreaks cresting the horizon. Ditches. Fields of wheat and corn.

Nothing that looks like a wetland. No glint of water. No ducks. No shorebirds. Just row crops and the round footprints of pivot irrigators stamped across the landscape. As I drive to the office of the Rainwater Basin Wetland Management District, I see signs with the national wildlife refuge's flying blue goose announcing Waterfowl Production Areas (WPAs). The WPAs are shaggy squares and rectangles amid the tightly plowed and planted section quilt. I stop at one and look at a green and white sign. It takes me a second to decipher the symbol because it is so out of place: a boat on a trailer. A boat ramp in this rough, grassy expanse?

Before European settlement, this plain between the Platte River and the Republican River was covered by prairie grasslands interspersed with an estimated 11,760 shallow ephemeral playa wetlands, called rainwater basins. Sealed off from groundwater by a claypan, the basins would fill with rain or snowmelt in the spring and produce bumper crops of protein-rich invertebrates for the migrant cranes, ducks, geese, and shorebirds. During the summer, annual plants sprouted and grew, bearing crops of seeds that birds depended on for their fall migrations. Wildfires, as well as bison trampling across the plains, kept trees from taking over. But the area was—and is—prime agricultural land. Farmers drained basins, routing water off the fields or into deep irrigation pits. Today the Rainwater Basin is covered by farms growing corn and soybeans. The tons of waste grain left in the fall fields after harvest are a boon for migratory birds, especially waterfowl and sandhill cranes. But the rainwater basins are now few and precious. Ninety percent of the basins have disappeared, most drained for farming. But one hundred publicly owned Rainwater Basin sites protect twenty-nine thousand acres of this wildlife habitat. It is less than 20 percent of the historic habitat, but it is better than nothing.

At the recommendation of a friendly USFWS employee, I head toward the Atlanta Waterfowl Production Area (WPA). Like other WPAs in the USFWS Rainwater Basin Wetland Management District, the property was purchased with Duck Stamp dollars. The WPAs are scattered across several counties: small squares of refuge in a sea of agriculture. She tells me that they have just finished the restoration on Atlanta by reseeding with a mix of 140 native grasses, flowers, and plants. While I'm there I should look for the prairie dog town in the upland grasslands. "It is one of our successes," she says as she smiles and waves.

I drive to the WPA and park near the road. Stepping out of the car, I have a moment of vertigo. After the uniform monotony of the croplands and straight-line section roads and the sterility of air conditioning, I am temporarily overwhelmed by the light and heat, the rustling cacophony of wind and birdsong, and the smell of crushed plants and drying mud. A truly horrible screech rises from a clump of dense grass and sunflowers.

I think of rusty oven doors, unoiled hinges, or the protesting cry of an old iron gate.

A ring-necked pheasant rooster flushes and breaks skyward as I duck down into the grass, startled. My heart is pounding and I laugh out loud as the iridescent and flamboyant bird, as gaudy as a feathered Mardi Gras reveler, flies away.

After I catch my breath, I walk into what was the wetland and is now a shallow mud pan patterned with bird prints, crazed with cracks, and sprouting with grasses and plants. At every step I see a different plant. In the distance I see the pale prairie dog mounds, grasses clipped close around their burrows. A movement catches my eye on the far side of the basin. I raise my binoculars and there is a big coyote looking back over her shoulder at me. We watch each other for a moment. She finds me less than interesting and turns to walk on. She is larger than her Texas cousins in my home county. Her thick pelt is russet with cream undertones and black accents, and I remember that in previous centuries, she would have been called a prairie wolf. She pauses after a few steps, turns her head, and looks at me again. She abruptly sits, facing my direction. Two can play this game, she seems to say. She idly scratches her side and then slaps a paw on a grasshopper or other small prey that she nips, then chews and swallows; she scratches her ear with a hind foot. She stands and, starting at the tip of her nose, sends a ripple down her body that ends with her hindquarters shivering and her tail wagging. She yawns and trots away without another look.

An adult male northern harrier soaring overhead disappears into the sun's glare, leaving only dark wing tips against the sky. He swoops down in a steep glide toward the earth but pulls up sharply to sail over the dry wetlands, his cool gray back and wings clear against the dusty green.

I have to take it on faith and a few footprints that ducks, geese, and shore-birds flock here by the thousands. I sit on the ground, leaning against a tire in my car's penurious shade. Common grackles prance and preen, males flashing glossy purple, their small prints overlying the dry wedges of duck and goose prints. Brown thrashers swoop down to a puddle, look over at me, and dart back to hide in scruffy bushes.

A virgin prairie looked like nothing more than a cow pasture to me. A rain-water basin and surrounding native grasslands looks like an overgrown, shaggy field. Is the problem with my idea of what I'm supposed to see? Or am I just ignorant of what is there, unrecognized and consequently undervalued? I know that if I were here during migration and could see the birds that flock to these rainwater basins, their importance would be obvious. The numbers of birds seem fictional: half a million sandhill cranes, three to six million snow geese, four million mallards, nearly a million white-fronted geese, nearly as many pintails, plus millions of shorebirds and songbirds. The bird list for the Rainwater Basin stands at 337 species. I've seen ten bird species, without a twinge of effort, in thirty minutes. Not bad, but for now I have to take the numbers of the feathered migratory hordes on faith.

Sandhill Crane Central

> These cries, which I cannot compare to the sounds of any instrument known to me . . . and strange and uncouth as they are, they have always sounded delightful in my ear.
>
> —Whooping Crane, *Ornithological Biography*, vol. 3

I dust off my butt and head toward the town of Kearney. My goal is the Big Bend Reach of the Platte River, eighty miles of waterway that stretches from east of

Kearney to just northeast of Grand Island and rims the top edge of the Rainwater Basin.

I cross the Platte's shimmering channel once and think, *Well, that wasn't much*. Then cross another channel. Then another. How many channels does this river have? I'm used to Texas rivers that are contained in tight valleys and lined with bottomland forests that buffer and absorb floods. When I cross the main channel there is no mistaking the wide, shallow river that sprawls out across sandy beds riven and sculpted into sandbars, shores, and rippled riffles. The river that early settlers described as "a mile wide and an inch deep" has been the rest stop for migrating cranes for tens of thousands—if not millions—of years.

It is breathtaking. I pull off next to a bridge to stand on a wildlife watching platform. Rough mud-brown cliff swallow nests bead the bridge seams. A wave of swallows erupts with every vehicle that drives over the bridge. They swirl over the sparkling current and then return to their nests, only to fly again as the next car or truck rumbles overhead. Shorebirds bow and keen, forage and skim from sandbar to sandbar.

Historically, the multiple streams of the braided Platte were surrounded by wet meadows and backwater sloughs bracketed with prairies that provided sustenance for migrating ducks, geese, shorebirds, and cranes. But such abundance was too tempting for settlers to ignore. They drained the wet meadows, plowed the grasslands, filled in the backwater sloughs, and pulled water from the river to irrigate their crops. Over time, upstream dams and reservoirs curtailed the river's flow in order to supply citizens and industries with water. Irrigation drained more of the river. Today more than 70 percent of the river's flow is diverted before it reaches this stretch. Spring floods no longer scour the shallow bed clear of sediment and vegetation; the reduced flows trickle through channels narrowed by invasive plant species as woody brush claims the sandbars and banks. And sandbars, it turns out, are extremely important.

This section of the Platte River valley hosts one of the largest gatherings of cranes in the world. Over half a million sandhill cranes—80 percent of the world's sandhill population—and most of the world's whooping cranes stop here for food and refuge along their migrations up and down the Central Flyway. During the day the cranes glean waste grain from farmers' fields, and every evening the sandhills return—splitting the sky with their bugling—to roost in the shallow-flowing waters of the Platte. Along with the cranes, the Platte and the Rainwater Basin host up to ten million waterfowl and millions more shorebirds each spring. White-fronted geese, mallards, pintails, wigeon, redheads, canvasbacks, avocets, whimbrels, godwits, peeps of all stripes—they'll all be here as the flyway pours birds into this narrow stretch of land and river.

It wasn't always so. The 1930s and 1940s saw sandhill crane populations at all-time lows across the country. The same unregulated hunting and loss of wetlands that devastated waterfowl populations also crushed sandhill crane populations. Their recovery was thanks to the same laws and conservation programs that benefited ducks and geese. Sandhill cranes flourished in the wildlife refuges, nesting among the preserved and restored wetlands and prairies. The big birds (three to five feet tall) have also demonstrated a remarkable adaptability when it comes to human developments. The cranes not only helpfully clean up tons of waste grain in farmers' fall fields but will return to methodically pluck sprouted corn seed from newly planted fields. Conflicts between farmers and cranes grow as grasslands are converted to agriculture and the birds become pests, decimating

Sandhill cranes

acres of corn.[14] The gregarious birds also happily forage in suburban spaces. One winter day, I sat in a car and watched sandhill cranes feeding in a drainage ditch behind an apartment complex in Rockport, Texas. Although my car was less than fifteen feet away, they were unconcerned with my presence or the nearby traffic.

By 1961, populations of sandhill cranes had rebounded.[15] When it became clear that crane populations in the Central and Pacific Flyways were stable or increasing, hunting resumed in fifteen states. Nebraska, however, is the only state along the Central Flyway that doesn't permit the hunting of sandhill cranes.

I stop at the Iain Nicolson Audubon Center at Rowe Sanctuary—a migration mecca for crane watchers. I'm the only visitor in the long, low building. Broad windows look out over the Platte. It is an odd feeling to be in a building at river level and just yards away from the shoreline. A woman in a camouflage sweatshirt with her hair tucked into a ball cap is watching birds at feeders just outside the window. I sign in and she looks over to see where I call home. She's clearly bored—all the excitement of migration is over and school groups are gone for the summer.

"Texas, huh?" she says and asks what has brought me to Nebraska and the Platte.

"I'm following the ducks up to the Prairie Pothole Region," I say.

She nods, unruffled by my announcement. Looking out at the birds clustered on and below the bird feeders, she asks whether I am a hunter.

I pause. Here I am in one of the world's epicenters of avian migration—in an Audubon sanctuary, no less—dare I admit I'm a hunter?

"Yeah, just learning," I say. "I'm a bird hunter." Without intending to, I lower my voice to nearly a whisper.

As we continue to watch the birds squabbling over seed, she introduces herself as Wendy and tells me that she was the hunter education coordinator for Nebraska Game and Parks. She needed a job closer to home and is now the director of community outreach for the Audubon Center.[16]

I introduce myself and ask, "How is that going?"

Wendy looks at me and smiles. "The director and staff are great," she says. "They're professionals and understand that birdwatching and hunting are both pieces of the conservation jigsaw puzzle." She shrugs. "Some of the volunteers, though . . ."

She looks at me ruefully. "There are a few that see hunting as a threat to all wildlife, so they see me as being on the wrong team." She goes on to tell me about an encounter with a volunteer who wanted to rescue a young crane injured during spring migration. Despite explanations that their job was to protect the entire ecosystem and that they could not rescue and rehab individual birds, the volunteer was not convinced that nature should be allowed to take its course.

Wendy shakes her head and looks out at the river and says that she told the volunteer that coyotes have to eat too. A hint of a smile crosses her face as she finishes the story. The volunteer had a conniption because she believed that the cranes were way more important than coyotes.

I nod. It is a familiar story, one with a moral that isn't always easy to embrace. While a single dead sandhill crane can look like a conservation failure, saving biodiversity is not about individual animals—it is about preserving and restoring functioning ecosystems. An injured sandhill crane scavenged by a coyote is part of the natural cycle. Preserving this length of river benefits the migratory birds and all the other plants and creatures that depend on this unique habitat.

I look around the center, at the sandhill crane information plastering the walls. She smiles when she notices me inadvertently raising an eyebrow.

"Cranes bring people in," Wendy says and then tells me about the importance of crane tourism to the communities along the Platte. Rowe Sanctuary gets twenty-five thousand visitors a year, and twenty-four thousand of those are during crane season. The big noisy birds are charismatic and bring in donations that support all the birds and wildlife. She adds that they get huge numbers of ducks and geese on the Platte and in the Rainwater Basin, but waterfowl just doesn't bring in birdwatchers and tourists like cranes. She looks up at me. "Unfortunately, we're losing our hunters. You do know about Pittman-Robertson Funds and the excise tax? And the Duck Stamp?"

I nod.

She pauses, looking out at the Platte streaming past the center. "Hunting and hunters are crucial to conservation in Nebraska. And everywhere, honestly." We talk for a few minutes about waterfowl hunting and she tells me about her former job recruiting hunters, teaching archery programs, and working with kids. The conversation dips and weaves until we are talking about rivers, water, and the Platte.

She tells me, "We've got a bunch of organizations working to protect and maintain this stretch of river." She fires off a list of names that I scribble down: Audubon, Crane Trust, International Crane Foundation, Ducks Unlimited, The Nature Conservancy, USFWS, NRCS, Nebraska Game and Parks Commission, Pheasants Forever, National Wild Turkey Federation, native plant groups, Master Naturalists, and the towns that depend on tourism. "But the politics about getting water down the river are incredibly complicated," she says. "It costs millions to keep this stretch of river alive and healthy. It just couldn't be done without everyone pitching in and working together." She shakes her head and we look back out at the feeders and the river swirling and flowing past.

⟡ 15 ⟡

The Ephemeral Landscape
The Prairie Pothole Region

I linger on the Platte River, sitting on her sandy shore watching cliff swallows drinking water and collecting mud for nests. They flare their wings and squabble with each other. A green heron walks across grass and sand, then crouches to stalk along the river edge to hunt. The compact silhouette makes me think of an Edward Gorey drawing. The heron turns to regard me, pinning me with its eyes as if it knows what I'm thinking. A yellow warbler floats across the river on the air currents like a bright butterfly. Only feet away from me, a mourning dove waddles down to the water on bright pink feet and sips daintily. The damp sand is patterned with raccoon, deer, and turtle tracks. I bask in the sun and breeze, blissfully free of ticks and mosquitoes.

The duck factory awaits me. I haul myself to my feet and point my car north toward the Prairie Pothole Region. If my information is correct, there will be nesting ducks and troops of fluffy yellow and brown ducklings paddling all over the place. I can't wait.

I cut through the edge of the Western Corn Belt. Steep rolling hills of dark brown soil patterned with sprouting green crops border the two-lane highway. I have plenty of time to contemplate the landscape while stuck behind a convoy of trucks carrying sections of wind turbines. They block the highway as they try to maneuver the outsized pieces down a narrow side road. Once this was all tall-grass prairie; now it is one of the most productive areas of corn and soybeans in the world. It has fertile soils, abundant rain, and now a forest of wind turbines

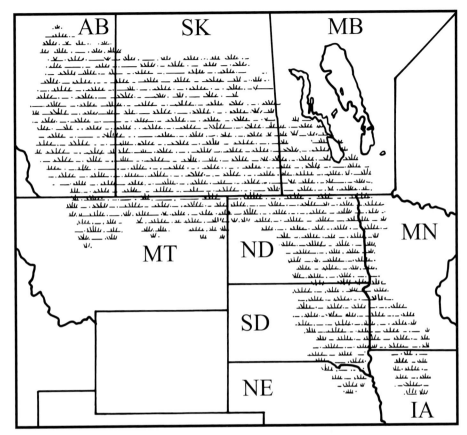

Historical extent of the Prairie Pothole Region.

spinning overhead. Maybe the turbines will blow some of the cattle feedlot fragrance away, I muse.

Cresting a lightly forested ridge, I drop down to the wide-open Missouri River valley. Just below the dam for Lewis and Clark Lake I cross the fabled Missouri only to discover that it has been reduced to a stream. Yet I've made it to South Dakota, and I'm just a few miles away from the duck factory.

South Dakota
Dog and Duck

> Now and then . . . [they] whistle out with great effort, often varying into a straining squeak, as if using their utmost endeavor to make some kind of noise in token of sociability.
>
> —Yellow-headed Troupial [yellow-headed blackbird], *Ornithological Biography*, vol. 5

"It's all about the dog," Jim Weisenhorn tells me. We stand next to a pond outside Watertown, South Dakota. "Without the dog, I wouldn't hunt ducks or ditch chickens." I wave helplessly at the cloud of leggy mosquitoes crowding my face and look at him. "Pheasants," he tells me, "the South Dakota state bird." He snorts. "Introduced and definitely not native. It fits."

Q, a fox-red Lab, bounds through the water toward us, a dummy in his mouth. He drops it in Jim's hand and then peers up, his entire body vibrating with expectation.

Jim is working on hand signals with Q, basic communication so he can direct his dog toward out-of-sight birds. He throws out a couple of dummies. Q leaps forward, landing with a great splash, then bounds through the shallow water until he finds a dummy. He returns with what can only be described as pure joy and confidence radiating from every hair and his toothy smile.

Jim lines Q up and sends him after the second dummy. The dog's absolute trust propels him on a beeline across the pond and into the tall grass. All I can see is a vigorously waving tail above the bright green blades. "Looks like he overshot it," Jim says. He gives a short blast on a whistle; Q pops up like a giant prairie dog to look at Jim. I laugh at the sight. Jim grins and waves Q to search to the right. The retriever hustles, working and searching for the scent of the dummy. "He's still young," Jim remarks. I see Q pounce on the dummy and he prances back, head held high, to sit at heel and deposit his prize at Jim's feet. But his excitement is too much to contain; at a word of praise, Q leaps up and bounces around Jim, jumping for joy. It is infectious and I stand laughing under the broad blue South Dakota sky while slow mosquitoes dance around me.

Jim and I were cautiously introduced by his cousin, my good friend Martha. She wasn't at all sure how her left-leaning birdwatching-environmentalist friend would get along with her red-blooded, NRA-supporting, former US Marine Corps cousin.

I arrive at Jim's home late, dusty and disheveled from my drive. He comes out to greet me wearing a big smile. When I stand up from rummaging in the back seat, his smile dims for a split second as disappointment slides across his face. *Well, there's the problem with having a decade-old author's photo floating around the internet,* I think. Clearly, he is expecting a younger, blonder woman, not the tired, wind-whipped, gray-haired version who has descended on his home.

He recovers and I'm introduced to Q, his fourth (Quatro) Labrador retriever. Q is a dark, reddish gold with a broad skull and intelligent brown eyes that watch Jim with an adoration dangerously close to worship. Jim and Q show me to the guest room. Jim has bought groceries for me, made dinner for me, and gone out of his way to make sure I'm comfortable.

Such kindness nearly overwhelms me.

He tells me over dinner, "I am a retired cop and self-confessed avid duck hunter. It doesn't mean I'm a good duck hunter, but I'm an avid duck hunter." While strongly opinionated, Jim is also a talented and engaging storyteller. We sit late into the night while he tells me about his life, work, and duck hunting. It turns out that Martha didn't need to worry; we get along fine. With duck hunting as a common interest, our conversation flows from one topic to the next.

The next morning, we load into the truck for a tour of Jim's neighborhood, the Crocker Hills geological formation of the Prairie Coteau ecoregion. Jim shows me pond after pond: water on private farms; ponds on Waterfowl Production Areas bought with Duck Stamp dollars; State Game Production Areas (funded by Pittman-Robertson Funds); and lakes both public and private. I am entranced by the smoothly rolling hills with wetlands nestled like jewels in the décolletage of a plump woman. Yet I can see for miles in every direction. Here I am, finally, in the midst of the famed Prairie Pothole Region (PPR) in the heart of the Great Plains—the landscape pocked with water that is nesting home to more than 50 percent of North American migratory waterfowl, 96 species of songbirds, 36 species of waterbirds, 17 species of raptors, and 5 species of upland game birds. Plus, the pollinators and unique plants in the PPR's 173 million acres.

Canada geese and goslings

Every small pond seems to have a pair of mallards and a few blue-winged teal paddling around. Migration is over, Jim tells me, and these are resident birds. He identifies most ducks at a glance—he doesn't need binoculars—but has no interest in the shorebirds and land birds. I laugh at a bill-popping ruddy duck drake as Canada geese herd fluffy yellow and brown goslings around a pond perimeter, keeping an adult between my camera and the young at all times. Everywhere we stop, the cattails, bulrushes, and tall grasses ring with the shrieking warbles of red-winged and yellow-headed blackbirds. A nesting coot in a thicket of reeds demurely tucks her bill by her wing and regards me from her nest.

"Where are the ducklings?" I ask Jim. "I'm looking for ducklings!" We both laugh at the absurdity of a fifty-eight-year-old woman on the prowl for ducklings. He explains that an unseasonably late snowstorm pushed spring back by a couple of weeks. "In a 'normal' year we'd have ducklings out, but . . ." He looks over at me with a raised eyebrow and a mischievous grin. I can almost see the baited hook of a global warming argument dangling in front of me. Jim delights in controversy and never hesitates to make his opinion known. I take a breath, listen to my better angels, and ignore the temptation to start what could become a heated exchange about climate change.

At each pond Jim shows me where he sets up his blind and explains how he sets up decoys for different weather conditions and the predominantly northwest winter winds. He talks about ice eaters and ducks dropping out of the stratosphere during migration. I'm looking for water, for cattails, those ubiquitous symbols of marshes, and birds. I hear frogs and wrens calling in the gaps between the South Dakota wind that slips over the land. Jim looks at the same landscape and sees something entirely different. He approaches a pond or field and analyzes the best spot to shoot from, gauges how much natural cover a hunter and dog could find, what type of blind, if any, is needed, what decoy spread would work best, and how far he will need to drag his decoy sleds. During hunting season, he hunts nearly every morning and scouts for the next day's hunt in the afternoon. "I've been hunting the area for over ten years but I learn something new every day," he tells me. I've never seen the world through a hunter's eyes, and it is both foreign and surprisingly familiar. Jim's knowledge about the habits and preferences of different ducks and geese is astonishing. I don't know many birdwatchers who have such an intimate understanding of birds and their natural history.

"Stop!" I say. "Was that an animal in that tree?" Jim and I are driving past a windbreak of tall cottonwoods on an old farmstead where he hunts and trains Q. We get out and look up at a large gray mass huddled next to a trunk fifteen feet up.

"Is that a porcupine?" I ask. I look out over the rolling pastures and fields running to the horizon and wonder whether there are enough trees in the prairie landscape to sustain a tree bark-eating mammal.

"I think it is," says Jim. "I'm sorry but I'm going to have to shoot it. I don't know if you've seen what a porcupine can do to a dog, but I can't risk leaving it here." I silently stand back as he pulls his .22 revolver out of a shoulder holster, braces himself, and fires. It takes several shots but the animal falls silently, landing in thick grass where it softly moans and twists. It is an enormous raccoon, a pregnant female. Her distinctive black-and-white tail and bandit face were hidden as she slept, curled on a limb and leaning against the tree trunk. Jim stands over the raccoon and fires two more shots, and she finally relaxes into death.

I am stunned. I wouldn't have pointed out the animal if I'd known that my curiosity would result in death. I hadn't objected when he said he was going to shoot it—I'm a visitor and I believe that when in a foreign country (which Jim and the South Dakota landscape seem to me), I should abide by the local customs. But the violence disturbs me. The raccoon wasn't bothering anyone, and it feels as though Jim went out of his way to shoot the creature. *At least he didn't seem to enjoy the killing*, I think.

And we have no shortage of raccoons, I remind myself. Without larger predators to keep them in check, growing populations of raccoons are devastating ground-dwelling and nesting birds (including ducks) and turtle populations all over the United States. Was I really upset about the death of a raccoon, or was it that I felt complicit?

In the truck I ask Jim about his gun. He pulls it out. "It is a Smith & Wesson Airweight twenty-two caliber revolver. It's made out of a lightweight alloy and I always carry it with me." He casually hands me the revolver. It is, as he said, surprising light.

It is the second time in my life I've held a handgun.

I look at the matte silver surface of the revolver. A few drops of bright red raccoon blood dot the metal. A .22, I think. Small yet deadly.

The sound of my ragged breathing rattles in my head. I hold my breath and feel my heart slow. "Where is the safety?" I ask Jim. He cuts his eyes at me, clearly surprised. "It's a revolver," he tells me. "Just don't cock the hammer and we're fine." I push the latch and the cylinder opens. Then I click the cylinder back into place, moves I've seen on television and in the movies. The gun's grip fits comfortably in the palm of my hand.

I look down and notice blood smeared on my fingers. I freeze, resisting the impulse to throw the gun to the floorboard, and then very deliberately hand it back to Jim. While he checks the cylinder and stows it, I scrub my hands against my jeans. *The same caliber handgun used to kill Nancy*, I think. A rising tide of rancid emotion fills my chest. Q leans over the seat and puts his chin on my shoulder. Jim looks at me but says nothing. I realize that I'm holding my breath and clenching my hands.

"My step-grandmother was murdered with a twenty-two," I say into the silence. Q's nose nestles against my neck and I reach up and rub his ears. "I was seventeen," I start.

In 1976, I returned home just in time for my free-spirited mother to uproot my brother, sister, and me from our comfortable uptown New Orleans house and move us to the Texas countryside. We'd landed in a free-school and hippie commune in the sandy post oak woods of Bastrop County. Air-conditioning and flush toilets were soon a distant memory—as were jobs, classes, and homework. We scattered to live in primitive cabins and rough buildings tucked into the woods. I slept in an A-frame building on a plywood bench, in a tiny room partitioned off with bookcases that were filled with the books, albums, and photographs we brought from New Orleans. One year passed. Then, just days after the calendar rolled over into 1978, when no one was there, a five-year-old boy struck a match and held it to a curtain. A slender tongue of flame licked up the fabric and the building was eager fuel. Within minutes the shredded paper insulation bloomed sheets of fire and flames reached up into the night sky.

The A-frame blazed hot and burned unbelievably fast. With no running water to quench the flames, nothing was saved. I watched as the fire incinerated all my belongings and my hidden savings. A carpenter's tools melted into twisted metal surrounded by ash; a young family's clothes, diapers, and toys disappeared into smoke; the ever-shifting gang of teenage boys who lived in the loft watched their guitars, amplifiers, and clothes burn. When the local volunteer fire department showed up, the building was already gone. Their only task was to stomp out stray flames in the surrounding woods.

The next morning I dug through the layers of ash, looking for something— anything—to salvage. The fire starter and his mother walked up and I heard him tell her, "Look at what a big fire I made." I stood up. He smiled as he touched the cracked iron skeleton of an upright piano. She looked at me and then told him clearly and slowly, "Be nice or you will have bad karma." I stood there, ash streaked and stunned. All I owned was a basket of dirty laundry left at the main building, a pair of combat boots, and a few journals.

In the coming days the boy's mother defended him, again and again, as blameless. Yet he insisted it was his fire. "My big fire," I remember him saying. She insisted on innocence, even as she buckled a dog collar around her son's neck and clipped on a leash.

A few nights after the fire, I was curled up on a couch in the main building, trying to stay warm and sleep. It took only the slightest whiff of woodsmoke for me to wake in dry-mouthed, heart-pounding panic. As I dozed, a door slammed and someone called, "Wake up! There's been a murder!"

A frantic call to the only phone had asked for my mother. "Come quick," someone whispered down the line. "You have to come right away."

It was the unthinkable. My step-grandmother, Nancy, had been shot to death. The elegant woman I remember as surrounded by hand-colored prints of birds and flowers had been murdered in her Garden District home. My grandfather was in critical condition from multiple gunshot wounds. My mom and I drove to New Orleans, shock compressing the drive into a memory of burning eyes, refineries glowing along the coast, and endless headlights. We knew who was responsible, even if we had no details and the police hadn't made any arrests. For years, my mother's stepbrother had threatened to murder his mother and stepfather. While his words were vile, his actions had never escalated beyond smoke bombs and vandalism. The police were impotent, unable to stop the escalating danger.

By the time we arrived, New Orleans' rival newspapers professed horror in bold headlines above the fold, speculated theories in twelve-point type, and gloated over the murder of a wealthy Garden District socialite. Matricide, it seems, sells papers. While police stood guard outside my grandfather's hospital room, detectives built a case against my step-uncle and the boyfriend who had fired the shots.

When the detectives confronted my step-uncle, he laughed. "I'm glad the bitch is dead!" Then he taunted them, announcing his innocence and wielding an alibi like a banner. But his accomplice, realizing too late that he was a pawn, sang like a lark, telling the detectives everything they wanted to know and more. They both landed in prison with life sentences.

"Not a blood relation," I'd insist whenever someone learned of my connection to the scandalous case. I worked, as I had in previous years, for the Jazz Fest and slept (when I could) on a couch in a friend's shotgun house. I remember sitting alone, trying to find a focus, a reason, some framework to make sense of the feelings that kept churning and erupting into rashes and blinding migraines.

Without a gun, no one would be dead, I reasoned. Neither man had the guts to kill without a bullet to do the work for him. The years of threats against my grandfather and Nancy didn't go anywhere—until my step-uncle got his hands on a gun. Desperate to make sense of an impossible situation, I focused all my grief, pain, and rage onto the handgun. Without questioning why, the revolver became the symbol of those horrible months.

"I vowed that I would never own a gun," I tell Jim. "Or shoot any kind of firearm. I wouldn't even touch guns; I made my husband move them whenever I needed something in the gun safe."

"I'm sorry about your grandmother," Jim says. "Step-grandmother," I reply automatically.

"Well, I've always been a cop. First a Marine, then Border Patrol, Immigration Service, and the Federal Air Marshal Service," he says. "I basically shot guns for a living."

A pair of pheasant hens dash across the road, immediately turn back, and then dodge and bow in a panic before finally disappearing into the grassy verge.

"Did you ever have to shoot anyone?" I ask.

"Yeah," he replies, shifting in his seat. "It was a them-or-me kind of situation. I'd do it again if I had to, but I hope it never comes to that."

Q moves his blocky head over to Jim's shoulder and licks his cheek.

"What do you hunt with?" he asks. I tell him that I'm shooting a 12 gauge semiautomatic made by Fabarm specifically for women. "I can finally fire a gun without it turning me black and blue. My first gun didn't fit and it got to the point where I dreaded pulling the trigger."

He tells me he isn't surprised, that guns are made for someone his size. He's six feet tall, with a solid frame and an ample belly. "I can pick up just about any rifle or shotgun and know that it's going to fit."

We drive past ponds full of ducks, but he tells me again and again that this is nothing compared to the numbers during migration. He calls ruddy ducks clicker-tails and says canvasbacks are the best-tasting ducks. "John James Audubon would agree with you," I tell him. As we bounce along a grass track, I look over at the plowed field next to me. The clods of dirt shift and I'm looking at a flock of American golden-plovers. They are stunningly beautiful with gold- and black-streaked backs. They melt away into the chocolate monotones of turned earth.

He stops the truck and a curtain of mosquitoes rises out of the grass to bump against the windows. He grins at me. "Time to work the dog." Q launches out of the truck, springing and boomeranging around while Jim waits for him to calm down. With every step in the tall grass, a wave of big, slow mosquitoes floats up and swirls around my face. Fortunately, they aren't as aggressive as their southern brethren, but the sheer numbers flying around my face make it hard to see. I accidentally inhale a few and Jim laughs as I snort and sneeze.

Frogs Unlimited

> Few birds are more shy or vigilant than the Great Marbled Godwit. It
> watches the movements of the gunner with extreme care.
> —Great Marbled Godwit, *Ornithological Biography*, vol. 3

Late that afternoon Ducks Unlimited's South Dakota conservation director Steve
Donovan stops by to take me to see one of the organization's restoration projects.
He is tall and has the sort of attractive and kind features I've always associated
with the Midwest.

We head east out of town, and the land ripples into undulating hills interspersed with ponds, pools, and wetlands. As we drive, I quiz Steve with serious
questions about Ducks Unlimited's work in South Dakota, but halfway through
I blurt out my burning question: "Where are the ducklings?" He laughs. The
Prairie Pothole Region is supposed to be the place for nesting ducks, but I have
yet to see a nest or a duckling. He kindly explains that what I've been seeing is
typical. Hens are secretive and protective of their nests and young, he tells me.
And adds that nesting has been pushed back by the late spring snowstorm. The
ducks are spread out, just a few to each pond because ducks are territorial. Lots
of small wetlands are better, he says, than a few large ponds because of this ter-
ritoriality. I'm feeling better until I learn that broods aren't territorial like their
parents, and once the ducklings hatch, it isn't unusual to see big groups together.
I silently imagine a couple of dozen fluffy ducklings paddling around a South
Dakota pothole and sulk, for just a moment.

The prairie sky turns violet and rose pink just as we walk into the site. It
is underwhelming at first glance: two quarter sections of land (320 acres total)
with concentric rings of brown earth and ocher stubble embracing a number
of small wetlands. I can't even call them ponds—they are just shallow depres-
sions holding water, with mucky borders of rushes and a few thickets of taller
dead grasses. Blackbirds sing from last summer's bulrushes and a trio of marbled
godwits stalk through the stubble, poking and prodding the ground with their
long bills. A chorus of frogs starts up and overwhelms the raucous trilling of the
blackbirds. Steve quietly jokes, "We should be called Frogs Unlimited because,
number-wise, we raise more frogs than ducks."

Waving his hand across the tidy squares of land, he tells me that restoration
means restoring the hydrology and walking away. My eyebrows shoot up. In
Texas, restoration of wetland or prairie sites usually means years of killing invasive grasses and planting native species. Steve glances at my face and registers
my disbelief. Smiling, he tells me that in the Prairie Pothole Region, the wetland

Pothole and canvasbacks

seeds and invertebrates are viable in the soil for as long as a hundred years. He adds that invasive grasses like the brome that ranchers prefer for cattle grazing can be a problem in the uplands, though.

He points up the slope and describes the work of restoring the hydrology: filling in a four-foot-deep gully and numerous ditches that cut across the land, resculpting the wetland margins so they hold water, and removing all the plastic pipes that drained the wetlands.

"Is that tiling?" I ask. He gives me a swift and surprised glance but smoothly launches into the basics of draining wetlands. Tiles, originally clay pipes but now plastic, are used to drain a wetland or pond from a single point. The drainpipes run to ditches that lead to larger ponds or local streams. The water that drains off is often contaminated with pesticide, herbicide, and fertilizer residues that continue downstream via our rivers to contribute to the Dead Zone in the Gulf of Mexico. In this heartland of the continent, the mention of the faraway Gulf jars me.

Steve points to irregular patches of darker soil on the neighbor's fields and explains that they are from drained former wetlands. He describes the wetlands as sitting on a lens or layer of fine clay that has collected over thousands of years. Even in a good year, he tells me, the soil is marginal for crops.

"But what is amazing," he says, "is that even after plowing and getting drenched with herbicides and fertilizers, one of those old wetlands can still produce plenty of invertebrates and plants for ducks."

"Just add water?" I say. He nods, looking into the distance.

The thing is, he tells me, 90 percent of the work Ducks Unlimited does in South Dakota is on private land—because 90 percent of the ducks are on private land. He warns me, "We're losing more of these small wetlands every year than we can restore. If we lose the wetlands—well, it's game over for the ducks."

A canvasback drake has appeared in the nearby wetland. The water doesn't look deep enough, but he happily paddles around. The godwits spook and, protesting loudly, fly away.

"What can we do?" I ask.

He is silent for a moment. Then he turns to me and elegantly lays out the issues. At this point in time, agriculture just isn't profitable enough to support conservation work—even when the landowners want to do it. Farmers and ranchers need to make income from every acre in order to survive.

He tells me that it all starts with the soil. If farmers can improve soil health—through techniques like planting cover crops, no-till planting, and rotational grazing—they will get better yields and more income from their land and, with any luck, will be able to leave the seasonal wetlands alone.

The sun is below the horizon. The wetlands reflect the sky and glow bright in the muted umbers of the stubble. Frogs are still bellowing and the canvasback turns his elegant silhouette to us.

"In the face of habitat loss and climate change, how do you stay optimistic?" I ask. Steve considers my question. "Seeing restored wetlands like this makes me happy." He goes on to tell me that DU will sell this land with conservation easements to protect the wetlands in perpetuity, and that makes a huge difference to him. But what he really likes is working with young people with new ideas. That is why he is so interested in DU's Soil Health Program and the agronomists they have hired. He believes they are a huge part of the future.

"We don't have to choose between agriculture and ducks—we can have both," he tells me as we leave.

"Growing ducks from the ground up," I say.

He smiles and nods.

The return trip to Jim's house is quiet. I ruminate over what I have learned. In the midst of all this agriculture—all this dirt—what happens impacts the streams, tributaries small and large, and finally the grand dame, the Mississippi River. In all the years I've heard about losing topsoil, and runoff from agricultural chemicals and its impact on water all the way to the Gulf, I'd never considered how difficult it would be to comprehend. I say something to Steve about trying to think about the Dead Zone in the Gulf of Mexico as linked to ducks in prairies.

"We're trying to get folks to understand just how far their actions reach,"

Steve says. A hint of weariness colors his quiet words. It isn't just preventing fertilizers, pesticides, and herbicides from flowing downstream to the Gulf of Mexico, he tells me. He is quiet for a moment and then continues by listing wetland benefits: they filter water, replenish aquifers, sequester carbon, help prevent downstream flooding by holding water on the land, reduce topsoil runoff, and increase plant diversity, which is important for the pollinators that many farmers rely on.

Frogs, ducks, and the Gulf of Mexico. Oh my, I think as the land streams past.

Jim is still up when Steve drops me off. Q quickly herds me into the living room (he prefers all his humans to be in the same room). We sit and talk quietly about life and ducks while I sip on bourbon and Jim has rye. We occasionally lean over to nab a scrambling tick from the other's arm or neck, pointing out the pests where we are hesitant to touch. We are virtual strangers and, in so many ways, opposites. While we are both high school dropouts, he joined the marines and served two tours, thriving within the structure and discipline. I'm so allergic to authority that I dig my heels in when I tell myself I should or shouldn't do something. He's a full-bore supporter of the NRA and as politically conservative as the summer days are long on the South Dakota prairies.

With a wicked grin he leans forward and says, "I got to blow up Mount Rushmore." I raise an eyebrow. "It was part of an emergency management scenario. My team played the part of insurgent forces that infiltrated the site and planted 'bombs.'" He makes air quotes with his fingers.

"Flash bangs all around the national monument. It was a blast," he says and looks simultaneously so pleased and mischievous that I start laughing. And then Jim starts laughing. Q comes over wagging his tail to see what the fuss is about, and I'm bowled over by an unbidden thought: I would trust my life to this man, in an instant and without hesitation.

Canada
Whitewater Lake, Manitoba

> During autumn they hunt for food over the wet prairies, passing low, and picking up the insects as they proceed without alighting.
> —Black Tern, *Ornithological Biography*, vol. 3

I fly out of Jim's place before first light with a bag of homemade duck and goose jerky and a promise to return in the fall to hunt. I mash the gas pedal down and cut across North Dakota like I am running away from home. I have three and a half days to see the Prairie Pothole Region (PPR) in Manitoba and look for ducks before meeting Bill in North Dakota.

At interstate highway speeds, the land streams past in a nearly featureless blur. I am blazing past prime duck breeding habitat, including some of the first national wildlife refuges for waterfowl and the first land purchased with Duck Stamps, but I want to get to Canada.

I turn north out of Rugby, North Dakota. The straight, flat road hiccups once, twice, and settles into a ripple of hills with small wetlands and ponds nestled into low spots. Trees appear and then there is forest and the road loops over hills and curls down into creek bottoms. I'm in the Turtle Mountains—not that they would be called mountains anywhere else, but here the elevation is surprising.

I cross the border. The Canadian border agent is professionally courteous. "Purpose of your visit?"

"I'm looking for ducks," I tell her.

"You know it isn't hunting season." No smile. Not even a lip twitch or eye twinkle. If she's being funny, she has a bone-dry sense of humor.

I assure her that I'm really a birdwatcher and point to my binoculars on the front seat. She asks whether I have alcohol or firearms. I confess to a bottle of bourbon but no guns.

"You are from Texas and you don't have any guns?" she chides. "Not even a handgun under your seat?"

"No, you're welcome to look," I say and we both look at the jumble of clothing, hiking boots, rubber boots, folding chairs, cooler, suitcases, cameras, and field guides that presses against the front seats, threatening to take over the entire car. I'm carrying Bill's luggage, boots, tripod, snake hooks, and snake tongs as well as my own gear.

She raises an eyebrow and waves me through into Canada.

Ducks couldn't care less about international borders. The drake's share of the Prairie Pothole Region lies on the north side of the US-Canada border, as do the boreal forests—two essential breeding habitats for waterfowl (and other migratory birds) in North America. Ducks fly south to winter in wetlands and coastal marshes that run from Texas to the Yucatán and beyond, skimming over borders. Blue-winged teal, one of the most abundant nesters in the PPR, winter as far south as Peru. Northern shovelers waddle around the Caribbean, and non-migratory mottled ducks inhabit the Gulf Coast from Florida to the Yucatán.

Western grebes

In the 1980s, a severe drought hit the PPR. Waterfowl populations plummeted. Meanwhile wetlands were being lost at a staggering rate across the continent from Mexico to Canada. The men and women responsible for managing ducks and geese—the biologists, refuge directors, researchers, and other professionals—recognized the need for a continental system of conservation. An international plan to manage waterfowl was hatched. In a collaboration across partisan lines and international boundaries, their vision resulted in the 1986 North American Waterfowl Management Plan (NAWMP). The international conservation plan to protect ducks and habitat from Mexico to Canada relied on Joint Ventures, voluntary regional partnerships that pooled public and private resources to protect waterfowl habitats.

Now there was a visionary plan—but no money. Yet just three years later, President George H. W. Bush quipped that "Christmas came early" as he signed the North American Wetlands Conservation Act (NAWCA) into law to fund the waterfowl management plan and pledged a new policy of "no net loss of wetlands." Once again, the desire to protect habitat for waterfowl and other migratory birds resulted in an extraordinary collaboration between political parties, hunters, scientists, wildlife lovers, and the federal government.

Since 1989, NAWCA grants have been the single largest source of US federal funds for wetland habitat work. While the grants are funded with interest from the Pittman-Robertson account along with fines and forfeitures collected under the Migratory Bird Treaty Act, one of the keys to NAWCA's success is that the act requires that every federal grant dollar be matched by at least one nonfederal dollar. Local support for the wetland habitat projects often results in matches of two to one or even higher. The partner contributions, as they are called, come from nongovernmental organizations like Ducks Unlimited, Ducks Unlimited Canada, Ducks Unlimited de México, The Nature Conservancy, and the National Audubon Society; private foundations; state and provincial fish and wildlife agencies; indigenous peoples; and individuals. To date, $1.9 billion in federal grants has been matched with partner contributions to result in more than $6 billion for conservation.

NAWCA and its ideal of continental collaboration based on ecoregions changed the way conservation is approached and how it is funded. In the thirty-plus years since it was signed, it has also shifted from a purely waterfowl-centric focus to supporting habitats for all the other birds (and creatures) that depend on wetlands. NAWCA isn't just for birds anymore. Wetlands replenish aquifers, filter water, sequester carbon, and reduce the impacts of flooding—all significant benefits for people and communities. In the past three decades, over 6,500 partners have conserved over 31.5 million acres of wetlands and grasslands in every state, province, and territory in North America. That ain't chicken scratch.

Waterfowl populations have slowly rebounded since the 1980s, their numbers steadily climbing over the years (with snow geese becoming overabundant). Today, forest birds, shorebirds, and grassland birds are in a precipitous decline, but once again, waterfowl have proved the exception. In an analysis published in the journal *Science* detailing the gut-wrenching loss of over three billion North American birds since the 1970s, the graphics and tables show, again and again, the one stubborn line that bucks the trend: waterfowl. Instead of loss, there are gains for many web-footed birds. The experts agree that ducks and geese have thrived in large part because of established programs like the Duck Stamp, the extraordinary vision of the continental management plan (NAWMP), and the funding from NAWCA, and especially because of the partnerships and collaborations that reach across political, geographic, and sometimes ideological borders.

In moments I am out of the Turtle Mountains and in the midst of a broad, flat plain. Whitewater Lake Wildlife Management Area, a self-contained alkaline basin and a designated Important Bird and Biodiversity Area (IBA), is out here somewhere. Several biologists and birders told me I should visit because waterfowl flock here during migration as do tundra swans; thousands of Arctic-breeding shorebirds use it as a staging area; and there are nesting Franklin's gulls, eared grebes, and black-crowned night-herons.

Again and again, I get close enough to see the lake but can't seem to reach it. Gravel roads peter out into marshes or end in fields. The directions I have are worthless; there are no signs, nothing that points the way. With gritty eyes and aching back, I slip past a "road closed" sign to follow a track that seems to run straight into the lake.

Standing on the shore of Whitewater Lake, I can't help but wonder why I was so determined to make it here. Remnants of an observation deck dangle from a small asphalt island offshore. The air has the same sticky humidity as the Gulf Coast and the wind whips the waves into dirty brown foam. Franklin's gulls and black terns twist and sail over the shoreline. Pairs of western grebes bob their heads to each other, then preen as the waves toss them around. The drying alkaline crust on the rocks smells caustic and rancid. Spent shotgun shells litter the ground. A few ruddy turnstones flash bold patterns as they flare their wings and squabble on the muddy shoreline. I see no sign of the freshwater cells installed by DU Canada along the edge of the lake. This place has the desolate and shabby feeling of an off-season seaside resort.

I jot down the birds. A fat striped ground squirrel poses for me, then panics when the camera shutter clicks. When I get back in my car, the sudden silence echoes after the relentless onslaught of wind.

As I drive the back roads to the town of Brandon, I see a pair of pheasant hens standing in the rows of a golden-stubbled field looking the way I feel— decidedly confused. A shallow wetland in the center of the field has no cover, no cattails, just a rim of low green plants. A coyote watches from the far side of the water, shifting his gaze from me to the birds. I frame birds, water, and coyote within the straight cultivation lines in my viewfinder. Just as I press the shutter, the pheasants spook, the coyote leaps, and I end up with a photo of tan blurs against an empty brown field.

Perfect, I think, *that sums up the entire day*. Exhausted and grumpy, I know that just because I didn't see masses of waterbirds at the lake doesn't mean they aren't there. And just because it wasn't aesthetically pleasing, that doesn't mean it isn't biologically and ecologically essential. *Buck up*, I tell myself. It is easy to appreciate lovely landscapes filled with wildlife and agree with their importance and need for preservation; it is harder when the place feels onerous to reach, dull and bleak.

Minnedosa Canvasbacks

> During their stay, they are wont to alight on wet prairies and muddy ponds in all open places, feeding on the seeds of various plants.
> —Canvass-back Duck, *Ornithological Biography*, vol. 4

After a night in Brandon, Manitoba, I drive from the Assiniboine River bottom-lands up into the hills around the town of Minnedosa to look for nesting can-vasbacks. In the rolling hills, fields of shorn wheat stubble create mesmerizing patterns that shift and change as I circle small farms and poke along back roads. A giant flying canvasback statue at a highway rest area confirms I'm in the right area. I pass a pond rimmed with dead cattails. Perched on a nest of dead leaves near the middle of the pond, a red-necked grebe bows her head at me. Canada geese graze on tufts of bright green grass in plowed fields shadowed with the dark stains of former wetlands. Every road I drive has pond after pond after pond. Some wetlands are heavily vegetated, others lightly plant rimmed, some medium sized, and many surprisingly small. Each has a pair of elegant canvasbacks with their aristocratic profiles along with blue-winged teal, mallard hens, and others. In a small wetland, surrounded by a wall of brush, mallard drakes, blue-winged teal drakes, and female canvasbacks swim away from me, disappearing down a small creek. Another pond yields a bufflehead drake who is beating his wings and raising a ruckus. I laugh, and canvasbacks, mallards, and blue-winged teal look at me briefly, then ignore both me and the bufflehead. Brilliant American goldfinches flash yellow and black. My list of warblers grows, and I spend ridiculous amounts of time stalking sparrows just because I can. The few people who pass me are plainly curious but simply wave and keep driving. No one asks what a Texan is doing standing on the side of the road with notebook, camera, and binoculars. No one seems to worry that a stranger is lurking at the edge of their

Bufflehead drake

property. I wish, not for the first time, that I had a magnetic sign to slap on the back of my car: CAUTION Birdwatcher—Frequent Stops.

Delta Marsh

> Few Hawks will venture to approach the farmyard while the King Bird
> is near.
> —Tyrant Flycatcher, *Ornithological Biography*, vol. 1

Delta Marsh, where Lake Manitoba seeps into the earth to create the largest freshwater marsh in Canada, is nearly forty-five thousand acres of freshwater wetlands interspersed with prairies and forested upland ridges. Delta Marsh is also the site of the Delta Waterfowl Research Station and where Delta Water-fowl, the Duck Hunters Organization, was founded.

As is usual for this trip, I am the only visitor. I park next to the recycling bins taking up most of the parking lot and wander down the "Taking Flight" interpretive trail.

The Delta Waterfowl Station was a wealthy American's dream. First, James Ford Bell, founder of General Mills, bought land and built a hunting lodge. Then, following one of the popular ideas of the day, he built a hatchery to hatch duck eggs pilfered from wild nests. The plan was to repopulate the skies with captive-raised and released waterfowl. Later he invested his money and vision into the wildlife management ideas of Aldo Leopold, consequently founding the research station that he deeded to Delta Waterfowl. Young men and women put the writings and theories of wildlife management into practice, studying waterfowl in the wild and working in the marshes.

The boardwalk stops next to the Delta Decoy, a replica funnel trap patterned after European waterfowl traps that use the birds' innate curiosity against them. It seems that if you wave a white kerchief—or wag a fluffy tail—above the grass, ducks just can't help themselves. Audubon wrote about tolling: "The nearest ducks soon notice the strange appearance, raise their heads, gaze intently for a moment, and then push for the shore, followed by the rest. On many occasions, I have seen thousands of them swimming in a solid mass direct to the object." The research station used a tolling dog to lure the ducks down the tunnels of the traps and into holding pens where they would be weighed, measured, and banded.

The research station is shuttered now, closed since a damaging 2011 flood. The marsh no longer brings in waterfowl in the spectacular numbers it once did. During its heyday, the rich and famous flocked to take part in the fall staging of millions of ducks and geese. Photos of all-white, all-male hunters include a youthful Clark Gable, a testament to just how long ago it was. A placard covered with long white streaks details the demise: dams and invasive species are the culprits in this degradation. Delta Marsh was once rich with sago pondweed, a tuber beloved by canvasbacks, as well as a rich assortment of other wetland plants and invertebrates. Since 1961, Lake Manitoba's dam-controlled constant level has suppressed duck-preferred plants and invertebrates. Invasive carp root up the remaining sago pondweed, relentlessly mucking up the water until nothing can grow in the cloudy depths.

The sun blazes down. My canteen is in the car and thirst converts to despair like a mouthful of ash. The millions of birds gone, the habitat destroyed, and the beauty and vitality lost crowd onto my shoulders until I sag onto a bench. Resentment coats my throat with acidic reflux. Who is to blame? Progress? The anonymous mass of people all striving for a better life? I put my head in my hands and give up, feeling like I'm being pulled earthward, down into the shadowed primordial muck of my own heart.

Bitterness coagulates into an exhaustion so complete I'm ready to slump onto the boardwalk and sleep. The sun is heavy on my back. An insistent murmuring, snapping, and crackling intrudes. It is the voice of the marsh and of

Eastern kingbird

cattails heating up in the sun. Somewhere a common yellowthroat throws its song skyward, a bright ribbon of sound that winds through the stems. A bird flies close enough that I can hear air against its feathered vanes. I look up. An eastern kingbird darts past me, pulls up at a nearby cattail, and glares at me. A duller version of the tidy tuxedoed bird overshoots his cattail perch and flaps frantically to stay upright. I look around. White streaks run from the railing, down the bench, and to the seat. Another adult flutters nearby, as if uncertain where to go. I stand and relinquish my seat. Almost immediately, five birds congregate on the rail. A tyranny of kingbirds that nudge me, push me out of their way.

A pair of Canada geese accompany their yellow gosling trio in lazy circles around the station pond. A henhouse, a hay-lined tube of fencing wire, is stuck on a post in the water. It is designed to keep a nesting duck hen, eggs, and ducklings out of reach of predators, and the survival percentages I read for ducklings in natural nests versus henhouses make it clear that predators love to eat ducklings. According to Delta Waterfowl's research, the henhouses greatly increase duckling survival. I've seen a number of these odd structures across the prairies, but nowhere near enough for all the duck hens.

I think back to the raccoon Jim shot, the untold numbers of turtle eggs eaten and the birds' nests raided by the wily and engaging creatures. But taking on the responsibility of top predator and managing all the other predators—well, it never ends, does it? As soon as one raccoon is trapped and killed, doesn't another raccoon, skunk, coyote, or red fox just take its place? We've disrupted the balance by building dams, introducing carp, draining wetlands, and fragmenting habitat; putting our finger on the scales by adding hen tunnels and killing predators makes a sort of hubris-saturated sense. We broke it; we'll fix it.

I remember Jim's emphatic statement: "Delta Waterfowl is the Duck Hunters Organization. I'm a member of Delta because they are all about hunting. All Ducks Unlimited cares about is habitat."

Delta Marsh is more than Delta Waterfowl and hunting, I remind myself. It is tens of thousands of acres of protected land—marshes and prairies set aside as Wildlife Management Areas (WMAs) by the Crown for ducks, birds, and other creatures.

The next morning, I return to drive down long, straight gravel roads across the marsh's platter-flat land punctuated with ponds, prairies, and cropland to look at the WMAs. At times the land south of Lake Manitoba seems more water than land. A pair of northern shovelers in a roadside pond bring me to a halt. The drake is nearly gaudy with emerald head, brilliant yellow eye, snowy chest, mahogany flanks, and a comically large black bill. The pair swim and strain food from the water. I nearly step on a nesting killdeer as I get out of the car. I freeze, slowly lower myself back into the seat, then drive down the road a dozen yards. The bird never moves, never cries, never wing drags to lure me away, and never flies. Yellow-headed blackbirds shriek and sway on cattails. A single striped garter snake eases out onto the road, then arrows across the gravel. A smaller snake follows. Suddenly I see them everywhere. White pelicans with flat horns protruding from their yellow and orange bills drift across a larger pond. It is beautiful, I'm fifteen hundred miles from home, and suddenly this summer land rippling with breezes and water feels astonishingly familiar. It feels like home, the way that the Texas Gulf Coast clicks into some part of my psyche and makes me never want to leave. On every trip to the Gulf Coast I convince myself, for a time, that I could spend all my days thinking about nothing but birds and fish and sun.

This must be what the Gulf Coast prairies were like before the freshwater wetlands were drained. A long, low land with tallgrass prairies and scattered oak woodlands. But there is another connection to Texas. Every year the Texas Parks and Wildlife Department (TPWD) sends money to Canada for nesting duck habitat. I don't know why it surprised me when I learned about it. The money comes from the Texas Migratory Game Bird Endorsement (required to hunt any migratory game bird and in addition to the federal Duck Stamp). Every dollar the TPWD sends north is matched once by Ducks Unlimited, and then those dollars are matched again by NAWCA grants. It's a nifty trick, turning one dollar into four. Factor in a favorable exchange rate and the total adds up. In 2021, forty-three state fish and wildlife agencies contributed $5.2 million. After matching by DU (with help from Delta Waterfowl and the Manitoba Habitat Heritage Corporation) and a bit of NAWCA magic, the result is US$21 million ($27.4 million Canadian) for protecting breeding habitat. Over the years, contributions from state fish and wildlife agencies from across the United States have resulted in more than $100 million to help conserve over 6.5 million acres of wetland habitat across Canada. These massive dollar amounts are heartening. Surely it is enough to save this vital land?

A trio of garter snakes rocket across the road in front of me, moving so fast that they seem to flicker like an old film. Impulsively I turn my car northward and head toward the Narcisse Snake Dens.

Google Maps lies about how long the drive is and I don't arrive until noon. The morning cool is long gone and it feels too hot for anything to be out but insects. Yet when I stop to drink water in the shade of a wooded trail, I hear a rustling. It is a sound I know, a noise that makes me pause and search for a creature no matter where I am in the world: the susurration of leaves against scaly bodies. The woodland floor stirs as if a breeze were moving through the trees, but the air is still as red-sided garter snakes glide away from the dens. At one of the pits, I lean over a guard rail and look down at the entrances to the winter dens in the labyrinthian bedrock limestone. Hundreds of the garter snakes writhe in the pits as males seek out the robust females, creating knots and tangled skeins. Even as a stray breeze rustles through the trees, I can hear the rasp of scales against stone. Other visitors stare into the pits, exclaim at the serpents, and then walk away, oblivious to the thousands of snakes dispersing through the woods and back to their summer homes in the surrounding marshes and lakeshores.

Oak Hammock Marsh

> They used only the bill, tossing the garbage from side to side, with a dexterity extremely pleasant to behold. In this manner, I saw these four Turnstones examine almost every part of the shore; after which I drove them away, that our hunters might not kill them on their return.
> —Turnstone, *Ornithological Biography*, vol. 4

I turn south, determined to reach Oak Hammock Marsh Wildlife Management Area, home to Ducks Unlimited Canada's national office and the Harry J. Enns Wetland Discovery Centre. I arrive just before closing and run in to see the educational exhibits before the doors are locked. I stand at a display, the worn edges and lightly chipped paint at kid level attesting to its use. This is no formal, cold museum but an inviting place designed for exploring, using all the senses, questioning, and learning. From history to hunting to the environmental benefits of wetlands, it is all here.

I want a center like this in Texas, I think. I know the perfect place for it, on Interstate 10, west of Houston and just outside Eagle Lake in the rice prairies. I daydream for a moment about an international wetlands center to pull unsuspecting tourists off the interstate into a world of history and futures; about hunting and habitat, birding and conservation, water and wildlife.

I spend the remaining daylight hours wandering the trails along the dikes that re-create a long-lost marsh. My ears ring with squawking, trilling, calling, and singing. Elegant marbled godwits in breeding plumage feed on a mudflat. Dunlins, American golden-plovers, and black-bellied plovers surround a mallard drake so self-satisfied, so gleaming, iridescent, snowy white, and chocolate brown that he hardly looks real. He lets out a rasping quack that sends the shorebirds skittering away.

I stand on an observation mound surveying the surrounding marsh that runs in streaks of gold and blue until it butts against feathery willow bluffs and the brown and green of fields and pastures. The sense of connection I feel between these northern wetlands and prairies and the Texas Gulf Coast is not imagined. They are parts of a whole. While nations and their laws stop at borders, the only allegiance birds hold is to habitat.

In 1937, the same year that the Pittman-Robertson Act passed Congress, a group of conservation-minded waterfowl hunters recognized that protecting land and restoring habitat in the States alone was not enough to save ducks from disaster. Even with the protections of the Migratory Bird Treaty and the hunting season regulations set by the Migratory Bird Treaty Act, ducks were still under fire. With over 70 percent of North America's waterfowl nesting in Canada, conservation had to cross borders. Under the name Ducks Unlimited, fund-raising began for habitat projects in the Prairie Pothole Region in both the United States and Canada. Ducks Unlimited Canada (DUC) formed the next year (with Ducks Unlimited de México, DUMAC, organizing in 1974). Today DUC is a substantial

Mallard drake with plovers and marbled godwit

organization with more than one hundred thousand supporters, but waterfowl conservation is still an intracontinental affair. Ducks Unlimited sends fund-raising dollars to both Canada and Mexico. With help from its international partnership and collaboration with a wide range of governmental and private partners, DUC has conserved 6.5 million acres, of which 3.4 million were restored to wetlands (like the one I'm wandering through), prairies, and forests. In addition to sequestering an estimated 48.5 million tons of carbon dioxide, DUC estimates that for every dollar invested in conservation, restoration, and wetland management, society receives twenty-two dollars' worth of economic, ecological, and societal well-being benefits. And that is something that you can, as they say, take from "the bulrushes to the bank."[17]

Ducks Unlimited organizations from Canada, the United States, and Mexico recently banded together to create a new International Conservation Plan. The plan prioritizes landscapes across North America, identifying which areas will yield the highest biological returns and generate the greatest positive impact on waterfowl. Ducks Unlimited, once again, is planning for the biggest bang for the duck buck.

Along the trail, tree swallows swoop past me to nesting boxes, their iridescent turquoise feathers surreal amid last season's tawny cattails and grasses. Red-winged and yellow-headed blackbirds shriek and trill. A common yellowthroat throws cascading notes over me as it flies up into the sky, then plummets back into the cattails and bulrushes. I walk the trails until the sun sets over the marsh and I'm forced to stumble to my car in the fading light.

As I drive south, I realize I haven't seen a single duckling. Consolation goslings, but not a duckling one.

North Dakota
Setting the Table

> At the foot of some tuft of tall strong grass you find the nest.
> —Meadow Lark or American Starling, *Ornithological Biography*, vol. 2

Bill and I stand on a windswept hill on Ducks Unlimited's Coteau Ranch with biologist Randy Renner. The Missouri Coteau, the watery heart of the Prairie Pothole Region, ripples around us. Blue sky arcs overhead while clouds the color of bruises rumble on the western horizon. Licks of cool air and the sweet zing of ozone waft past. Randy is younger than Bill and me, with a laid-back manner that puts us at ease. He doesn't make grand gestures; his hands don't fly around when he talks, but his words sweep over the landscape. He says, "Coteau means hill or hillside. This landscape was formed by the glaciers that covered the upper part of North America." The hummocks and swales aren't the result of erosion—the potholes are not remnant stream beds or oxbows—but the footprint of the last glacier that stalled on the Missouri escarpment. The ice slowly melted in irregular patterns beneath a mantle of sediment to produce the Prairie Pothole Region's characteristic topography of wetlands irregularly dotted between gently swelling and rolling land.

There is no rhyme or reason that I can make of the landscape. Without the dendritic patterns of erosion to define up from down, I feel a little light-headed.

"Any chance we'll see ducklings?" I ask. Randy laughs. "Usually this would be the time to see them, but we had a late snowstorm this spring that put everything back a couple weeks." My heart sinks a little. It is stupid but I really wanted to see ducklings, puffball evidence of conservation at work.

Under Randy's tutelage, the small wetlands scattered before us shimmer with life and possibility. On my journey I have ignored the shallowest potholes,

Western meadowlark

always looking for substantial ponds. More water, I thought, equaled more ducks.

Nope. We learn that the ephemeral or seasonal wetlands drying up isn't a problem—indeed, it is much of the reason that ducks flock here in spring. As snowmelt and spring rains soak into the shallow basins, invertebrates resurge to life: snails, amphipods, midge and mosquito larvae, mayfly and dragonfly nymphs, beetles, and small crustaceans. Creatures rich in protein and calcium, packed with the nutrients duck hens and female shorebirds need for producing a clutch of eggs. Calorie-dense food is essential for putting on fat for the long days of incubating until eggs hatch. Wetland plants sprout from seeds that have lain dormant, waiting for the right conditions to germinate into plants that ducks eat, plants that produce seeds for noshing on, and plants that insects need as the first links in spiraling food cycles. Randy reminds me that ducks become territorial during nesting season, and ten one-acre ponds are better for nesting pairs than one ten-acre pond. Small potholes that look no more substantial than a parking lot puddle each have a pair or two of ducks. Bachelor mallards are the only large congregations at this time of year. We pass a group that looks like a gang of bored teenagers halfheartedly picking on each other.

Randy gives the blue-black clouds on the horizon a measured look, then turns back to me. "When you are used to seeing birds all ganged up for migration or in overwintering flocks," he says, "it doesn't look like there are many. But there are a lot of birds spread out here—over half the ducks in the states nest in the US part of the PPR."

When he tells me that in some parts of the PPR, there are so many ponds that there can be fifty pairs of nesting birds per square kilometer, I suddenly imagine the skies raining ducks. Mallards, northern pintails, canvasbacks, redheads, gadwalls, blue-winged teal, northern shovelers, ruddy ducks, and buffleheads pattering in a steady downpour across the prairie and dispersing two by two into the ponds and grasses.

I'm trying to scribble notes as Randy gives me the basics of duck biology in the PPR, but the yellow-headed blackbirds, sparrows, and dickcissels keep getting in the way. A chestnut-collared longspur completely derails the conversation while Bill and I track it through the grass. I'm sketching a yellow-headed blackbird swaying on a bowed cattail and Bill is photographing a butterfly when I hear Randy say something about cattails choking out wetlands. "Cattails?" I ask.

Cattails, that ubiquitous symbol of wetlands, a problem? I'd spent much of my trip up the Great Plains looking for cattails as vertical signposts of wetlands in the sweep of grasslands and fields. I learn that the same hybridized cattails that cause problems in the Cheyenne Bottoms in Kansas are troublesome here as well. With tiny windblown seeds that can also travel stuck to the feet and legs of birds, narrow-leaved cattails have spread across the Great Plains from their native northeastern corner of North America all the way from the Cheyenne Bottoms up through the PPR. But it isn't the endemic cattail or the uninvited narrow-leaved cattail that is the problem; it is the hybrid offspring that refuses to leave home, sprawling and taking over the living space, carelessly discarding last year's strappy leaves, clogging small wetlands, and absorbing water and nutrients.

Bill and I follow Randy like goslings, hanging on to his every word yet continually distracted by birds, flowers, and butterflies, bumping into each other and nearly mowing Randy down whenever he pauses. He herds us to an ATV to take us out onto the prairie. I hold on as we jolt across the grasslands. He calls out the names of ducks, songbirds, and shorebirds as he sees them—or hears them. A flock of least sandpipers wings past us. He stops the ATV when he hears a western meadowlark. "We don't see so many anymore. I miss them." We listen and look. The bird finally turns on its shrub perch, flashing yellow so it is impossible to miss. "Preserving the uplands is good for the ducks, grassland birds like meadowlarks, native pollinators, and butterflies," Randy tells us. He nods at the plains rising up before us. "Before settlement there were elk, deer, bison, antelope, and plains grizzlies. It was the Serengeti of North America." And with those words, a lifetime of unrecognized bias is exposed. Why do I think of the plains as hostile and lifeless? Just because I'm a total wuss when it comes to the cold? Because I can't imagine anyone choosing to live here? Am I so timid that I can't imagine life without a tree canopy? Like so many nature buffs and birdwatchers, I've dreamed of visiting the Serengeti Plain of Africa with its herds of wildlife and unique creatures. Now I learn we had the same abundance and we've nearly lost it all.

"The Great Plains is the most altered ecosystem in the world." He says matter-of-factly.

The numbers are brutal. The acres of prairies plowed and wetlands drained mean little because the numbers are so large that they become unreliable, unrelatable. How many acres of prairies plowed and converted to cropland translates to—what? City blocks? How far I can drive on an interstate at seventy-plus miles per hour? The island of Manhattan? Dallas Fort Worth Airport times fifty? Times a thousand? It is impossible to comprehend on a personal scale. The numbers pummel me until I feel bruised and bloody. I've never felt data as a physical onslaught before.

Grasslands in the Great Plains have been steadily plowed under since the European settlers first started arriving en masse in the 1800s. Every year, millions of acres of native prairies are converted to cropland. The land has been plowed black, with grasses and herbs torn up and turned under until there is no sign of the former prairie, only soil exposed to the sun and wind. In the ten years from 2009 to 2019, over 98 million acres were plowed black. The numbers go up and down a bit because some plowed acres are returned to grassland and a few hardy souls attempt to restore prairie to its original diversity. Yet less than 1 percent of the tallgrass prairie that ran from Manitoba to southeastern Texas remains. Three-quarters of the mixed-grass prairie's 140 million acres, which include the Missouri Coteau, have been plowed and converted to croplands.[18]

More than 80,000 acres of wetlands are lost nationwide every year, with 16.8 million acres drained since the 1950s and more than 2 million acres just since 1986. In regions of the PPR, at least 50 percent and up to 90 percent of the potholes are gone or seriously degraded.

"You know about Swampbuster?" Randy asks. I shake my head. I've heard of it, but Bill doesn't know about it. Randy explains to us that while Ducks Unlimited and other groups were trying to protect the wetlands for ducks and the USFWS was buying wetlands for WPAs and refuges, the government was subsidizing the draining of wetlands for farmers. It wasn't until the 1985 Food Security Act (better known as the Farm Bill), with the Swampbuster provision, that the government stopped paying for the tiling and ditch drainage of wetlands.

There was an immediate effect. In the ten years between 1986 and 1997, loss of wetlands plummeted 80 percent per year from the astronomical rates of the previous decade. The latest reports actually show a small gain in wetlands. Good news until you realize that commercial fishponds and cattle tanks are now considered wetlands. While created stock tanks can keep cattle watered and out of emergent wetlands (particularly in the PPR), I can't help but think that a muddy-margined pond in a Texas cattle pasture is a long way from a native wetland.

"When biologists first started waterfowl management in the 1930s," Randy tells us, "we used to just manage the wetlands. The goal was to drought-proof the prairies by preserving the wetlands."

The 1930s were the era of big conservation. By the time the Great Depression and a massive drought steamrollered the country, leaders such as Aldo Leopold, Jay "Ding" Darling, FDR, and countless other hunters, ornithologists, and politicians recognized a public responsibility for the wildlife held in trust for the American public. There was a shift toward active wildlife management by trained professionals based in science and research. In the first flush of funding during the New Deal, the US Biological Survey (predecessor of the USFWS) focused on the Prairie Pothole Region, buying up thousands of acres of river corridors, shallow lakes, and pothole-riven prairies. A few years later, with funding now secured by Duck Stamp dollars, Pittman-Robertson Funds, and state hunting license revenues, wildlife managers got to work saving habitat and species. Protected by hunting seasons and bag limits, waterfowl species began to flourish. Success after success rolled in as land and waters were protected. For nearly fifty years the paradigm held, but an extended drought caused waterfowl numbers to plummet. The ducks began disappearing. Again.

The drought from the late 1970s to 1980s proved that preserving just the wetlands wasn't enough. Randy waves at the rippling prairie. "All the ducks that nest in the uplands, their populations took a nose dive. Pintails were hit really hard." The initial reaction, he tells us, was to put money into intensively managing habitat for ducks. Hen tunnels and predator fences were installed to protect nesting hens, specialized seed mixes for nesting cover were planted, and annual surveys tracked the falling numbers of ducks across the continent.

"What about predator management?" I ask. "I know they do a lot in South Dakota and when I visited Delta Marsh in Manitoba, Delta Waterfowl had displays that made it sound like it is the only way to save ducks."

Randy all but rolls his eyes, but he is too professional to trash-talk another conservation organization. He tells me that in the short term, predator management can make a big difference in nesting success and reducing hen mortality. A hen spends twenty vulnerable days on the nest. But as with predator fences, nesting cover, and other costly and labor-intensive management techniques, time has proved that predator management is nearly impossible to sustain on a landscape-wide scale. Once you take responsibility for one cog in the machine, you have to juggle all the other parts too. He shakes his head. "And there is always something that wants to eat duck eggs. And ducklings."

Randy cuts his eyes at me. Am I one of those tenderhearted women who will become indignant at the idea of darling ducklings gobbled by a raccoon or coyote?

"Everybody likes duck eggs," he continues. "Coyotes, badgers, raccoon, skunks, and fox. Red foxes are really good at finding nests." I flinch a little. The day before, Bill and I had been charmed by a trio of fluffy red fox kits. They romped on a roadside boulder while we snapped dozens of photos.

Randy explains that the current idea is to pay attention to the landscape as a whole and "set the table." The goal is to preserve the best habitat possible, habitat

Mallard hen on nest and red fox kit

like the PPR here and in Canada. If we can preserve, restore, and manage healthy wetlands and upland habitats, the ducks—and other birds, butterflies, plants, and pollinators—will be able to survive droughts and other climate variables.

If anyone can save the region, it is Ducks Unlimited. It is a powerhouse of an organization. With 653,000 members, DU's 2020 annual revenue (membership, gifts, donated conservation easements, and federal and state habitat support) surpassed $230 million. Of that money, 83 percent went directly to fund conservation programs.

In 2012, it started the Rescue Our Wetlands campaign. Its members dug deep into their own pockets and raised $2.34 *billion* in seven years. According to its annual report, that campaign alone has conserved 2.2 million acres of the more than 15 million acres that DU reports as conserved and restored. I feel a surge of pride that I'm a member. I am helping to protect this land, I think. With my Duck Stamp, hunting license, and gun and ammo purchases, I'm part of the solution.

I'm scribbling away while Bill snaps photo after photo of the murmuring prairie and cloud-filled sky. Randy continues, "The issue is that a full ninety percent of waterfowl in the US nest on private property." My pen drags to a stop. My pride fizzles into panic.

I have heard it before. This time it hits me. We are in trouble. The federal government cannot possibly buy up all the habitat required for healthy migratory bird populations—not even a landscape as important as the Prairie Pothole Region. No matter how many Duck Stamps are sold. Nor can DU, regardless of

how astonishingly robust its member support has proved to be, buy up the large, contiguous tracts needed. No single entity, not Audubon, The Nature Conservancy, or any other nonprofit, has the resources to purchase and manage habitat on such a scale.

"Conservation easements are the tool of the day. And of the future," Randy pronounces. I stand with pen poised. He's looking a little tired but soldiers on with the lesson. Ducks Unlimited works with the USFWS to set up grassland and wetland easements with willing landowners. He makes it clear that this is no land grab by the government. It is a willing exchange in which the property owner receives a cash payment for a percentage of the going land value for the grassland or wetland acreage.[19] In turn, the owner agrees to three things: never plow the prairie, never fill or drain the wetlands, and never cut hay until after July 15, when the birds have finished nesting. DU acts as the matchmaker between the landowners and the USFWS, who hold the easements in perpetuity.

We end our day walking up to the DU Prairie Program dedication site on a hilltop overlooking the Coteau Ranch's 3,700 acres and the neighboring 8,000 acres of The Nature Conservancy's Davis Ranch. There is an attractive sculpture of burnished duck silhouettes on a frame of steel cattails. Donors' names are inscribed on the ducks in flight. Randy is giving me the history of the ranch, pointing out the donors who bought parts of the ranch for DU.

"How do you get along with The Nature Conservancy as a neighbor?" I ask.

"Our goals are pretty similar," he replies.

"What about hunting?" I'm thinking about my experiences with the Texas Nature Conservancy. Its preserves are not open to the public except for a few days a year, and I can't imagine that it would allow hunting. In fact, years ago I'd been visiting a TNC property on the Gulf Coast when a professional hunter was scheduled to cull feral hogs. The staff panicked when they realized I was a writer and begged me not to say anything—if donors knew they were shooting animals, even destructive feral hogs, they said, the public backlash would be severe.

Randy replies that The Nature Conservancy allows hunting on all its North Dakota properties. I'm stunned. He looks at my expression, grins, and tells me that because of state laws, conservation groups in North Dakota work together closely, both because of shared goals and out of necessity.

North Dakota has the most restrictive laws in the nation regarding conservation. Conservation land sales aren't simply a matter of willing seller and willing buyer. The proposed sales require public hearings and approval by an advisory committee, and ultimately the governor needs to sign off on each sale. No matter the size of the acreage. No matter the uniqueness or importance of the property for wildlife. No matter what the seller wants. Conservation easements in North Dakota are restricted to ninety-nine years. Because federal law supersedes state law, easements signed with the USFWS are permanent.

Gusts of wind swirl around us, smelling of rain and petrichor. The storm rumbles blue-black against viridian hills and the archipelago of silvery wetlands. In the distance curtains of rain fall, tearing the clouds' smooth bellies into ragged lines. The storm is only a fraction of the sky but Randy suddenly tells us it is time to leave. He all but jogs down the hill, looking over his shoulder at the coming storm.

As we are leaving, I ask what he wants people to know. He pauses, considering my question.

"Ducks need more than the wetlands," he says. "They need the uplands for nesting." He goes on to remind me that duck reproductive strategies require at least 15 percent of hens to nest successfully to maintain the population. Fragmentation of habitat is as much an issue here as anywhere in the world. Even though many ducks can and will happily nest in crops, hayfields, and even ditches along roadways, the fragmented habitat poses a real danger for ducks and other grassland-nesting birds because of predators. "The gold standard," as Randy calls it, is a mosaic of wetlands and prairies. But it is clear that from a duck standpoint, wetlands are the most important factor in survival. If we lose the wetlands, we lose the ducks. But as we learned in the 1980s, without the prairie, the ecosystem has no resilience, no ability to adapt and reframe during drought or other crisis.

As we drive away from the ranch and toward Bismarck, the fields look like lace. Even the no-till squares and rectangles reveal the dark soil in concentric patterns. The patches expand until the whorls and lines of cultivation drape over the rolling hills. The Coteau Ranch, for all its pristine beauty, and The Nature Conservancy's Davis Ranch next door—one of the largest remaining tracts of native prairie in the US Prairie Pothole Region—are small, jagged rectangles in a vast ocean of private lands.

Prairie Smoke

> The earth was warm under me, and warm as I crumbled it through my fingers. I kept as still as I could. Nothing happened. I did not expect anything to happen. I was something that lay under the sun and felt it, like the pumpkins, and I did not want to be anything more.
> —*My Ántonia*, Willa Cather

> How strange it is, Reader, that birds of this species should be found breeding in the Fur Countries, at about the same period when they are to be found on the waters of the inland bays of the Mexican Gulf!
> —White Pelican, *Ornithological Biography*, vol. 4

Bill and I duck through a wire fence on one side of a gravel lane. Small wetlands glint in the distance as we walk through thick grass and plants on a federal Waterfowl Production Area near the Chase Lake NWR. The land looks lush, and intensely sweet blooming silverberry perfumes the air. Then we cross the road, bend our bodies to fit through the wire strands, and climb the opposite hill. Standing beside a boulder I run my hands over its cool surface, the coarse stone buffed to a glassy smoothness by the rough heads of bison rubbing and scratching. Neil Shook, USFWS manager, says, "Listen." We pause, standing like pioneers at the crest of a hill, overlooking an ocean of prairie. The rustling, clicking, chattering of a thousand creatures simmers around us, rising up and drenching us in a rolling boil of life. It is the contrast that is stunning. The winnowing of a snipe slips past us. Birdsong threads melodies through the wind. Wildflowers, the sentinels of prairie diversity, lace the air with splashes of color and wisps of fragrance. We are no more than two hundred feet away from where we'd stood fifteen minutes before. And yet this land sends a shock through me, an electric current that runs up my spine and burns through me like joy. For a second, I am a husk, ready to blow away and shatter. All that is real about me drains into the earth and I am as fundamental as the snipe, meadowlarks, and the red buds of prairie smoke flowers.

The rolling hills seem as immense as monuments, no longer static land-forms but rippling life in towering waves that are set to crash over us at any minute. This immense haunting beauty of the rolling Missouri Coteau is so much grander—and yet more primal—than any other landscape I've experienced. It is not as majestic as the Rocky Mountains, or as mysterious as the cypress swamps and bayous. Although the land ripples away like ocean, it is not as unyielding as the Gulf of Mexico and definitely not as familiar as the cattle pastures of central Texas. Yet somehow it is all these things and more.

Neil pulls me back into the world. "This section is leased for grazing." I look down and notice dried cow patties among the grasses and wildflowers.

With rolling grasslands extending in every direction from our hilltop vantage, Neil Shook tells us, "This prairie is vanishing." We look at him askance, trusting our eyes over his words.

But I can recognize a man (or woman) with a mission. I've watched my step-father endlessly repeat his account of restoring his ranch in the Texas Hill Country. It is a story with a beautiful arc that starts with debilitated, overgrazed land and, through hard work, ingenuity, and nature's resilience, results in meadows of native grasses, flowing springs, abundant wildlife, and robust livestock. He has inspired untold numbers of people to look beyond what they see before them—impoverished soils and abundant cedar (Ashe juniper) trees—and imagine what was and what could be again.

But here, it isn't a matter of restoring land to a previous abundance; it is preserving what we have before it is lost. Neil Shook is a crusader with a simple plea: Save the Prairies.

I don't know how much of our time with Neil is scripted, or how many others he has honed his words on. It doesn't matter because he is smart enough to let the prairie speak to us. The land tells us all we need to know and Bill and I are converts long before we know the how or the why.

Then Neil takes us to the people who know this land the best. The men and women who hold the future in their hands because Duck Stamp dollars can't buy up all the wetlands and The Nature Conservancy can't buy up all the prairie: farmers and ranchers.

As we drive, Neil waves his hand toward the rolling prairie and tells us that for decades conservation professionals operated under a false assumption. The

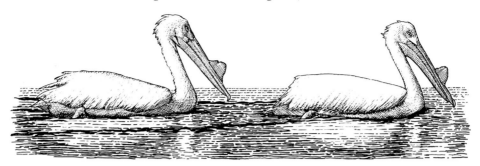

White pelicans

thinking was, he said, that as long as we had land—refuges and WPAs and ease-ments—set aside for conservation, things would be okay. But in 2012, a perfect storm of expiring Conservation Reserve Program[20] contracts, plus GMO[21] crop advances for Roundup Ready crops, record commodity prices for corn and soy-beans, renewable fuel standards (ethanol), rising land prices, and longer grow-ing seasons prompted a massive change up and down the Great Plains as prairie grasslands and wetlands were converted to cropland. Neil's jaw clenches as he works to get the words out. "It was a real eye-opener for the conservation groups and conservation-minded people. Over one hundred sixty thousand acres of native and planted grasslands right around Chase Lake were plowed and con-verted to crops." In the five years from 2006 to 2011, over 1.3 million acres of grass were converted in the Prairie Pothole Region. Overall, 43 million acres of grasslands in the northern Great Plains have been plowed under, with more than 22 million in the last ten years alone. It is a smothering weight.

Once again, I am confronted with the simple fact that the majority of land we need for both conservation and agriculture is held in private hands.

Neil reminds me that these are not our enemies; they are people who have to make a living. It all comes down to profit. He tells us that in 2012, local farm-ers looked at the commodity prices and realized, "I can plow up this grass and make money on corn." Or, "I can afford to run drain lines and ditches to dry up those wetlands and plant soy."

We drive through a gate and up to a collection of barns, sheds, silos, and pens. Bawling cattle churn up clouds of dust as a woman, two younger women (who must be her daughters), and an older man yell and sort the cattle. A slen-der girl who looks like she is all of twelve pulls up in a truck with a huge livestock trailer and jumps out. Off to the side, a Chevrolet Trailblazer sports a custom license plate: LV2RANCH.

Brent Kuss is a tall, rangy man wearing rubber boots and a hoodie. Except for a few graying whiskers, he could be in his twenties. He speaks directly, honestly, and rapidly. I struggle to keep up as a flood of history, family, work, and the future pours out of him.

"We crop, run cattle, and run sheep." He pauses, laughs, and tells me that sheep, or range maggots, control the brush and weeds. Cattle eat the grass. They run cattle on land that is marginal for crops and plant crops on the best soil. They have converted to no-till cultivation and use it whenever possible.

He tells me that everything they do is to make the place better. He leans forward and watches as I write down his words. His philosophy is simple: he has to leave the ranch for his daughters in better shape than it was when he started.

He points to the corrals and tells me that there are three generations working the ranch. One of his daughters flashes a smile at us. His wife, Cody, frowns at him but smiles and waves at us as she pushes cattle around. He continues, telling me that ideas about ranching and farming keep changing, and, as he puts it, the goals keep moving. He illustrates with an anecdote. When his father-in-law returned from the war in Vietnam, he took out all the property's cross fencing because bigger pastures with continuous grazing were the trend. Now Brent has installed cross fences so they can intensively graze and rotate pastures to avoid overgrazing. Brent glances over his shoulder as if his father-in-law were standing there. He laughs and shakes his head. "My father-in-law looked at the new fences and remarked that they were just about exactly where he'd pulled out the old fences."

Brent continues, telling me that resistance to change is natural; people want to stick with what worked for them in the past. On the farm they use no-till cultivation, but his father-in-law plowed fields black, turning the soil until there was no trace of the sod or previous crop. He knows his daughters will force him into new ideas and new ways of doing things.

"We'd all love to live in Happy Land," he says with a wry grin, "but North Dakota is a tough place." He goes on to describe droughts, fires, and floods. He tells me that you can either be positive, for instance regarding lightning-set prairie fires as a positive management tool, or fight against nature. Brent tells me that he and his family are always looking for ways to make marginal land more productive and healthier.

Brent looks over at Neil, who is studying his boot tips. He then turns back to me to say that they are grazing their cattle on national wildlife refuge land. While they were ambivalent at first, Brent says that once the family put their cattle out on the refuge, they were impressed. They could see the change in plants and diversity almost immediately. The refuge was improved and they benefited with quality forage for their cattle.

Brent goes on to explain that he has known the past managers of Chase Lake

NWR and each had different styles and agendas, but Neil is the first to allow haying and grazing on refuge lands. "Neil is interested in helping the prairie and the ranchers." Neil paws the ground and gives an aw-shucks kind of response. He and Brent spend a moment complimenting each other's vision and dedication. Bill wanders away. I clear my throat.

Brent turns back to me. "Everything is all about time and efficiency or inefficiency." They farm the best land, hay or graze the marginal land. Put wetlands in easements. To his surprise, the number of bushels produced in the row crops has stayed similar, but they now have more good grazing land.

Brent's wife, Cody, shouts out a question. While he's been talking to us, his wife, daughters, and father-in-law have continued to work. He bids us goodbye and calls over his shoulder as he heads to the corral, "You have to have livestock, though. Without cattle and sheep, we couldn't do what we do. Or keep the grasslands."

As we drive away, I ask about grazing.

"The prairies need to be grazed," Neil tells us. The northern Great Plains ecosystem developed under particular stresses: herds of grazing bison, browsing deer and pronghorn, frequent natural wildfires, ripping winds, and droughts. The native prairie has extraordinary resilience when it is stressed by natural cycles. Not only would bison herds graze and crop the grasses, but their hooves would cut into the ground, opening channels for water to be absorbed. Woody brush would be burned out by wildfires while grasses and plants would resurge in a burned area. Because the native prairie is famously one-third aboveground and two-thirds an extensive root system, even in extreme droughts the soil holds in place. But without grazing or fires, woody shrubs take over the grasslands. The number and variety of plants diminish, and with them the insects, birds, and mammals.

Neil pulls the truck off the road and kills the engine. We've reached the next stop on the prairie tour, Chase Lake Pass in the center of Chase Lake National Wildlife Refuge.

From our vantage point, the 2,000-acre alkaline lake spreads out before us. The white pelican rookery is a pale smudge on the far side. Through my binoculars, the blur refuses to segregate into individual birds. Neil tells me that there are over thirty thousand pelicans, ten thousand gulls, several thousand herons and egrets, and lots of cormorants nesting down there. It is the largest breeding colony of white pelicans in the United States. It is a little surreal to think of white pelicans, a bird I intimately associate with the Gulf Coast, up here in the middle of the Great Plains on an alkaline lake. Why are they here?

Neil points out old pit blinds built by market hunters. The nearby town of Woodworth was a mecca for hunting, he tells us. Grouse, prairie-chickens, waterfowl, upland game, and of course pelicans. "People ate pelicans?" Bill asks. I look away and let Neil answer as I think of Audubon's opinion: "Its flesh is rank, fishy, and nauseous, and therefore quite unfit for food, unless in cases of extreme necessity." Neil smiles easily. "No, the Chase Lake area was settled in the late 1800s. On Sundays after church, families would go to the lake to picnic. Family time included shooting pelicans. In 1908, President Theodore Roosevelt established the refuge with an executive order. By that time the population of pelicans had declined to fifty birds."

"If it is an alkaline lake, what do the pelicans eat?" asks Bill. "No fish could survive."

"Tiger salamanders," says Neil. Bill's eyebrows shoot up. "Not in the lake!"

Neil laughs. "The birds take turns leaving the nests to feed in small wetlands and ponds across the prairie. There are some fish in larger ponds and lakes, but studies show that the pelicans' main food is salamanders."

Meanwhile Bill has spotted a leopard frog sticking its head out of a grassy burrow on the hillside and is sprawled in the grass, snapping photos. Neil tells me, "Ducks have gotten us to this point in conserving the Great Plains, but we need to preserve more for the future. Habitat loss for grassland birds is massive. It is a sad picture; the majority of species are in decline. And these aren't birds that need a tiny, highly rarified niche. We're talking about meadowlarks and sparrows."

The National Audubon Society's list of the top threatened grassland birds does not include any of the brightly colored songbirds that frequent bird feeders. There are no easily recognizable cardinals, blue jays, or goldfinches on the list. Shunning flashy colors, these denizens of the grasslands wear finery designed

Tiger salamander

to melt away into striated shadows of brown and green. A meadowlark shields its sulfur-yellow belly with cryptic browns and golds, baring its bright underside only when calling to other meadowlarks. Grassland birds of all stripes, I learn, are as dependent on the Prairie Pothole Region as ducks.

More than 150 species of sparrows, swallows, nighthawks, raptors, woodpeckers, wrens, grouse, flycatchers, warblers, and game birds nest in the prairies and wetlands. One-third of the continental population of American white pelicans nests in the PPR along with a number of gulls, grebes, bitterns, soras, and terns. At least thirteen species of shorebirds breed here including the threatened piping plover,[22] American avocet, upland sandpiper, marbled godwit, long-billed curlew, and Wilson's phalarope. Plus, there are the migrating birds, including whooping cranes, that rely on these lands for food, water, and stopover sites on their journeys.

I think about my trip up the flyway and my search for water and ducks. Here I am talking to the manager of a refuge of 4,000-plus acres that is half water and half land, a refuge at the center of a Wetland Management District, and we're talking about the prairies, not the wetlands, and about a lot more than ducks.

"So," I ask, "how does one save the prairie?"

Neil looks at me with a wry smile, but his eyes are sharp as he decides whether I'm being serious or sarcastic. He shrugs like someone with nothing to lose and starts talking.

When he finds a rancher or farmer who is willing to talk, Neil tells me, he has a toolbox of USFWS programs and funding to help the landowner protect the wetlands and grass. But there are limited funds, he stresses. It requires creativity, trust, and respect on both sides.

I nod my head.

He continues, telling me that there is a lot of distrust between the agricultural community and the conservation community. Fish and Wildlife's main tool is easements, but there are programs to help with cross fencing, getting water to livestock for rotational grazing, and of course grazing leases on the refuge itself. Plus, there are all the USDA programs (he spews out an alphabet soup of acronyms), but they have their own guys. Finally, there is carbon sequestration to consider. Neil tells me that an unplowed prairie holds tons of carbon, and there are a number of people and organizations trying to establish carbon markets that would pay landowners to keep their lands in grass and wetlands.

He's looking off into the distance, avoiding eye contact as he rattles off the grocery list of benefits I hear and read again and again: Wetlands filter water.

Help prevent downstream flooding by holding water. Replenish aquifers. Increase plant and wildlife diversity. Sequester carbon. Reduce topsoil runoff. Prevent fertilizers, pesticides, and herbicides from flowing downstream to add to the Dead Zone in the Gulf of Mexico.

It is all very important and I want to toss away my pen and paper, lie down in the grass, and turn into one of Willa Cather's pumpkins soaking up sun and prairie, staring up into the sky. Purposefully not thinking about how what happens here on the plains impacts the rest of the country—no, the entire continent—from the Gulf of Mexico to the Arctic. More than ducks are depending on the PPR.

Neil nudges us back to the truck. At that moment he reminds me of an Australian heeler, nipping at our heels as Bill and I plod along, cowlike, more interested in the grass and water in front of us than anything else.

As we drive, I ask Neil how he copes with watching the prairie go up in smoke.

"All of this," he waves his hand from one shoulder across the windshield to the other, 270 degrees, "this is my life . . . and what I know." He trails off, anguish roughly edging his voice.

"In 2013, at the height of the conversion, the plumes of smoke rising from the burning fields reminded me of Kuwait, when the oil wells were all on fire. I started photographing the fires and conversion but it became too hard." He shakes his head. I'm struck by a sudden vision of skin being flayed from Neil's body. With each acre and section of native prairie plowed black, another square of skin is peeled from live flesh, leaving muscle exposed to air with no protective skin, nerves exposed, and tissue drying to hard, cracking scabs. The image disturbs me.

"Now I'm refocusing my energy. I'm doing my best to build bridges—that is what will save the prairie, helping people understand what it is that they have and its value."

I see a few slender plumes of smoke on the horizon. Neil turns his head away, refusing to acknowledge the fires.

Bill and I stagger away from the USFWS office, burdened with information overload and the ongoing prairie losses. As we drive, we look for squares of grass, of prairie in the miles of cropland. I'm still looking for ducks, but now I know that this vast land is not empty. It is not soulless, but it doesn't reveal its richness unless you stop and step into the prairie grasses. There, if you have learned how to see, is one of the most dynamic and endangered systems in the world. It is bitter and glorious, sweet and terrifying, and awe inspiring in a way that humbles all men and women. But you have to silence the noise, the preconceived ideals of trees, forests, mountains, and streams that rattle in your brain. For those willing to accept this almost monastic reverie, it is the most exciting place in the world.

16

Make Way for Ducklings

The whole of the prairies as well as the hills have been so trampled by them [buffalo] that I should have considered it quite unsafe for man to travel on horseback. The ground was literally covered with their tracks.
—May 22, 1843, *Audubon and His Journals: Missouri River Journals*[23]

As we drive west away from Chase Lake and south to the Missouri River, the squares of prairie are subsumed by croplands. As we descend the Missouri slope, the silver gleam of wetlands becomes increasingly rare.

"I had no idea," Bill says.

"Nor did I," I answer.

"But I've been a hunter all my life. I didn't know half of this stuff," he says, looking out at the land streaming past.

I started my flyway trip looking for water. Ducks—and other migratory birds—need water, right? So, I hopscotched from wetland to wetland and discovered year-round marshes and seasonal wetlands important to migratory birds of all kinds. But once I reached the Prairie Pothole Region, I kept looking at water, unable to understand the prairies or recognize their importance. Ducks don't have the obvious connection to prairies that they have to wetlands, but we now know that prairies and upland grasses are as essential to pintails as they are to meadowlarks. Long term, you can't have one without the other. Just as early proponents of duck hatcheries discovered, wild ducks without their habitat just don't thrive.

By the time we reach the former tallgrass prairies on the eastern side of the

Great Plains, it is a world of corn and soybeans. There are a few cattle pastures, but nothing I would identify as a prairie. I would have to work to find tallgrass prairie and wetland remnants tucked away in the Corn Belt's patterned hills of tillage. Yet working lands like these held by private landowners are the future of conservation.

Over half of the land in the lower 48 states is made up of working lands: ranches, farms, and parcels of forest that add up to roughly a billion acres of agriculture. Most of that is privately owned. What has become clear to me as I drive up and down the Great Plains is that without the help and collaboration of our farmers and ranchers, the future of conservation—our future—is uncertain at best.

The single largest source of funding for conservation on private lands is the Farm Bill. The US Department of Agriculture has hundreds of millions of dollars available to private landowners to keep wetlands, grasslands, and other fragile lands protected. Every year that the programs are funded, millions of acres of wildlife habitat are improved.

But the gargantuan and yet bipartisan legislation commonly known as the Farm Bill relies on congressional appropriation of taxpayer money (every five years or so) to fund conservation programs through the USDA's Natural Resources Conservation Service and Farm Service Agency. Popular programs include the Conservation Reserve Program (CRP), which pays farmers to retire highly erodible or environmentally sensitive land and plant it with grass, pollinator mixes, or trees; and the Environmental Quality Incentives Program, which helps farmers and ranchers with projects ranging from creating wildlife habitat to building ponds to reducing erosion. Taxpayers' money pays for administration, technical help, and cost sharing on projects. It isn't preservation of pristine wildness, but conservation comes in all shapes and sizes and the USDA programs are crucial for our future.

Relying on the government for so much conservation honestly makes me uneasy. True, we've had some successes, but with so many species of birds and pollinators plummeting, can we wait for the slow-grinding wheels of partisan government to catch up?

What if there was another way to pay for conservation on private lands? Instead of relying on Uncle Sam to pony up tax dollars, is there a strategy that could send my money directly to help ranchers and farmers conserve and preserve soil, wetlands, prairies, wildlife, and their way of life? A way I could help private landowners create habitat for ducks, imperiled grassland birds, monarch butterflies, native bees, and other pollinators, and ultimately protect the Gulf of Mexico?

The oldest program that fits the bill is the Duck Stamp. Yup. Not only is it unique because, by law, 98 percent of the stamp's purchase price goes directly to the "perpetual conservation of critical habitat for migratory birds," but the Duck Stamp's secret weapon is acquiring perpetual wetland and grassland easements on private land in the Prairie Pothole Region. This is in addition to acquiring land for national wildlife refuges all over the country and securing Waterfowl Production Areas for migratory birds of all kinds.

The funding for the conservation easements comes from the Migratory Bird Conservation Fund (MBCF), where the revenues from Duck Stamp sales are deposited. But Duck Stamp sales provide only about half the money. Import duties on foreign guns and ammunition pour tens of millions of dollars into the fund per year (yet another major source of conservation funding from firearm sales). In 2019 alone, $80 million from the MBCF permanently protected more than seven thousand acres of wetland habitat in migratory bird refuges and nearly fifty-four thousand acres in the Prairie Pothole Region.

I'd never bought a Duck Stamp before I became a duck hunter. I associated the stamp with hunting, and honestly, I didn't want to support killing birds. I was fully ignorant of the Duck Stamp's importance to wetland and prairie conservation. Duck Stamps, I decide, will make dandy gifts.

A second way to promote conservation on private lands is to support organizations that work with landowners. Ducks Unlimited, the National Audubon Society, and Quail Forever are just a few of the many groups working on private lands conservation. Programs like Ducks Unlimited's Soil Agronomy, the World Wildlife Fund's Sustainable Ranching Initiative, Quail Forever's Farm Bill Biologist, and Audubon's Conservation Ranching Initiative help farmers and ranchers with land management techniques and practices to benefit both wildlife and landowners.

"Conservation in the US has always been policy and land acquisition," Marshall Johnson, Audubon Dakota's executive director, tells me.[24] "In my opinion, we need to reach for the third rail—market-based conservation."

We're on a Zoom call. He takes off his white cowboy hat and leans toward his computer. "I really want people to take back their superpower. And in this society, that is the power of purchase. One of my favorite quotes is 'Every dollar you spend, or don't spend, is a vote you cast for the world you want.' Everyone hears about clean water, wildlife, and nature. What is missing is that day-to-day connectivity to their life. I want to empower people to make everyday choices that directly impact bird populations. And I think that way is through market-based conservation."

He's talking about the National Audubon Society's Conservation Ranching

Initiative. A private lands project, it has a twist: Bird-Friendly Beef certification for ranches. Audubon created the program to benefit grassland birds but also to reward ranchers for their work. Working together, ranchers and Audubon create a management plan for each ranch that can include stocking rates, pasture rotation or reduction, alternative pesticides (no neonicotinoids are allowed), and ways to increase plant diversity. Because beef from Audubon-certified lands garners a premium price, it benefits the rancher directly (instead of a sale barn or feedlot reaping the final profit). And you or I (the consumer) know we are getting hormone- and antibiotic-free, ethically raised beef that supports birds and grassland conservation. With over a hundred ranches and 2.5 million acres enrolled, the program presently includes nearly every type of historic grassland: shortgrass prairie, mixed-grass prairie, tallgrass prairie, Chihuahuan grasslands, basin desert steppe, western Gulf Coast grasslands, Texas's Edwards Plateau, and California grasslands. It is an encouraging beginning. While a number of retail outlets are local to the ranches, a variety of sellers now ship nationally to deliver Bird-Friendly Beef directly to consumers. Someday it will be available at local supermarkets.

Imagine being able to choose to support grassland birds when you buy dinner.

But for years I've heard that the only way to save the planet is to eat less meat. If you do an internet search about the sustainability of cows and beef—be prepared. You will end up with a nearly overwhelming amount of information that, at first glance, makes cattle ranching seem profoundly unsustainable for the planet. There will be charts that show the tons of methane cattle burp during their life span, and the carbon released into the atmosphere by the beef industry. Graphics tally the gallons of water required to produce a pound of beef versus a pound of soybeans. Should I eat nothing but tofu and locally grown produce? But most of these articles and studies are looking at global trends (which include cutting down rain forests for cattle), and corn-fed finishing in industrial feedlots.

We have 370 million acres of native grasslands remaining. That includes the Great Plains, the Gulf Coast coastal plain, the California Central Valley, and the Chihuahuan Desert. The vast majority is held by private landowners and native nations. Much of the land is marginal for cropland, either because of poor soil or because it would require intensive irrigation from limited water supplies.

"What those grasslands are good for—and what is good for it—is grazing," Johnson tells me. "We don't have herds of bison anymore, but we do have cattle. And, if the land is grazed and managed properly, there are all these vital ecosystem services that can benefit millions of people." He rattles off benefits: "An acre of native prairie can sequester five to fifteen tons of carbon—the equivalent of sixty to one hundred cars' emissions annually. Prairies replenish aquifers, reduce water runoff, and create ecosystems that are resilient to drought. Native pollinators thrive in prairies—and one in three bites of food we take depends on insect pollination."

An acre of soybeans or corn, even organically grown, just doesn't have the same benefits as native prairie. But finding ways to help our ranchers, farmers, and wildlife thrive together—I'll vote for that any day.

Once we hit the interstate, the landscape becomes a distant abstraction. From the highway, one town looks like another, a procession of big-box stores, franchise restaurants, and gas stations as we drive south. By the time we arrive home, the prairies, the potholes, and all I'd seen seem distant and dreamlike. Confronted by stacks of mail, bills to pay, chores, weeding, and washing, I feel the thrumming life force of the prairie slipping out of my grasp.

I last two days at home before I hop back in the car and flee to the Gulf Coast. A phone call from a fledgling environmental nonprofit seduces me (it doesn't take much) with a proposal interweaving art, Matagorda Bay, and, of course, birds. Over lunch in Palacios the conversation ranges from rice fields and birds to farmers and wildlife, art and education, and birds, birds, and more birds. We drive to see the model wetlands created next to the public pavilion, and then to a redfish farm.

As I stand on a grassy shore, watching ponds full of farmed redfish roil with flashes of silver, a movement catches my eye. In a small overflow pond black-necked stilts and yellowlegs troll through the shallows. Behind them, the streaky browns of a mottled duck separate from the shadows. I watch as she slips from the grassy verge into the water. A small yellow and brown fluff ball follows. Then another. And another until there are four ducklings paddling after their mother, darting after insects, and bumping into each other.

I'd driven to Canada and back looking for ducklings. I'd been certain that the wilder the land, the more ducks I'd see. And yet here, in the middle of a fish-farming operation on the Texas coast, a mottled duck hen is showing me just how little I know.

Make way for ducklings, indeed.

PART IV
Hunting Season

⟡ 17 ⟡

Opening Day

Whilst the etherial [*sic*] motions of its pinions, so rapid and so light, appear
to fan and cool the flower. . . . They are quarrelsome, and have frequent
battles in the air . . . twittering and twirling in a spiral manner until out of
sight.

      —Ruby-throated Humming Bird, *Ornithological Biography*, vol. 1

Migration has started. Unlike the drama of spring migration, which takes place
in just a couple of weeks, fall migration lasts from the end of June until January. Species head south when their fledglings have taken to the wing, when the
weather shifts and food supplies decrease. In July, purple martins roost in mid-
sized oaks in an urban parking lot in front of a megastore. At dusk they swirl
into cauldrons of iridescent purple and dark gray that settle like shadows into
the trees, then spook back into flight. I watch with my grandniece, a five-year-
old who reminds me what magic it is to sit and watch thousands of birds whirl
overhead. It is rare nowadays to see such large congregations of birds other than
grackles and starlings. I think of the historical accounts of flocks of birds, not
just passenger pigeons, that darkened the sky and filled the air with the sound of
their beating wings: Eskimo curlew, snipe, American woodcock, dickcissel. Birds
diminished or gone. The list goes on and on.

    The August days roast to over 100°F and it feels like summer will never end.
A flock of blue-gray gnatcatchers descend on our post oaks and the woods ring
with their shrill cries. I fill hummingbird feeders once, sometimes twice a day

as ruby-throated hummingbirds guzzle the nectar. It has been a long, hot, dry summer with little rain, so insects are scarce, as is anything in bloom. Our resident hummers try to defend their feeders from the transients, but they are overwhelmed. I've put a feeder outside my studio window and I stare, distracted by the dramas and triumphs occurring just a few feet away.

Bill and I hunt on his family farm on dove season's opening day. We set our stools down next to a muddy-rimmed pond where mesquite trees cast their filigreed shade over us. Red-eared sliders lift their heads out of the water to look at us. Fish hit the surface gulping insects, and swallows carve Vs in the water as they drink on the wing. Birds fly in and out of the trees rimming the pond: eastern phoebes, eastern kingbirds, mockingbirds, and a Cooper's hawk after one of many sparrows. Mourning doves speed over the pond, nearly too fast to see in time to raise my gun. But when I start listening for the whistling sound of their wings, I have forewarning of birds approaching from behind. I watch birds and clouds, spend too much time observing blue-black wasps rolling up pellets of mud to build nests, and try to stay focused enough to shoot at the doves as they blow past. I hit one and it spirals down to the pond. It is out of my reach unless I plunge into hip-deep mud. I watch it struggle briefly before it goes limp. I want to hold it, to see it up close. I keep an eye on it as the wind pushes it across the pond, hoping it will get close enough to the far shore for me to scoop it up. One minute it is there, and then it is gone. I search the shoreline and scan the water but I suspect a snapping turtle is behind the disappearance. *My bird*, I think, *it ate my bird*. My possessiveness is a surprise. Why should I begrudge a turtle a meal? I end the day squarely hitting a mourning dove with my last shell. I find it in a patch of grass, its wings folded and eyes closed, the long light of evening setting its iridescent neck feathers aflame. It is small, and a single bird seems meager. I am wondering whether I can justify the killing since it isn't enough for a meal, when Bill arrives with enough birds to fill a pan. We sit on the truck's tailgate, plucking birds as the sun sets.

The idea of eating birds that I've killed still seems foreign. I've cooked and eaten plenty of doves (and a particularly ill-tempered rooster that ended his rebellion as coq au vin), yet I expected that eating the first dove I shot would be different somehow. It isn't. The bird has the same dry powdery scent as all the other mourning doves. The feathers pull out of the skin as easily on the bird I shot as on the ones Bill shot. When we get home, I stuff the plucked birds with dried figs and cook their tiny bodies low and slow with a splash of port as red as their flesh.

They all taste the same—some younger and more tender—but there is no flavor of bitter recrimination or salty tears. Just the sweetness of the figs and

Northern mockingbird

the dark, oxygen-rich meat of the doves enrobed in gravy. We gnaw on the tiny drumsticks, nibble the tender meat off the delicate bones, lick our fingers, and swab up gravy with chunks of bread.

If I'm honest, I feel a connection with the land, a sense of being part of a great whole. As if by eating the dove, I've bitten into something vital, something nourishing and sustaining that runs deep into the earth.

As I wash up, a lead pellet rolls off a plate to rattle around the sink. We are careful when we clean doves and work to remove all the pellets, but we do miss some. It concerns me; I don't like the idea of eating lead pellets in birds or fragments of lead bullets in other game. For all waterfowl hunting, steel shot is required by federal law. Not because lead was poisoning the people who harvested the birds, but because it was killing ducks, geese, and swans.

By the mid-1870s, improved shotguns made hunting waterfowl surprisingly easy. By the 1890s, the mass production of shotgun cartridges, repeating shotguns, and later, Browning's patented semiautomatic made guns and hunting affordable entertainment. Hunters carried 8 gauge, 10 gauge, and light (at the time) 12 gauge shotguns into the field. The massive large-bore guns used by market hunters, the 2, 4, and 6 gauge guns, were too heavy to shoulder and were mounted onto punt or sneak boats where they could fire up to half a pound of lead shot at a time. Hunters blasted lead pellets over shallow lakes, corn and rice fields, wetlands, and marshes. Wherever waterfowl congregated, hunters followed and showered the landscape with toxic metal.

As ducks, geese, and swans fed, rummaging in muck for vegetation and invertebrates, they could pick up and swallow pellets. Some of the pellets passed through, but the birds also picked up shot along with the sand and other grit they swallowed to help with digestion. Lead pellets poisoned the birds as gastric juices, muscular contractions, and grit pulverized and dissolved the lead in their tough gizzards. The birds died slow deaths as the toxins destroyed their organs.

Forest and Stream published one of the first accounts of lead-poisoned waterfowl in 1894 (incidentally just below its editorial calling for banning the sale of all game). While abundant anecdotal evidence of lead poisoning in waterfowl was around for years, it wasn't until the 1960s that research proved, repeatedly, that millions of ducks were suffering and dying every year from lead shot poisoning. Not just waterfowl were dying, but birds of prey were becoming ill and dying after eating poisoned ducks.

Ammunition makers and hunters balked at the idea of switching to nontoxic shot. Steel shot, hunters argued, would ruin the barrels of their fine old shotguns. Many hunters were convinced that because steel shot lacked the range and power of lead shot, it would leave more crippled ducks to die lingering deaths. The ultimate excuse was cost. Lead shot was cheap and shotgun shells made from steel shot were initially pricy. While the debate raged, hunters scattered an estimated three thousand tons of lead shot across the landscape every season.

In 1976, the US Fish and Wildlife Service took the first steps toward phasing out lead shot, but it took another ten years before there was "scientific justification for a ban on the use of lead shot."[25] After a bit of waffling, and a few lawsuits, federal regulations were put in place in 1986 to start phasing out the allowable use of lead shot for waterfowl hunting—the same year the Safe Drinking Water Act was amended to require lead-free plumbing. By 1991, there was a complete ban on lead shot for waterfowl and coot hunting. Cases of lead poisoning in waterfowl have slowly dropped over the last three decades.

There has been additional research about lead shot and upland birds, poisoning of raptors and scavengers by lead bullet fragments, and loons and other fish-eating birds harmed by lead in fishing tackle. So far, California is the only state to require nonlead ammunition for all hunting. But there are indications that lead fragments in game are a serious concern to anything—or anyone—that eats the meat.

Bill and I have decided that we are going to switch to nontoxic shot for all the birds we hunt. Yes, some of the cartridges can be more expensive, but it seems like a small price to pay for our health and the continued health of our wildlife.

It seems a little hypocritical to worry about the type of shot I use when I hunt birds. My intent is still to bring home doves or ducks for dinner. But is the death I deliver with a shotgun fundamentally different from a natural death? For a duck, which is better—death by shotgun pellets (whether steel, bismuth, tungsten, or corrosion-inhibiting copper), by being snatched off a nest, or by disease? Is a slow death from exhaustion, dehydration, or starvation preferable? What happens when, after miles of migration, ducks circle farmlands and suburbs, looking for wetlands that are drained or dried up? When habitat is limited and waterfowl are overcrowded, plagues of avian botulism result in gruesome mass deaths. The first birds die from eating botulism-infected snails or other invertebrates. Then maggots writhe in their corpses and more birds die after feeding on the toxin-laced larvae. The cycle continues with raptors, shorebirds, gulls, loons, and other wetland birds dying.

To the list of natural dangers that each duck faces, add new human-made dangers: wind turbines, power lines, tall buildings with reflective windows, unnaturally bright lights, open oil pits that look like water, oil spills, and chemical-laced water.

"Ducks are short-lived birds," Kevin Kraai, waterfowl program leader for the Texas Parks and Wildlife Department, tells me when I ask about natural mortality. "And nesting mortality is very high, so hens have a higher mortality rate than males. Juveniles have a higher mortality rate than adults." I'd hoped to compare natural mortality with hunting totals but there isn't an easy answer. After I quiz Kevin and pore over reports, it looks like less than 10 percent of the total population is harvested each year. In 2019 about one million hunters harvested 12.4 million ducks and geese. I'm stunned by the numbers. *Nearly ten million ducks harvested? How can this be sustainable?* I wonder.

It may not be. The ninety years of dedicated, systematic waterfowl research combined with wetland preservation and restoration on public and private lands may have only postponed the inevitable. The waterfowl data amassed by federal and state agencies alone—not counting the information gleaned by cadres of scientists—probably physically outweigh the data sets for any other creatures. Every year breeding bird surveys, habitat surveys, midwinter surveys, Harvest Information Programs, and banding data are used to set waterfowl hunting regulations. The men and women charged with setting the regulations juggle the existing data, tossing in weather predictions and jet stream patterns, numbers of hunting licenses, and habitat loss—all to balance existing resources with future desires. Will there be enough ducks to satisfy the duck hunters? Will there be enough ducks to retain the hunters so they continue to buy licenses, Duck Stamps, and ammunition?

Not shooting a duck or dove doesn't prevent its eventual death. All birds die. Without the money provided by Duck Stamps, Pittman-Robertson Funds, NAWCA, and conservation organizations like Ducks Unlimited, ducks wouldn't stand a chance against habitat loss and fragmentation, nor would the hundreds of other species, including ourselves, that depend on the wetlands.

18

On the Texas Rice Prairie

They are the first ducks that arrive in that part of the country, frequently making their appearance in the beginning of September, in large flocks, when they are exceedingly fat.
—Blue-winged Teal, *Ornithological Biography*, vol. 4

I sit on the edge of a small levee in humid velvet darkness, damp grasses and sumpweed arching over my head. Decoys are thrown out into the flooded stubble of a harvested rice field and we wait while the sky, thick with clouds, brightens slowly. The water gathers light and gleams like rippling quicksilver. A flock of dark birds spins over the decoys and disappears, silent except for the flurry of wings through humid air. Slow mosquitoes buzz languidly in the morning cool— the repellent is working but the insects hover near. My shotgun rests across my thighs, pointing toward the water.

It is my first teal hunt and an early-season opportunity for Bill and our host, Andy Sansom. Brian Center, manager of the Bucksnag, a venerable private hunting club in Garwood, Texas, is our guide. Pam LeBlanc, a journalist and first-time hunter; her husband, Chris; and a photographer for *Texas Parks and Wildlife* magazine round out the group. They sit at the far end of the levy with Andy. A few birds silently drop into the decoys while we wait for the clock to tick over into shooting hours. I can hear Andy whispering instructions to Pam on the 28 gauge shotgun he is loaning her. His elderly Labrador, Scout, moves restlessly, her stiff joints and clouded eyes forgotten in anticipation of ducks. Brian's Lab waits, focused and intent. I'm happy sitting in the dark, tucked into the weeds, listening to the September night creep toward dawn. Whistles and peeps drift across the water. Sparrows rustle through the grass around us. Over the chuckling of leopard frogs, I hear the plop and splash of a nutria hurrying away. A bullfrog starts to groan, stops, then begins again and I laugh to myself. Brian will call the shots and warns us, once again, not to shoot an early pintail; we are hunting the September Teal Only Season. As if on cue, a quartet of pintails swoop past, their wings flickering in the early light. "Don't shoot," warns Brian.

Soon enough a sextet of blue-winged teal zoom over the flooded field, out of range but eyeing the decoys. We sit quietly. I'm intensely aware of the smell of damp soil, the musky smell of sumpweed, the repellent smeared on my hands and neck, the metal and oil smell of my shotgun, and the funk of waterlogged mud.

The birds circle back, this time close enough for Brian to call, "Shoot that duck!"

It is like a damned artillery barrage, shotguns going off and birds scattering. Only one bird is hit; Scout goes after Andy's downed bird, floundering through the decoys. I hold my breath as she stumbles back, teal in mouth, head high and tail wagging. Unbelievably, the birds circle back. This time we wait for Brian's call, try to pick a bird, and follow it before firing. Andy and Bill both bring down birds that the two dogs, one old, one young, run to retrieve.

As flocks of blue-winged teal circle the decoys, Chris, Bill, and I take shot after shot, missing again and again. Brian groans in frustration. "We should be getting a lot more ducks, y'all." Meanwhile Andy picks off teal that drop like shadows into the water. Two drakes and a hen dodge the fusillade to land in the decoys. I prop my gun on my shoulder and sight in on the drake, following him as he paddles along. When the trio springs into the air, I fire and the drake drops. "Nice shot," Brian says. A few minutes later I shoot at a quartet of fast-flying teal and a wounded hen spins down to the water. Remorse and anger crash together and I berate myself for not making a clean shot. The hen, holding her shattered wing high, swims past a great egret and black-necked stilts to the far side of the water where she disappears into tall grass. Brian's dog lopes across the pond and snuffles through the plants, easily finding the hen and bringing it back. If I'd had to retrieve my own bird, would I have ever found that hen? Cliff swallows twitter as they skim through the decoys, sipping water on the wing and ignoring us.

The stack of teal slowly grows next to Brian. The compact bodies of the hens and drakes look particularly fragile in death. Yet these small ducks may be just partway through a continental journey from their nesting grounds to their wintering grounds. The third most common duck in North America, blue-winged teal nest as far north as Alaska. While some will spend their winter along the

Texas coast, 80 percent of blue-winged teal either spend the winter in Mexico or pass through on their way to Central and South America.

Long before the first European explorers traipsed across the Gulf prairies, teal winged their way across the continent. But as explorers and, later, settlers changed the face of the land, teal and other waterfowl were forced to adapt.

First there were prairies. An arc of rolling coastal plain up to a hundred miles wide ran from west of the Mississippi River to south of where the Rio Grande formerly emptied into the Gulf. Tallgrass prairies rippled—nine million acres' worth—pocked with seasonal wetlands and cut with densely wooded river bottoms and slow bayous and creeks that flowed to the Gulf of Mexico. Freshwater flowed into salty bays and the prairies and freshwater wetlands merged with the salt marshes rimming the Gulf of Mexico. Dr. Ferdinand Roemer described his first encounter in 1854: "I had my first view of a Texas prairie. The long grass was yellow and dry, and because of the heavy spring rains, the water had collected in numerous puddles. The only living things we saw on this broad expanse were Canadian geese (*Anser canadensis* L.), a chattering flock of which were grazing in the wet grass" (Roemer, *Roemer's Texas*).

Ranchers ran cattle on the aristocrats of prairie grasses: Indian grass, big bluestem, and wild rye. Farmers burned the prairies, then plowed the soil to plant crops. Some thrived, others floundered.

Then came the railroads and technological advances. Rice had been grown for decades in small, impounded fields in river bottoms in Texas and Louisiana, but the 1880s and 1890s brought irrigation pumps, harvesters, threshers, and improved processing and mills that pulled the industry away from the rivers and onto the prairies of Louisiana, Texas, and Arkansas. Railroads brought new settlers and hauled crops to market. The irrigation infrastructure needed for rice sprouted and grew, creating a network of ditches and canals that elbowed its way across the plowed prairies between lakes, creeks, rivers, and fields.

In 1886 on land near Beaumont, a trio of farmers harvested the first commercial rice crop in Texas. Ten years later Colonel William Dunovant pumped water from Eagle Lake, a shallow oxbow lake next to the Texas Colorado River, onto a test crop of rice. The heavy soil that cracked in the summer sun proved perfect for growing rice: sturdy enough for heavy plows (and later massive combines), it held water and yet was easy to drain. Within just a few years, rice crops sprouted up and down the Colorado River. Every year, farmers planted more acres of rice, and soon the irrigated fields displaced native wetlands from western Louisiana to just west of the Colorado River in what became known as the rice prairies.

At Eagle Lake, the combination of water and rice proved irresistible to waterfowl. But long before the railroad-stop town dubbed itself the "Goose Hunting Capital of the World," the lake (and later, the town) was famous for its birds. Lesser prairie-chickens, cranes, greater Canada geese, and mallards thrived in the prairies and seasonal wetlands as well as on the lake and along the Colorado River. The lake itself, shallow and thick with cattails, cut-grass, and bulrushes, was ideal for dabblers: rich with invertebrates and plant food, and lots of cover. The ducks roosted on the lake during the day and fed in the prairies at night—until they discovered the ripening rice fields. According to historian R. K. Sawyer, "rice field hunting did not start as a sport, but as a necessity to reduce crop destruction." (Sawyer and Kaminski, *A Hundred Years of Texas Waterfowl Hunting*).

Wintering ducks migrated south and arrived in time to destroy the just-harvested grain. Farmers stayed up all night with lanterns to protect the shocks of harvested rice, even sending their children out to patrol night fields with shotguns to shoot feeding ducks. But the ducks were wild about rice. And hunters were wild about ducks. Local hunters began offering guide services, and private hunting clubs like the Eagle Lake Rod and Gun Club and Jimmy Reel's Lower Lake Club were started. There were so many mallards, pintails, teal, and gadwalls that old-timers remember the ducks darkening the skies, thick as flocks of blackbirds over the prairie.

Upstream of the rice prairies, a contentious battle erupted over a series of unfinished dams on the Colorado River, left behind by a bankrupt electrical utility. In 1934 farmers along the lower river banded together and supported the creation of a state agency to complete the dams and manage the river. In exchange, the new Lower Colorado River Authority promised the farmers irrigation water to grow rice.

Meanwhile, the geese began to notice the rice buffet. There had always been small groups of geese on the prairie (like the greater Canada geese seen by Roemer) and small populations in the coastal marshes. But there wasn't enough food or habitat for big flocks. That all changed with thousands of acres of rice cultivation. By the 1930s and 1940s, the geese, especially snow geese, started moving down to Texas to take advantage of the bounty. The hunters and guides may have been thrilled with the influx of geese, but not all the farmers were happy. A flock of geese could quickly gobble up acres of freshly sown seed or turn a field of sprouting seed into a muddy wasteland. Some farmers went so far as to intentionally poison ducks and geese by broadcasting rice seed soaked in pesticides (chlorinated hydrocarbons). The indiscriminate use of pesticides (many now banned) between the late 1950s and mid-1980s poisoned thousands of waterfowl, shorebirds, songbirds, and birds of prey every year in the rice prairies.

By the peak of the snow goose migration to the rice prairies, between the 1950s and 1970s, the greater Canada goose had disappeared from Texas. Mallards, once one of the most populous ducks on the upper coast, dwindled to uncommon by the 1970s. Canvasbacks, which used to frequent inland lakes, were rare. Fulvous whistling-ducks, once numerous, vanished from the Texas coast.

Regardless, there were geese. Unbelievable numbers of geese: specklebelly (white-fronted), Ross's, and snow geese, both white and blue (a dark phase). Geese travel in big flocks—up to twenty-five thousand birds—and need concentrated food sources. The rice fields were perfect and in the 1970s and 1980s up to a million geese and half a million ducks annually descended to feed and winter on the hundreds of thousands of acres of Texas rice fields.

But even as the geese were discovering the rice fields, the prairies and wetlands continued to disappear, subsumed by crops, gravel pits, and the cities and towns that flourished along the Texas coast.

Jimmy Reel, a hunting guide famous for devising the Texas rag spread to decoy snow geese, was one of the first in the area to start actively managing habitat. In the 1930s he noticed that the natural roost ponds in the prairie were disappearing. Reel and his friend, Eagle Lake philanthropist David Wintermann, came up with the idea of flooding fallow fields or harvested rice fields to create roost ponds for ducks and geese. Hunting wasn't allowed; the ponds were for the birds to rest. The shorebirds, wading birds, and other waterbirds took notice and moved on in. Reel built a hunting club on the land where Colonel Dunovant planted his first rice crop. In two hundred acres of shallow water Reel started growing food for ducks by broadcasting seed and planting aquatic bulbs and roots. By this time there were federal limits on duck harvests and finite seasons for hunting. Nevertheless, Reel insisted on further restrictions: shoot only drakes, and, following Wintermann's lead, no afternoon hunting to give the ducks time to feed and rest. Reel's club was renowned for the numbers of ducks and geese, so his clients complied with the added restrictions.

By the time Reel and his partners started Garwood's Bucksnag Hunting Club (originally intended as a dining club) in 1969, the waters of Eagle Lake were no long a duck magnet. When farmers began pumping the lake full of Colorado River water for irrigation, it drastically altered the ecosystem, decimating the plants and the flushes of invertebrates the ducks loved. Introduced nutria chomped down the remaining plants, further changing the lake. Meanwhile, Reel continued to experiment with building habitat for the ducks and geese, working with local farmers, teaching young men to guide, and welcoming hunters from all over the country until his death in 1975. By then, improved strains of rice were harvested earlier, and profitable ratoon, or second crops, were grown from the same plants. Some farmers harvested the ratoon crops, leaving waste rice in the field; others left the plants for the arriving waterfowl. Irrigation canals and ditches delivered Colorado River water to Matagorda, Wharton, and Colorado County rice fields. For a few more years, the geese would throng the rice prairies.

To this day, almost no one hunts in the afternoon.

And here I am, in Jimmy Reel and David Wintermann's old rice prairie stomping grounds, hunting a flooded field outside Garwood. We are just a few miles as a mallard flies from Eagle Lake and the Attwater Prairie Chicken National Wildlife Refuge. The geese no longer flock here in the same dramatic numbers—they go to Arkansas, where the rice fields have not been dried up by drought, upstream demand, and politics. A tiny population of Attwater's prairie-chickens, one of the most endangered birds in the world, lives in a small coastal prairie remnant just north of town. The world's largest flock of endangered whooping cranes winters at Aransas National Wildlife Refuge, a coastal sanctuary crisscrossed by gas pipelines and cut by the Intracoastal Waterway. Barges loaded with a witch's brew of chemicals chug past, skirting disaster and tragedy every day. Yet there are still ducks. And geese.

On a fall visit to the historic Pierce Ranch, Andrew Armour tells me, "We used to farm rice. Now I guess I farm ducks." He grins and points out smartweed, sedges, and duck potato in one of their intensively managed plots. "Without the hunters," he tells me, "there would be little to no habitat left anywhere on the coastal prairie. Rice fields are still the most abundant wetland habitat around here, but irrigation water from the LCRA has gone up in price to the point that, with recent trade wars, growing rice is less than profitable." He waves out at the field. "We couldn't afford to do this without the waterfowl hunters."

Trailing behind Andrew, I learn in short order that a duck farmer needs to be a bit of a botanist, an agronomist, and a hydrologist, as well as an engineer. Mud, sun, sweat, and mosquitoes are a given. There are long days of preparation for a future entirely dependent on capricious weather and nature. Plus, the coastal prairie is chock-full of invasive species just waiting to aggressively overwhelm unattended land: tallow trees (a USDA trial crop), McCartney rose (introduced by a homesick Englishman), King Ranch bluestem (a South African import), and giant cane, plus destructive nutria and feral hogs.

"Seeing the birds come in makes it all worthwhile," Andrew tells me. His eyes shine as he looks over the field seeing future flocks. "We take one year at a time and try to make the best of whatever comes. I grew up with this and it's in my blood.

Blue-winged teal drake

"Really," he says as he gives a short laugh, "I honestly wouldn't know how to act without ducks and geese and hunting."

Andrew, like other wildlife managers, starts preparing land for winter waterfowl in late spring. He creates habitat, seasonal wetlands, that go by the distinctly unromantic name of moist soil units. He builds levees, discs soil, and waits to see what grows. If he's lucky, the area will green up with nosh-worthy plants. If not, he uses the tools of fire, grazing, and chemicals to bring invasive plants to heel, sometimes planting Japanese millet, a duck favorite. In early fall the area is flooded with shallow water (from rain or irrigation) to produce crops of invertebrates for the birds. Other fields are flooded for roost ponds where no hunting is allowed. While ducks and geese feed and rest, long-legged wading birds pluck frogs from the water, shorebirds plunge their bills into the mud to pull out wriggling treats, coots squawk, rails hunt, and songbirds glean insects and seeds from the shorelines.

Rice fields are still among the most abundant wetlands on the Texas coastal plain. Studies estimate that the rice fields along the Colorado River and in the surrounding prairie supply at least half the food that wintering waterfowl in the area need. Even though rice fields don't have the extraordinary diversity of a native wetland, they still provide a home for the frogs, snakes, insects, crawfish, snails, and other native wildlife that feed a pyramid of other creatures.

Just a few months earlier, I stood in the middle of a Matagorda County field surrounded by the golden seed heads of ripe Texmati rice. The late July sun hits my head and shoulders with an intensity astonishing for early morning as a scent like toasted popcorn drifts off the plants. I run the fronds of rice though my fingers like strings of rough beads. As the sun heats the plants, the crisp green leaves and stalks crackle around me.

Stewart Savage stands beside me in a turquoise shirt that would verge on garish elsewhere but is of a piece with the pale ocher rice shimmering over green leaves against a backdrop of rustling tallow trees and blue sky. He's telling me about rice, but I haven't heard a word; I'm too entranced with the ripe grain. Under the stalks the bare dry soil is cracked, fissures splintering in intricate patterns. I wonder where all the crawfish, insects, frogs, and snakes that lived in the rice field have gone.

As I walk, I try not to crush or break the plants, but there are no rows to place my feet between. My *National Geographic*–inspired ideas of hand-planted flooded rice paddies pop and dissipate with a sizzle as Stewart describes seeding rice fields with trucks or airplanes in late March. With a little rain or irrigation, the seeds germinate and send out a slender green leaf. Then the battle between blackbird and farmer begins.

Where did the idea come from that the rice tossed at weddings would kill or sicken birds? When I'd asked Laurance Armour of the Pierce Ranch about this idea he'd laughed at me. "If only!" he said and then, glancing at my face, became serious again. "No, I don't know of any birds that get sick from eating rice. We feed enough red-winged blackbirds with our seed rice, and of course the ducks and geese eat the waste rice left after harvest." Standing hip deep in the field, Stewart describes the blackbirds pulling up the seedlings to eat the sprouted seed. I imagine a flock of dark birds descending like smoke into a pale green field and prancing along, plucking the green threads out of the ground.

"Once the rice seedlings are about ten inches tall, we flood the fields. Then the rice grows in standing water until we drain it off about two weeks before harvest," Stewart tells me. "Lots of creatures in the fields. We don't mind sharing with the wildlife." He pauses, a grimace rolling across his sunny face. "Except feral hogs. They strip rice heads and what they don't eat, they wallow and crush. And they root up the levees." I think but don't say out loud—and eat bird eggs, fledglings, and any other creatures they can catch.

During the summer months when the rice is growing, resident birds use the flooded fields for nesting and foraging. King rails, common and purple gallinules, and yellow rails nest in the fields. Mottled ducks, the mallard-like regional ducks found only on the Gulf Coast, like to nest near rice fields. Yellow-crowned night-herons hunt the fields.

Just about the time that the first crop of rice has ripened and is ready for harvest, shorebirds start their southbound migration. In late July or early August, long-billed curlews return from the western and northern plains, either passing through or staying the winter. Ditto for a bevy of sandpipers, dowitchers, killdeers, Wilson's phalaropes, black-bellied plovers, black-necked stilts, avocets, willets, and yellowlegs. The shorebirds scatter across the coastal prairie, foraging in grasslands, natural and managed wetlands, and rice fields. Because most farmers alternate rice with row crops and grazing, the idle rice fields sprout grasses and forbs. It isn't pristine native prairie, but these surrogate grasslands, part of the rice-growing cycle, are potential nesting and foraging habitat, nevertheless.

At Stewart's invitation, I clamber up into the cab of a massive combine to ride along while he harvests a field of organic rice. Perched in the trainer seat, I'm mesmerized watching a thirty-foot-wide swath of grain sweep into the combine's scissoring blades. The machine lumbers across the field, cutting grain, blowing chaff and weed seed out one side, and shooting rice into a bin. The flocks of red-winged blackbirds and cattle egrets play a dangerous game, darting in front of the machine to snatch grasshoppers and frogs. I watch a pair of white-faced ibis both latch onto a crawfish and rip it into two pieces. A great blue heron flaps down, grabs a massive bullfrog, and wedges it into its throat before flying off. We pass a drainage ditch and Stewart points out a mama gator and a dozen banded babies floating next to a culvert.

After harvest, this field will get fertilized and reflooded, stimulating the rice plants to grow, flower, and set seed for the ratoon crop. This second crop, unique to the Gulf Coast's longer growing season, is harvested just about the time that migrating waterfowl arrive. Some fields are left unharvested, the grain a bounty to the just-arriving waterfowl. Other fields are idled or prepared for row crops. Matagorda, Colorado, and Wharton Counties are still the most prominent rice-producing counties on the Texas coast, but Stewart doesn't know how long that will last. "Every year the number of acres is lower," he says. "In the 1970s there was forty-five to fifty thousand acres of rice in Matagorda County alone. Now we are down to under eleven thousand acres." He looks out at the field, steering the combine over levees. "My great-grandfather was one of the first in the area to start rice farming. I hate to say it, but I believe that eventually, likely within my lifetime, the price of irrigation water from the LCRA will be so high that it will end all rice farming—and possibly all irrigated farming—in the lower

Colorado River valley." We're quiet, the loss of his family's heritage a sudden and unwelcome passenger in the cab. The competition between Austin's urban population and the downstream farmers and wildlife managers has been going on for years. With increasing demand for water and land, booming populations, urban sprawl, and few young people willing to become farmers, the future is frightening.

But this issue is not unique to Texas. Over half of North America's dabbling ducks winter in one of three regions that were formerly rich in natural wetlands but are now rice lands: California's Central Valley, the Mississippi Alluvial Valley, and the Texas and Louisiana Gulf Coast. Yes, water is precious, but so are heritage, culture, and wildlife. Nowadays I bandy numbers about: acres of wetlands lost, acres of prairie plowed under, NAWCA dollars appropriated by Congress, PR Funds, and Duck Stamp dollars. Yet quantifying the value of wetlands, even surrogate wetlands, is hardly attempted. A number of years ago, the USA Rice Federation suggested that replacing existing rice fields with managed natural wetlands would cost more than $3.5 billion. It is an astonishing sum and yet sounds like nothing. How do we put a value on the ecosystem services that benefit wildlife, downstream residents, and the Gulf of Mexico? How can we convince people that the way we use water, and think about water, has far-reaching and long-lasting impacts? In this period when questions about the sustainability of global food production abound, can we afford to lose our regional farmers? During the COVID-19 pandemic, rice producers in the Colorado River basin pitched together, donating eleven thousand pounds of rice to food banks to feed Texans.

I'm waiting for the teal to circle back, watching shorebirds, and listening to an anonymous sparrow twittering in the grass, when the wind suddenly kicks up. Within minutes dark clouds clot over the sun and the temperature drops. Fat splats of cold rain pelt us and we collect decoys and shoulder our gear bags in the downpour. We are soaked by the time we reach our vehicles, just in time for the sun to break through the clouds. The dead teals' wings glow in the suddenly bright light, and, just as Audubon said, "the blue of their wings glistens like polished steel." The photographer lines up Andy and Pam to take photos with the morning's harvest. She forces a smile, clearly uncomfortable with the string of ducks hanging around her neck. Just before we leave, the photographer assembles Bill and me with Andy and Pam. The four of us laugh with arms draped over shoulders and around waists on a beautiful morning afield with friends.

♪ **19** ♪

In the Big Dog's Yard
South Dakota

The amusement of duck-shooting is probably one of the most exposing to cold and wet.
   —Canvass-backed Duck, *Ornithological Biography*, vol. 4

"When in the big dog's yard, play by the big dog's rules," I tell Bill as we drive north to join Jim Weisenhorn for a week of South Dakota duck hunting. We laugh. These words of wisdom are from Frank, a fellow tourist on a hellish ecotour to Brazil's Pantanal. Long haired, bearded, and covered with tattoos from a former life in motorcycle and prison gangs, Frank got along fine with the ill-tempered and oversensitive tour leader. Bill and I had taken Frank's words to heart. It made that trip enjoyable, and we hoped it would work on this trip as well. I was a little nervous about how Bill, Jim, and I would get along for an entire week.

I'd never imagined that Jim and I would become friends. On my flyway trip, Jim started texting me every day or so, asking where I was and what I was seeing. I replied with photos (ducks!) and anecdotes. We fell into an easy pattern of texting and phone calls that became habit, and then friendship. He teases me, leaving voicemail messages in August (105°F in Elgin) that it is 65°F and raining in Watertown. I retaliate with my own weather reports when the tables have turned (Thanksgiving—we're wearing shorts!). We talk about cooking and great meals we've eaten, share jokes, and I call him with duck hunting questions. My circle of longtime friends has little interest in (and some are clearly repulsed by) my new pursuit. Jim accepts me. He sees me as both a hunter and a birdwatcher. It doesn't mean that it is always easy, but we learn from each other, share our stories, confide our secrets, and—surprising to us both—become fast friends.

Since hunting season started in South Dakota, I've been sharing Jim's almost daily text messages with Bill. The Duck Reports, as I call them, usually include a photo of Jim's dog Q posed with the day's ducks and geese, plus the number of Q's retrieves, and a weather report. Jim's original invitation to come back and hunt hasn't wavered over the summer. Bill's initial ambivalence about driving eighteen hours to Watertown erodes under the Duck Reports. I had already applied for, and received, nonresident South Dakota waterfowl hunting licenses. We stock up on hand warmers, stuff all the thermal underwear we own into our duffel bags, and load up guns and ammunition. We are on our way.

Thirty-six hours later, I'm up to my waist in icy pond water holding a shotgun and wondering what I was thinking. It is thirty minutes before sunrise at Geidd Waterfowl Production Area. Bill and Jim stand thigh deep and crouched behind cattails and bulrushes. I'm on tippy-toes trying to keep my shotgun out of the water and see over the plants. The cold water presses around my lower body but the multiple hand warmer packs I dumped into my waders are helping. Q sits expectantly in his hide, nose showing, ready to leap out after ducks. The sounds of coots murmuring and ducks quacking and whistling drift across the water.

We wait. The light grows until I can see the ice crystals blossoming on my gun, my clothes, and the plants around me. The sun cracks the horizon and sets the glassy water and cloudless sky on fire. Groups of green-winged teal, gadwalls, spoonies,[26] and a few pintails wing past us, just out of range, to land in a growing raft of ducks at the far end of the pond. I wish I had my binoculars. We persist until midmorning, willfully optimistic, but our luck never changes.

As we haul decoys and gear back to the truck, Jim apologizes for our bad luck and claims responsibility for our duckless day. "And I didn't realize the water was so deep," he says, which I recognize as a polite way of saying, "I didn't remember that you were so short." I never think of myself as small; why would anyone else? My fingers are numb with cold and I haven't felt my toes for the last thirty minutes, my stomach is growling, I'd kill for a cup of coffee, and yet I'm ridiculously happy. The sun sparkles off the frost riming every blade of grass and leaf while a pure blue sky soars overhead.

"Hey," I say, "it's duck hunting. I'm having a magnificent time." I'm serious; it is a beautiful morning and I've gotten to watch the sunrise on the prairie. I look up in time to see Jim raise an eyebrow, likely at my choice of words. "Though I did have to wonder if you were hazing us when the water reached my waist."

Jim's look of horror at the idea of hazing a couple of hapless Texans by partially submerging them in a duck pond makes me laugh. He shakes his head.

But spending a morning cold, wet, and waiting for ducks isn't just my idea of fun. The North American Waterfowl Management Plan's 2017 survey of waterfowl hunters discovered that a majority insist that they'd continue to slog through mud or ice before dawn regardless of the length of the season and no matter the bag limit. In fact, about one in four hunters admitted that the minimum number of ducks harvested on a hunt in order for him or her to be satisfied would be zero. That's right: even with freezing temperatures, mud, mosquitoes, wind, rain, snow, hauling decoys, and all the other work required for a hunt, most waterfowl hunters would be out there anyway. Of course, quite a few admitted that bagging two ducks, just enough for dinner, would be very nice.

Clearly, duck hunters are tougher than mail carriers.

Back at his house, Jim fries up a big greasy feast of eggs, sausage, and hash browns. I wolf it down like a teenager and then stagger off to nap, dreaming of

Setting out decoys

reclining in frosty whorls of grass, of the South Dakota night's frozen clarity, and of watching constellations fade as dawn slips over the prairie.

In the five days Bill and I are in South Dakota, Jim arranges five hunts. Every day is different, with Jim's creative adaptations to changing weather and migration. Mornings we hunt; then we return home to clean birds, brining and freezing the breast fillets under the big dog's direction. We clean and put away decoys and gear. Afternoons we tag along as Jim scouts for the next day's hunt. Coming from Texas where public hunting lands are rare, Bill and I are in a state of wonder, amazed by the numbers of federal Waterfowl Production Areas, state Game Production Areas, and private lands open for hunting.[27] Where Bill and I see staggering numbers of ducks on countless ponds and lakes, Jim sees flocks roosting, puddle ducks feeding in shallow ponds, deeper ponds where divers float, and loafing ponds where ducks while away the afternoon. He makes plans while we gawk. Then we return to the house to assemble and pack the next day's gear.

One morning, Jim sets out mallard, gadwall, and teal decoys on a small private pond. As mist pools over the water, redheads and canvasbacks (diving ducks) come in to the decoys. So, the next day we set up at Long Lake 3 Game Production Area to hunt "big water for divers," but we are skunked when the wind kicks up. The ducks huddle in tight clumps across the lake and we are miserably cold. Jim remarks that the only advantage to not getting birds is that we don't have to clean birds. On my birthday, we hunt a harvested cornfield. Cocooned in a layout blind, we watch as the weather shifts from mist to rain to drizzle and back again as mallards, pintails, and Canada geese drop in to the decoys around us.

On our last morning we hunt public land again. We drive in thick fog, Jim relying on his GPS to find his way down the ruler-straight roads and make the necessary turns to Cottonwood Lake Game Production Area. In the foggy dark we load up sleds with decoys, sling our guns over our shoulders, and blindly tromp through tall grass. Bill and I have no sense of where we are going in the velvet-black fog; we stumble toward Jim's light at the water's edge. The afternoon before, we'd seen a number of mallards on the slough, so Jim sets out a smorgasbord of decoys. We pick out seats and sit on the ground at the water's edge, hidden by the tall grasses. In some ways it is my favorite hunt of the week. No blinds to mess with, just decoys, guns, dog, and the graceful arcs of dried grass framing my view of the water and sky. The wind abandons us, so Jim tugs the decoys on a jerk line to imitate paddling ducks. The fog fades away as the sun rises behind clouds.

Ducks tricked by Jim's decoys fly into range. A trio of green-winged teal drops in from the left, cutting close to me before veering away. I shoot a drake, which drops, and then I aim and fire at a hen. I see the hen dip in the air, but she flies away. Q retrieves the teal drake and then, ignoring Jim, splashes across the slough in great bounding leaps. Jim bellows. He blasts his whistle. Q ignores him. "Goddamn it, Q, you better not be after a raccoon!" Jim roars. He starts slogging through the shallow water and mud after his dog. Q comes prancing back with the teal hen. I had hit the second bird, but the only one who knew was Q.

"And that's why I always hunt with a dog," Jim tells me after he praises a wagging Q.

As the sun rises in the sky, the day warms up. Five days before, I'd stood waist deep in water with the air way below freezing while ice crystals bloomed on me. This morning had been foggy but a comfortable 38°F. All of our hunts, except for the field hunt, were within a twenty-minute drive of Jim's home.

The best part, after just being here, is watching Q retrieve. I have hunted with guides with retrievers, but this is the first time I've watched a well-trained dog at work for an extended time. Now I understand why Jim told me, "It is all about the dog." Jim and Q are an amazing team. Watching them work together, I realize they are bonded by their common purpose in a way that I will never achieve with our mutts. Biographer William Souter wrote about J. J. Audubon that "he was never happier than when he was lying in wait with his dog and gun on a reedy shoreline as ducks materialized out of the gloom and settled on the water." Now I wonder how much of his happiness was from working with his dog.

I'm waiting for Bill and Jim at the truck. I snap a photo of the Cottonwood Lake sign, and as I check the image, I notice Q sitting behind the sign looking at me in the photo. I raise my phone as if I'm taking another photo. Q spins and sits facing me. I lower the phone, and Q stands and turns away to look for Jim. Raise the phone, Q sits and stares at the camera lens. Later I'd look through the pictures from the trip and in dozens of shots, there is Q, politely sitting and waiting for me to snap a photo. Jim didn't teach Q to pose whenever someone raises a phone for a photo; he figured it out on his own.

As we drive back to Watertown, Jim turns to Bill. "Bill, you're a lucky man," he says. "You have a wife who shoots ducks. She cleans ducks. And she cooks ducks for you." From the back seat I can't see their faces, but I hear Bill's pleased "Yes, I am."

Little do they realize that I'm the lucky one. I suspect that for most hunters, the idea of inviting a wife or girlfriend along on a duck hunt would seem a foolish setup for disaster. Indeed, it seems that many men hunt and fish to get away from home and their wives. That Bill has encouraged my sudden about-face and exploration of duck hunting as conservation is no small miracle. That an avid hunter like Jim has invited us to hunt with him is astonishing. At my age, when I could be letting my life constrict, I'm having a blast and feeling my world expand by the day.

We drive home with a cooler full of duck and plans to hunt together in Texas.

On our first night in South Dakota, Bill and I raved over Jim's duck Italian sausage, so he pulled out his grinder and taught me how to make it. Ten pounds of sausage, five pounds of duck fillets, and a few whole roasting ducks are going home with us. We played by the big dog's rules and had an extraordinary time. Jim bellowed at us a few times; more than once we tried his patience as we stared at the landscape, watching birds and daydreaming. But we were all sad when it was time to go. Bill and I knew we would never be able to repay Jim, but we would try. When Jim fled the South Dakota snow for East Texas, we would meet on the Texas coast.

☙20❧

Redhead Redux

The Red-breasted Merganser is best known throughout the United States by the name of "Shell-drake." It is, like all the species of its tribe, a most expert diver, and on being fired at with a flint-locked gun generally escapes by disappearing before the shot reaches the place where it has been.
—Red Breasted Merganser, *Ornithological Biography*, vol. 5

Jim Weisenhorn and Q are on one side of me in the blind; Bill is on the other. I can't quite see over the mangrove branches tacked onto the blind's plywood sides. Fog curls over the surface of Redfish Bay. Strings of white-faced ibis fly over and ghostly great egrets stalk the edges of the salt marshes. I can hear the peeps and calls of shorebirds working mudflats somewhere close by. If I listen carefully, I can hear the horns of the Aransas Pass ferries as they chug back and forth.

There isn't a duck in sight.

Jim is unimpressed.

"I can't believe they didn't have any kind of safety talk before the airboat ride," he says. "And look at these, that's just dumb." He points at the spread of tired decoys that list sideways, their paint faded and worn. "And this blind, it's just a plywood box in the middle of the bay. Couldn't they even try to camouflage it a little or put it back against the marsh?"

Bill tries, once again, to explain that the decoys and blind wouldn't matter if it was a normal year. He tells Jim about redheads heedlessly splashing down next to hunters setting out decoys; mornings when wave after wave of redheads,

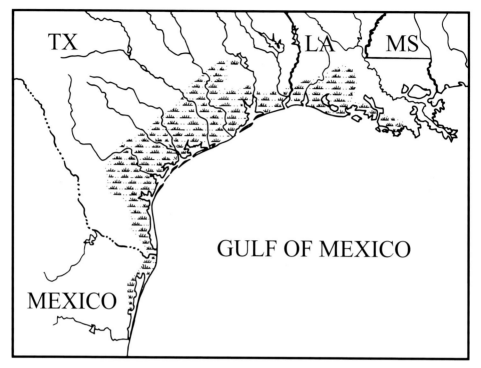

Historical extent of the Western Gulf Prairies.

scaup, and pintails dropped in to any kind of decoys; and flocks of redheads so large that they look like black clouds funneled down the Texas coastal bays.

Jim is having none of it. "That's a nice story, Bill," he retorts, "but there is no excuse for shoddy decoys." Bill shakes his head and looks away. I lean close. "Remember Rockport?" He smiles. Just over a year before, we'd seen a raft of over a thousand birds on Aransas Bay during the 2017 Rockport Christmas Bird Count. While our birding partners photographed a distant pair of common goldeneyes, Bill and I watched the redheads bobbing like a glossy living carpet on the rough surface of the bay. Behind us shattered live oaks, twisted buildings, and mountains of debris were reminders of Hurricane Harvey's destructive winds. I wonder whether Hurricane Harvey has anything to do with this season's paucity of ducks. Clearly something has changed.

We sit and wait, whispering and ducking down whenever one of the scarce ducks flies nearby. They appear suddenly out of the fog and disappear just as fast. A pair of birds flies in and drops into the mist at the far edge of the decoys. Before I can say "merganser," Bill and Jim have both fired. Q dashes out and retrieves one bird, and then the other. Jim looks at the red-breasted mergansers in disgust. "I'd never intentionally shoot a merganser," he says. "But at least Q got in a couple retrieves." They are the only ducks to come within range the entire morning.

The fog swirls away just before our guide shows up in his airboat. A hunter already on board notices the mergansers and tells Jim he nailed a ring-necked duck at fifty yards. Jim rolls his eyes and cups his hands over Q's ears. When we land, the marksman offers me his trio of ducks. "I have no use for these," he tells me. "I hunt every day and I don't eat duck." Jim and Bill both make about-faces and disappear, leaving me with the loquacious marksman. Looking past me for Bill and Jim, he reports the stunning accuracy and superior skill he utilized in shooting each duck at extraordinary ranges. I thank him for the ducks. "Worst hunting season in twenty years," I hear Jamie Spears tell Bill. The marksman echoes him. "Worst season in twenty years. Where are the goddamned ducks?"

That night, under Jim's direction, I breast the donated ringnecks and redhead, then sear the fillets while we wait for the feral hog green chile stew to heat up. Jim takes one bite of the duck and puts down his fork. "I owe you an apology," he says, taking a long pull from a beer. "I didn't believe you when you told me bay ducks had a fishy flavor. I thought you didn't know how to cook them. I was wrong." I smile and ladle out the stew.

The next morning, we say our goodbyes. Jim and Q are heading to a hunting cabin outside Mineola in northeastern Texas; Bill and I have to return to our work. As I stuff gear in the truck, I hear Jim say, "Well it wasn't like we had to watch ducks ignore us all morning." Jim and Bill laugh together. Bill swears that someday we'll all come down and hunt redheads again—when the ducks are back. "Everything is bigger in Texas, right, Bill?" Jim razzes him. "Flocks of a hundred thousand redheads? Sure."

Later I'll find data from the Texas Midwinter Waterfowl Survey (a joint project between the USFWS and TPWD) that confirm our experience. We weren't unlucky; the redheads really weren't there. From a high of eight hundred thousand redheads counted in 2017, in January 2018 the survey spotted only eighty-six thousand birds along the Texas coast.

Kevin Kraai, waterfowl program leader for the Texas Parks and Wildlife Department, tells me in a phone call, "Yes, the numbers from the Midwinter Survey are dramatic. But just because we didn't count redheads," he says, "that doesn't mean they aren't around. Continental populations of redheads have reached all-time highs in the last decade. They like to clump and you can have flocks of four hundred thousand to five hundred thousand birds."

"Did you just say *four hundred thousand ducks*?" I ask, trying to imagine such a flock.

"Yes," he laughs, "and if the survey transect [the designated line or pattern flown by the spotter airplane] doesn't happen to cross the main flocks, or the flocks are in the Laguna Madre de Tamaulipas, the data looks like there are no birds."

It seems that the redheads aren't gone, just gone to Mexico.

I knew that redheads wintered in the Laguna Madre, the shallow bay tucked behind Padre Island with its lush beds of sea grass. But in a typical Texas-centric fashion, I had never realized that the Laguna Madre doesn't end at the Texas-Mexico border. The fifth largest hypersaline lagoon in the world, the Laguna Madre stretches more than 250 miles along the Gulf Coast from Texas's Corpus Christi Bay south to Río Soto La Marina and the town of La Pesca in Tamaulipas, Mexico. The lagoon is only briefly interrupted by the Rio Grande/Río Bravo delta where the river once regularly flowed out into the Gulf.

Along the Laguna Madre's length, barrier islands separate the shallow bay from the Gulf. In the arid climate, and with no major rivers feeding the bays, the twin forces of sun and wind evaporate the bay's waters until they are concentrated, at times becoming three to four times saltier than the Gulf itself.

During the fall, over 80 percent of North America's redhead population migrates to the Laguna Madre of Texas and Tamaulipas, where they spend the winter noshing on the rhizomes of sea grass (especially the favored shoalgrass). The redheads are joined by pintails, American wigeon, hundreds of thousands of shorebirds (including threatened and endangered populations of piping plovers), reddish egrets, wood storks, brown pelicans, and peregrine falcons—just to name a few.

"I read that redheads could possibly eat their way out of the Laguna Madre," I tell Kraai. He laughs. "No, there are lots of sea grass beds in the Laguna Madre. But where they go is not just about food source. They also need freshwater daily." After feeding on sea grasses in the bays, especially the hypersaline waters of the Laguna Madre, redheads need freshwater to drink and purge the excess salt. Seabirds, including sea ducks, and many shorebirds have a pair of supra-orbital salt glands that allow them to thrive in saltwater environments. But the redheads, wigeonss, and pintails can't stay if there isn't freshwater nearby—no matter how much food is available.

In Mexico, agriculture has boomed along the coastal plains that back up to the Laguna Madre de Tamaulipas. Over three million acres of grasslands, brushlands, and freshwater wetlands have been converted to fields. And this is where, not surprisingly, Ducks Unlimited de México (DUMAC) is stepping up. With help from local conservation-minded property owners, Ducks Unlimited, TPWD, and private donors, DUMAC is restoring former wetlands and building infrastructure for new ponds and freshwater wetlands for all the migratory birds that winter in the Laguna Madre de Tamaulipas. North of the Rio Grande, the Texas Prairie Wetlands Project (a collaboration between DU, TPWD, NRCS, and USFWS) is working with the King Ranch and other property owners to ensure that there is freshwater for migratory birds along the Laguna Madre of Texas's salty bay.

Cheered by the redhead revelation (not gone, just out of sight), I ask Kevin Kraai about the Midwinter Waterfowl Survey's graphs with lines that skid downward, indicating fewer ducks along the Texas coast. I hear a sigh. "It's real," he tells me. "Every species is in a downward trend along the coast."

My relief disappears. I feel the familiar dread, a dark weight that increases with every unhappy fact and dire environmental prediction.

"There is a deficit of habitat on the Gulf Coast," Kevin tells me. It seems an oddly bloodless term for the loss of what was once one of the most productive wetland systems in North America.

The Gulf Coast is not just Texas and Louisiana, but the jagged rim of life-giving coastal prairies and marshes edging the Gulf of Mexico from Florida to the Yucatán Peninsula. It is the ribbon of habitat where land meets sea and freshwater meets salt. More than 90 percent of coastal wetland loss in the lower 48 states has occurred along the US Gulf Coast. The coastal prairies and marshes of Alabama, Mississippi, and Louisiana historically hosted 50 percent of the Mississippi Flyway's ducks. Over half of the Central Flyway's waterfowl population wintered along the Texas coast, frequenting the prairies, rice prairies, and coastal marshes. Once upon a time, more than fifteen million ducks and geese wintered along the US Gulf Coast.

Redhead drake and hen

I close my eyes and silently recite the joyless litany of coastal environmental issues: land subsidence, rising sea levels, beach erosion, saltwater intrusion into freshwater aquifers, tidal water infiltrating freshwater marshes, invasive species, oil spills, British Petroleum's Deepwater Horizon oil blowout, irresponsible development, hurricanes, reduced freshwater inflows, sea grass beds and oyster reefs smothered by silt from dredging, propeller-scarred sea grass beds, and the relentless erosion along channels cut for navigation and petroleum exploration. The result is a cumulative loss of more than 1.2 million acres of Gulf Coast wetlands. This is more than just a habitat deficit—it is an ecological disaster. And it is happening right in front of our eyes.

From the deck of Captain Tommy Moore's boat, the *Skimmer*, I am witness to the uneasy juxtaposition of endangered whooping cranes foraging in salt marshes with barges full of benzine, crude oil, and who-knows-what other petroleum products churning down the Gulf Intracoastal Waterway just yards away. I brace myself as the wake from yet another barge rolls our boat full of binoculars- and camera-clutching birdwatchers. The waves roll into the salt marsh of the Aransas National Wildlife Refuge and I watch the delicate curlicues of dissolved shoreline slip into the turbid muscling current of the navigation channel.

The Gulf Intracoastal Waterway (GIWW), the US Army Corps of Engineers' self-proclaimed "1,000-mile miracle," originally ran through the bays along the Texas coast. Then an engineer, concerned with freight, ships, and harbors (and not the benefits of marshes), rerouted the channel to cut inside the shoreline. Since it was completed in 1941, every passing barge has trailed a wake that slaps shorelines, both natural and engineered, across Texas, Louisiana, Mississippi, Alabama, and Florida.

I think about Mad Island Lake off the coast of Matagorda Bay. The lake once merged seamlessly with the surrounding prairies, creating freshwater marshes that slowly slipped to brackish as they neared the bay. Saltwater crept into the narrow mouth of the lake, where it mixed with freshwater and created a layered nursery in the grasses and bulrushes for shrimp and fish. Birds feasted on the plants, insects, crustaceans, fish, and other creatures that thrived in the gradient of fresh to salt. The Intracoastal Waterway changed that with its relentless waves of tidal water pushing inland, eroding and altering the shorelines, not just here at Mad Island, but along the channel's entire length.

As the salinity changes, so does everything else, from the smallest worms and snails to the plants, to the animals that eat the plants, to the birds that eat the plants and snails. The change is subtle at first but cumulative over time. As freshwater flows decline from creeks and rivers, and as less water flows off irrigated rice fields, salty water slowly backs into the freshwater lakes along the bays. The freshwater marsh plants die back. Sometimes they are replaced by salt-tolerant plants; other times, the now-exposed shoreline erodes. In Louisiana, the state itself is disappearing. The waterways and canals cut for navigation and oil exploration and production have fragmented the swamps and marshes. Intensifying storms scour the Gulf Coast with punishing waves and winds, and more land disappears, and with it the habitat that ducks, herons, egrets, rails, and an untold number of other creatures rely on for food, shelter, and nesting.

Shoreline once lost is rarely reclaimed.

Unless you let a river have her way . . .

Is there a river or stream that flows to the Gulf that hasn't been modified by the US Army Corps of Engineers? From the mighty Mississippi to small creeks, waterways have been schooled into dredged canals bound with levees and dock-lined harbors. For many, their nutrient-rich freshwater and sediments are shunted away from the marshes and into the Gulf. Distributaries that once split away to create bird's-foot river deltas have been clipped and blocked so they no longer feed freshwater into salt or replenish marshes with layers of sediment.

The Texas Colorado River's management could be an analogy for the Mississippi. Two hundred years ago it freely flowed into Matagorda Bay through an ever-changing delta made of winding distributaries. The bay was alive with oysters, fish, and birds. But in the 1920s the river coughed a logjam, long stuck in its craw, out into the bay. The clot of mud and logs collected more sediment and debris, rapidly creating a land bridge that grew across the bay. Because there was nowhere for the water to go, every river rise created a flood. Determined citizens dug a ruler-straight canal through the land bridge in the 1930s, thereby diverting the problematic river directly into the Gulf of Mexico and bypassing the bay. The US Army Corps of Engineers stepped in and took over the river canal, building floodgates and locks where the Gulf Intracoastal Waterway and the river crossed paths at right angles. Soon, the last of the river's distributaries were blocked and the Colorado's single stream was dredged into a tidy channel the right depth and width for cargo ships. The bottomland hardwood forests, essential to migratory songbirds, that once sprawled across the river valley to catch and slow floodwaters were trimmed into thin ribbons framing the banks.

Matagorda Bay languished without the Colorado's freshwater. For sixty years, fishermen and oystermen told anyone who would listen that the bay was dying. Finally, the corps dug another channel to solve the problems created with the first canal and the GIWW. Now, thanks to their continued interventions, the Colorado's freshwater flows into Matagorda Bay, where the river is creating a new delta and nourishing the estuary and oyster beds.

I have witnessed firsthand the birth of the Colorado's new land, where river-borne sediment mounds up into mudflats that transition into marsh as cordgrass takes hold. The delta is where the river and bay move from freshwater to salt, from flowing water to pudding-like mud to terra firma as colonizing roots reach down and hold fast. For as long as freshwater still flows downstream, the Colorado will create a new world in Matagorda Bay.

I am not surprised to learn that there are plans afoot to dig multiple diversion channels from the Mississippi River in the hopes of reinvigorating Barataria Bay and rebuilding the marshes and delta. By re-creating the river's natural distributaries, the plan is to restore Barataria Bay a little at a time by adding freshwater to salt for the fish, shrimp, and crabs and using the Mississippi's muddy water to rebuild the sinking land. History shows that no matter how carefully planned or designed, tinkering with natural systems has unintended consequences. Let's hope that this time the end results are at worst benign, or at best beneficial.

Some say we are too late to save our coast, that the issues of the twenty-first century will thwart our attempts at restoration. Will sea level rise, warming waters, intensifying storms (a record nine storms hit the Gulf Coast of the United States and Mexico in 2020), demands for freshwater, and rampant development outrace the work of the people and groups working to save and restore our Gulf Coast prairies and marshes?

The US Army Corps of Engineers directs the never-ending dredging of the GIWW to keep it from filling in. The spoils, the slurry of mud, sand, and water produced by dredging, were once considered waste. Nowadays, when given a chance—and the funding to cover additional expenses—the Texas Department of Transportation (the GIWW state administrator) and the corps will collaborate with conservation groups to use the spoils to rejuvenate marshes, stabilize bird rookery islands, rebuild lost shorelines, and replenish beaches. In Louisiana the corps works with the Louisiana Department of Wildlife and Fisheries, the state's Coastal Protection and Restoration Authority, Ducks Unlimited, the National Fish and Wildlife Foundation, the National Audubon Society, and the USFWS (to name just a few) to rebuild marshes and barrier islands. All along the GIWW, conservation groups like DU and the Coastal Conservation Association acquire permits from the corps to construct breakwaters to reduce erosion and saltwater incursion into the remaining freshwater lakes and marshes. The groups combine fund-raising dollars with NAWCA grants to protect public lands from our own best intentions.

Inland, the DU-spearheaded Texas Prairie Wetlands Project (in collaboration with TPWD, NRCS, and USFWS), has been working for three decades with private landowners to create wetlands and emergent wetland-mimicking moist soil units in the coastal prairie. To date, the project has created eighty-five thousand acres of primarily freshwater wetland habitat that benefits waterfowl, shorebirds, and resident waterbirds. The program's counterpart, the Louisiana Waterfowl Project, focuses a bit more on salt marsh restoration but also works with private landowners. Again, the focus is on waterfowl, but hundreds of other species benefit from their work. All along the coast, numerous groups work to mitigate the cumulative damage caused by the previous century's priorities of flood protection and navigation and the ongoing crisis of rising and warming seas. Money from the Deepwater Horizon oil spill settlement is earmarked to fund restoration, conservation of land, and enhancement of natural resources harmed by the spill.

I think about a raft of a thousand redhead ducks floating on a bay, flocks of shorebirds working mudflats, wading birds stalking prey, and whooping cranes hunting in salt marshes next to the Intracoastal Waterway. Is it too late to convince a public who prefers sandy beaches that salt marshes are vital? Or that the turbid waters of river deltas flooding into bays are visible signs of rejuvenation and healthy estuaries? How do we persuade anyone that mosquito-filled wetlands are key to protecting our future, and that those expanses of cordgrass that look uniform and unchanging from the window of a speeding car are not only full of life but also buffer homes and lands far inland from storm surges, while protecting Gulf waters by holding soil and filtering pollutants?

It is about so much more than ducks.

❧21❧

Birdwatcher's Brain

The flight of this species is remarkable for its speed, and the ease and elegance with which it is performed. The Wood Duck passes through the woods and even amongst the branches of trees, with as much facility as the Passenger Pigeon.
—Wood Duck, *Ornithological Biography*, vol. 3

I look ahead from my seat at the front of the poke boat. Catfish Creek slips silver through tangled thickets of winter woods and past a leaning shadowy hackberry tree. There, at the tree's base, a pair of wood ducks stand in perfect dark silhouette on a partially submerged branch. We drift closer and light floods the drake, his iridescent green crown glowing, his fiery red eye and chestnut chest all bracketed by white so pure it seems illuminated from within. The hen is a shadow at his side until she springs, squealing, into the air. The drake follows and I watch them fly up and clear the trees. Only then do I look down to see my 20 gauge clasped in my hands. I hadn't even considered taking what, in hindsight, I realize was an easy shot. One that even an unskilled marksman like myself could have made. It wasn't that I had any hesitations about shooting at a wood duck; I had simply forgotten about the shotgun in my hands.

I am here because my friend Andy called in a favor. Out of the blue, Scot McFarlane emailed me with an invitation to hunt wood ducks at his father's hunting preserve,

BigWoods on the Trinity. On the appointed January morning, I leave a grumbling and envious Bill to drive to Tennessee Colony in East Texas. I wind down the road into the preserve, 7,500 acres of bottomland hardwood forest, wetlands, and creeks. Over the years Scot's father, Dr. Robert McFarlane, has relentlessly assembled parcel after parcel to create this East Texas wildlife haven and duck hunter's dream. Now it is protected by a perpetual conservation easement with Wetlands America Trust, Ducks Unlimited's land trust partner. I park at a grand lodge that stands sentry over a collection of houses and apartments for hunters. This is no fly-by-night operation. I wonder how I will ever repay Andy, much less Scot, who is giving up a precious morning with family for me.

I sling my gun case and pack into the waiting truck. As Scot drives us down to the creek where we'll start our paddle, he warns me that we'll have to walk back to the truck. He easily hauls the ancient poke boat to the water's edge. His slenderness and quiet manner belie his strength. I hop in. Rondo, our retriever for the day, sits behind me, and Scot paddles in the stern. At first his reserve makes me wonder whether he wants to be out here with me at all. Perhaps I've taken him away from his wife and child for no good reason? But as we converse quietly, I realize it is simply his natural manner. A comfortable silence falls as we slip along the creek.

The day is warm, overcast with muted light. The winter woods and creek merge into a palette of tans and browns. Arching bare-limbed trees sketch gray against the pale sky, leafless vines snaking diagonally through the woods. Water seeps into the woods, and slender-branched thickets reach out from either side to tangle shotgun, hat, hair, and dog.

I slip into a state of wide-eyed observer submerged in the smells, textures, sounds, and sights of the world around me. I smell the mustiness of decomposing leaves, the acrid fragrance of willows and hackberries, and the lightly tannic creek water rippling through downed wood, plus wet dog, gun oil, and the funk of old cat pee somewhere in the boat. There is the gurgle of water against the fiberglass hull, the hollow thwack of the paddle against the side, the scrabble of dog toenails, and Rondo whining as I forget to take shot after shot—wood ducks, teal, and mallards unseen until too late. I'm mesmerized by their beauty as they explode into flight.

It's like my brain shifts into a different mode, I tell my friend Shannon. When I'm in watcher or observer mode, I seem unable to aim a gun and pull a trigger. It is uncannily similar to the disjunction I have between writing and making art. She's listened to me over the years as I puzzled my way out of frustration, until I finally realized with the help of my friend Carol Dawson, another artist and writer, that while I am both a writer and a painter, I simply cannot do both at the same time. It is as if each activity utilizes a separate part of my brain,

Wood duck drake and hen

different areas that don't communicate well with each other. When I'm making art, I pick up one of my books and have no idea where the words came from, no idea how they looped into sentences, paragraphs, and pages. When I'm writing, I look at my art and instead of my usual analysis of color and technique (which pigments did I use? which brush?), I stare, dumbfounded by color and texture. How did I do that? I inevitably wonder.

I'm not, I have learned, the only one to find that birdwatching and hunting have fundamentally different mental states. The revelation comes during a conversation about cattle ranching with Marshall Johnson, executive director of Audubon Dakota.[28]

We'd set up the call to discuss Audubon's Conservation Ranching Initiative, but my first question has nothing to do with cows. What I really want to know is how his fellow Auduboners regard his hunting. Johnson, a Black Texan living in

North Dakota, and a bird hunter working for Audubon, laughs out loud at my question.

"There are a few things I hunt that get a nasty look here or there from certain birdwatchers, but we don't have to agree on everything," he tells me. "I work with seven hundred fifty Audubon professionals. Our work is based in science. And science shows that hunting has very little adverse effect on regional or continental populations.

"Locally I don't need to reconcile hunting with conservation and birdwatching because both are accepted around here. Nationally, well, there is some lingering angst. But hunters and birdwatchers are both important pieces in the conservation puzzle," he says. I nod and make notes.

"Look," he says, "I'm a birder and the joy of birding is special, but self-reflective. Selfish but not in a negative sense. The culture of hunting is just so different." He goes on to talk about the camaraderie of the duck blind or hunting camp. "Plus, you harvest a duck, you know you are giving back with the Duck Stamp. Birders don't feel like they are taking anything, so the notion of putting something back isn't as strong."

I'm looking at him quizzically, not because I disagree but because it is the first time anyone has put my conflicted loyalties into words. He mistakes my expression and starts over, telling me that when he first started working for Audubon, they'd just done a valuation of their brand—surveys and studies of how the general public and their members felt about logos, brands, and values. For The Nature Conservancy (which is four times larger than Audubon and three times the size of Ducks Unlimited), the public's verb association was "to protect," with the accompanying association that "it takes a lot to protect." Ducks Unlimited's verb association was "to hunt," and the group was identified with both effort and teamwork.

Audubon's verb association was "to watch." "And that says a lot," Johnson tells me. "You can watch a bird feeder from a kitchen window or watch as you take a nice stroll down a city block. You don't have to work hard to watch." He shakes his head. "The difference reflects a deeper cultural impediment. Hunting and protecting are more active and watching is more passive. And that passivity can lead to a disconnect with the need to be an active participant in conservation and advocacy."

My head snaps up. He's not only just described the difference between my birding brain and my hunting brain; he's put a pin in the eel-like revelation that I've been trying to grasp since the start of my journey, the crux of why birdwatchers don't do more for conservation.

When visiting wild places, I've always obeyed the dictum "Take only photos, leave only footprints." And felt smugly virtuous doing so. I don't litter, I don't cart home river rocks to decorate mantels (well, maybe very small ones), I don't cut down trees for firewood, gouge or paint my name on rocks, or kidnap box turtles for pets—things that make me a good citizen of public and private land. That attitude naturally extends to birdwatching, where I do my best to only observe, not interact at all.

When I'm out birding, I'm looking at everything, absorbing all the sensory information around me. But being an observer is, without doubt, passive. I often slip into a trancelike state where I walk or sit, doing my best to let the irritating details of life, vanity, and self-importance fall away until I'm a sponge soaking up the world around me. I finish rejuvenated, often hopeful, and feel connected to the natural world in an overwhelmingly positive way. If I've seen unique birds or bird behavior, a quiet euphoria carries me home.

There are birders who will argue that birding and birdwatching are different activities, that birdwatching is passive, and birding is active. One is just observing birds you happen upon; the other is actively pursuing birds, whether a resplendent quetzal in Costa Rica or the warbler that just vanished into a yaupon thicket. Birders keep life lists; birdwatchers fill bird feeders.

When I'm hunting, I can't let myself slip into the role of passive observer. I have to be ready to participate fully, to engage with life and death.

I was an active member of our local Audubon chapter for many years, one of the hard-core volunteers who played musical chairs on the chapter's Board of Directors. We set up monthly meetings to entertain and educate our members with slide shows, arranged field trips, and helped with the local annual Christmas Bird Counts. Too many board meetings were spent arguing over the small sums we raised through T-shirt sales and donations. The membership got older and our numbers dropped. It never occurred to us to raise money for National Audubon or conservation projects outside our area. Indeed, I remember our outrage when the national office tried to curtail the chapters' share of membership fees.

Ducks Unlimited chapters have a different purpose. Yes, the local members of DU get together to socialize, but always with the same goal: raise money for duck habitat conservation, preservation, and restoration. Chapters compete to see who can raise the most money. There are auctions and raffles of gear designed to tempt (male) hunters. Membership premiums are myriad and geared toward hunting, with hats, blind bags, waterproof packs, thermal shirts, and coats (for men). No reusable tote bags for grocery shopping here.

Waterfowl, wild turkeys, pheasant, quail, and other game birds have benefited from a ready group of protectors, benefactors, and boosters. Hunters have poured their money and time into protecting and creating habitat. They have made their way to the halls of legislation and lobbied for laws and funding.

Yet birdwatchers outnumber hunters four to one by the latest count. With the shutdowns imposed by the COVID-19 pandemic, the number of bird-watchers has skyrocketed. But songbirds, shorebirds, waders, and land birds don't have the same intensive conservation work benefiting them and their hab-itats. Birdwatchers don't have federal or state stamps, hunting licenses, or taxes like Pittman-Robertson to fund conservation with our activities. We don't raise money locally to send to national organizations.

What birdwatching does provide is a nearly universal chance to connect with nature. Anyone can birdwatch, just about anywhere, without spending a dime. From pigeons in public squares to peregrine falcons nesting on skyscrapers to cardinals and chickadees in neighborhood parks, birds are everywhere.[29] While a pair of good binoculars is beneficial, birdwatching doesn't have to be expen-sive or require specialized equipment (like duck hunting). There is mounting evidence that contact with nature has profound physiological and psychological benefits. I'm not the only one who feels calm and rejuvenated after a few min-utes of birdwatching or walking through a park or woods. Doctors now prescribe walks in parks for patients. Studies measure stress hormone levels and blood pressure and test cognitive abilities in an attempt to quantify what we already know: being connected to nature feels good.

I'm thinking the quote for hikers and birdwatchers needs to be amended with a final clause: "Take only photos, leave only footprints, and donate money or time."

On Catfish Creek I'm stuck in birdwatcher brain and I forget how to be a hunter. Kinglets, chickadees, and cardinals tweedle and flit past. We paddle past a sleek herd of white-tailed bucks socializing down by the creek. They freeze, their heads creating a thicket of spreading antlers, then wheel and run into the woods. How can they run through the dense brush with those branching racks without tangling them? We pull the boat through snarls of vines and branches and carry it around a fallen tree that blocks the creek. Robins hop around the woods. Wood-peckers small, medium, and large bang on snags, flashing red like warning lights. Around another bend a sounder of hogs, a dozen small to medium in shades of brown and black, squeal and scatter. "Good eating size," I remark to Scot. "There are enough of them," he replies. Ahead of us a black vulture is perched on something in the center of the creek. The current pushes us past, but we look down into the water to see two bucks submerged, their antlers fatally locked. Scot backpaddles and we take a closer look. In life they would have been mag-nificent; in death they are a curiosity. Heads bowed, legs tangled, and breast to breast, they lie on their sides in the stream. Even in death they are graceful, their peeling skin waving like silk in the current. The smell of rotting flesh doesn't hit until we are downstream, and then it twists and turns, following us. A big beaver placidly munches on a twig and watches us paddle past. Before I have the wits to pull out my camera, he slips silently into the water. And there are ducks. Wood ducks, teal, and mallards. The wood ducks are usually in shallow water, deep in a thicket. I don't understand how Scot spots them. He whispers that they are ahead and I scan the woods, seeing nothing until the birds spring into the air. By then it is too late and nearly every time, I just watch them fly away. I remember my gun in time to make several hopelessly long shots after wood ducks. I aim for a pair of teal that spring up and quickly disappear into the canopy of winter-bare trees.

We pull up at the takeout spot (which looks like every other bend along the creek to me). Scot says, "Shots were fired. No ducks killed so no birds to clean. I'd call it a success." His words surprise me. I'm feeling mortified by my lack of skill and for wasting Scot's morning. I remember Bob McFarlane's words to me just before we left for the creek: "Wood ducks will make a fool of you." Boy, was he right.

We walk back to the truck, layers of mud sticking to my shoes until I'm skating on slabs of clay. We load the boat, scrape off mud, and return to the lodge where half a dozen bearded guides clad in camo stand around, looking like a casting call for the *Duck Dynasty* show.

As a hunt, it was a wash. The times I remembered to raise my shotgun, I was too late, too far behind the ducks. Maybe if I'd carried the recommended 12 gauge with 3½" shells I might have gotten a duck. But it is unlikely. I just couldn't switch from observer to participant, from birdwatcher to hunter.

But spending a morning paddling a creek through deep woods in a world-class preserve? Even as a lousy hunter, I knew it was a magical day.

22

Season's End

On the water, few birds exhibit more graceful motions than the Pintail Duck. There seems also a kind of natural modesty in it which you do not find in other ducks.
    —Pintail Duck, *Ornithological Biography*, vol. 3

Andy Sansom, Bill, and I sit with Greg, our guide, at the edge of an emergent wetland, a former rice field left fallow for ducks. A pair of pintails come in just as the clock ticks over into shooting hours. Bill and I fire at the same drake, missing completely in the cool dawn light. Andy hits the other drake with a clean shot, and at a word, Scout takes off to retrieve the bird. I can hear her splashing but, worryingly, she seems to be heading away from us. We wait as the rising sun paints the low clouds with lurid pinks, oranges, and reds. The sky turns lemon yellow as long shafts of light pierce the prairie. Scout is nowhere in sight. When she doesn't respond to calls or whistles, Andy goes to retrieve Scout (she had followed our track back to the truck). Bill and I wait quietly, watching the human-made marsh before us as its creatures stir with the rising sun.

The night before, we'd sat in rocking chairs on Bucksnag's porch in Garwood. Andy Sansom is a hunter-conservationist in the mode of George Bird Grinnell and Aldo Leopold. He has spent his career building bridges between disparate groups as the executive director of the TPWD and The Nature Conservancy, a member of Audubon, a writer, a teacher, and a mentor.

He leans back in the rocker, a glass of wine in hand. The Bucksnag is a grand old building, lovingly restored and maintained for the members of the private hunting club. At the other end of the porch a Houston lawyer is loudly telling his son stories about fast cars. Andy's voice is measured and I lean forward to catch his words. "Hunting is cultural," he says. "Most hunters learn from family, fathers teaching sons or daughters, so the traditions are passed down generation to generation. Especially waterfowl hunting." I wonder, briefly, if those barely remembered glimpses of my father's hunting set the stage, as it were, for my sudden about-face to be a hunter. Certainly, Bill's calm and steady approach was essential. "Texas is one of the biggest hunting states in the US," Andy continues, "but we've been losing hunters since the 1970s. And not just in Texas but all over the US the numbers of hunters are in decline." Our state and country's transition from rural to urban is a major factor, but even when someone is interested in learning to hunt, finding someone to teach you the skills and techniques—a mentor—is not easy. I've been extraordinarily lucky to have my husband, Andy, Dr. Ken Sherman, and Jim as mentors. I am not sure what I would have done if Bill hadn't been a hunter, whether I would have been able to traverse the unknown ground between birdwatcher and bird hunter. Fishing isn't in decline the way hunting is: it requires less gear, and fishing sites are easily accessible to nearly everyone, whether urban or rural. We sit in the cool night air, sharing stories, laughing, and talking quietly while Scout paces around us, excited to be back at the Bucksnag.

We wake early and follow our guide down dark roads, driving past the hulking shadows of a gravel mine to park near an old barn. Greg cranks up the ATV and I hear the motor putt-putting as he splashes through mud and water. Bill and I walk out in the dark, balancing on the low levees contouring the field, spooking the occasional snipe. A cluster of larger shorebirds fly off into the night, their piping complaints trailing behind long after the birds are out of sight. We settle at the edge of the field behind canvas panels that are dressed in mud and dried grasses.

After the initial excitement of the first pintails, it is a slow morning for hunting ducks. A flock of hundreds of pintails swirls high above us, appearing again and again. Only a few birds are tempted to join the decoys, their gregarious nature proving a fatal flaw. In the distance sandhill cranes fly over the fields, announcing to the world that they are on their way to breakfast. A juvenile bald eagle cruises past and I track its progress across the fields by the waves of birds that it spooks into flight. I pull out my binoculars and scan the usual suspects working the shoreline and shallow water. It is a quiet and peaceful morning. The ducks don't flood in to the decoys. We don't limit out in thirty minutes or worry about accidentally shooting a restricted species in the chaos. Instead, we end the morning with a total of five ducks. The shots fired were considered and intentional. After the echo of the gun blasts fades away, we sit in silence. Occasionally we whisper to each other but mostly we watch and wait. The long light of morning reaches across the field, illuminating every blade of grass in sharp detail as I listen to the rise and fall of our breathing and the murmuring of the marsh. I look at Andy. He sits with one hand on the stock of his shotgun, the other gently stroking Scout's neck, with a deeply tranquil expression on his face as he looks out over the decoys.

Bill and Greg have the same expressions. Focused and, yes, serene—although that word seems out of place among the beards, camouflage, and shotguns. Despite the mud, the chill, waking early, growling stomachs, and few birds, the three of them look as content as I feel.

As I sit with Andy, Bill, and Greg, I think about birdwatchers and ducks. Honestly, I've never met a birdwatcher who was deeply excited by ducks. I certainly wasn't. Bring together a flock of birdwatchers and you'll hear stories about Neotropical songbirds—the brightly colored jewels that flit through the oak mottes and bottomland hardwood forests along the Texas coast during migration. Falcons, hawks, and eagles are worthy of attention, as are woodpeckers, kingfishers, and cranes. Nearly always there are stories about travels to foreign lands to see antbirds, quetzals, puffins, macaws, and penguins. Some birders are passionate about shorebirds and have honed their skills to recognize the subtle plumage variations of miscellaneous peeps skittering on shorelines of fresh and salt water.

But excitement about ducks or geese? Not so much. Maybe waterfowl are too close to barnyard fowl. Has domestication of their brethren tainted their reputations so they aren't seen as so purely wild as a yellow warbler or an indigo bunting?

Today the divide between nongame species such as egrets and songbirds and game birds like quail and ducks seems solid and obvious. Yet it wasn't all that long ago that everything from dickcissels to whooping cranes was considered fine table fare. It is true that many of the birdwatchers I've spent time with seem to regard game species as somehow lesser citizens, less interesting and less desirable quarry than nongame species.

Like flocks of red-winged blackbirds that crowd the sky, is it the abundance of ducks and geese that makes them seem less precious? In my experience, a lake full of hundreds of gadwalls, blue-winged teal, coots, and northern shovelers does not elicit the same excitement from birders that a single peregrine falcon does. I certainly have been guilty of this nongame prejudice. Yet ducks have come back from a brink nearly as precipitous as the falcon's brush with extirpation.

Waterfowl's recovery from the population lows of the 1930s and our race to preserve their wetland habitats is a huge, astonishingly successful conservation story. In addition to the Duck Stamp and other legislation, the collaborative model of Joint Ventures set forth in the North American Waterfowl Management Plan has been so successful that it has expanded to include shorebirds and land birds.[30] Groups modeling themselves on the Joint Ventures have popped up across the globe, working to conserve wildlife and wild places. Between government funding and donations to Ducks Unlimited, Ducks Unlimited Canada, Ducks Unlimited de México, Delta Waterfowl, and others, waterfowl research has been a leader in avian research for over three-quarters of a century. Indeed, numerous bird species and studies have coattailed on waterfowl research funding.

But today's relative abundance of ducks may be obscuring a fatal flaw. I worry that ducks will become a victim of their own success and that past achievements have resulted in a stagnant complacency about the future of waterfowl and wetlands. I've been told that waterfowl are doing "okay now," "pretty good," or its equivalent from half a dozen duck biologists. Waterfowl populations are considered generally stable, and they are meeting the objectives set by the North American Waterfowl Management Plan. Evasive conditionals like "pretty good" and "generally" make me nervous. Kevin Kraai from the TWPD told me that because waterfowl are doing well ("for the most part," he added), there is a feeling that it is time to concentrate on other habitats and other species, that research and research dollars should focus elsewhere now.

The prospect terrifies me. Wetland habitats continue to disappear. It isn't just that they are drained and plowed up or built over, but if there is no water, there are no wetlands. Competing demands for water for cities, industry, and irrigation are leaving wetlands like Kansas's Cheyenne Bottoms and Quivira NWR gasping; rivers like the Platte and the two Colorado Rivers struggle to flow into their lower reaches; coastal marshes and estuaries wither as freshwater inflows diminish. The prairies continue to be plowed up for crops. And the numbers of hunters continue to decline. With that decline there are fewer licenses and Duck Stamps sold, fewer funds available through Pittman-Robertson, and less money for wildlife refuges and conservation easements. Conservation groups like Ducks Unlimited are working hard to recruit new hunters as the majority of their membership slips into retirement age and beyond. National legislation for conservation funding like the Recovering America's Wildlife Act is introduced again and again but has yet to pass.

I take a deep breath. Our society is dynamic and evolving. I've got a phone full of apps for birdwatching, weather, hunting in Texas and in South Dakota, iNaturalist, and even an app that connects to my Beretta 20 gauge and tells me how many shots I fired, when, and where. Climate change is real, regardless of whether one believes humans are the cause. The intensifying droughts and storms, shorter winters, and erratic frost dates affect everyone: people, plants, insects, animals, and birds. There is always a long list of environmental crises and species in peril that need funding.

Out of the corner of my eye I see a large shadow racing across the field. The bald eagle cuts close to a pair of green-winged teal that spring straight up from the water. The eagle veers one way, the teal the opposite direction. I raise my gun, aim, and fire. The drake plummets. "Wow, Margie, what a shot!" Andy says. I can't believe it was me. I look over at Greg and he smiles at me as he lowers his shotgun. I narrow my eyes at him and his smile broadens. I suspect Greg actually hit the drake and it makes me uneasy to get the credit for the stunning long shot. Scout joyfully runs out and circles. She splashes through the shallows and pounces on the drake. She wags and swaggers, as frisky as a puppy as she prances back. The four of us stand with matching smiles on our faces as Scout, radiating happiness like a small golden-brown sun, brings Andy the duck.

❧ 23 ❧

Back at the Vineyard

> Because hunting was central to his ornithology, Audubon never made much
> of a distinction between sport and science, and when it came to ducks, his
> blood ran hot.
> —William Souder, *Under a Wild Sky*

"I hope you like the show I arranged for you," Steve Balas says with a wry smile.[31]
I can barely hear him over the honking, quacking, trilling, whistling, and squeak-
ing. In front of us are three hundred acres packed breast to beak with geese,
ducks, waders, shorebirds, and blackbirds. Spoonies (shovelers), gadwalls, pintails, green-winged teal, specks, snows, blues, and a few Canada geese jostle each
other. White and white-faced ibis, egrets, and herons stand in contrast to the
browns and grays of shorebirds too numerous to count. Caracaras and vultures
hop and fly around the perimeter, waiting to clean up birds exhausted by migration or wounded by a hunter.

"Do you hunt?" I ask.

"I'm not opposed to hunting," he says, "but the only hunters allowed here
are the bald eagles. This pond is just for the birds."

I nearly laugh out loud. This pond was never intended to "lure in poor ducks
so some macho hunter can blast them out of the sky." I am back where my journey started, only to learn that the remark made by one of the birdwatchers—the
statement that made me confront my own bias—was wrong about the flooded
field's purpose.

"Why do you do it?" I ask Steve, genuinely curious about why he creates wetland habitat on this scale.

"Because someone told me to," he answers, smiling. "My father-in-law just loved seeing the birds and I promised that I would continue to take care of them. And I do." Ducks and shorebirds continue to drop into the crowded water. A northern harrier flies low over the pond, ignored by the birds below. A nearly full moon hangs lopsided above the eastern horizon, as pale as a cloud.

I look out over the roost pond and the rice prairie surrounding it as my ears ring with the cacophony of the birds, frogs, and insects. I am back in Eagle Lake where my quest started. In the interim, I've driven from Texas to Canada looking for ducklings and migratory birds. I've put aside a lifetime of ambivalence and fear to learn how to safely handle a shotgun. Now I own three. I've hunted on private lands; Texas Wildlife Management Areas and South Dakota Game lands paid for with Pittman-Robertson Funds; and Waterfowl Production Areas paid for with federal Duck Stamp dollars. I've watched birds and hunted on the shores of stock tanks, on the edges of flooded rice fields, in the middle of cornfields, from cattail clumps in waist-deep water, from riverbanks, and from the edges of both natural and created wetlands. We have harvested and eaten plump South Dakota ducks, ducks lean from fall migration, fishy bay ducks, and succulent young birds from the Texas rice prairies. I have simmered duck gumbos, braised duck in red wine until it is as earthy and rich as beef bourguignon, roasted ducks whole, made lean Italian duck sausage, and learned the absolute best way to roast the breasts. I have found beauty—and birds—nearly everywhere, but if I am honest, breaking dawn light seen from a duck blind gilds even the starkest landscape with 24-karat optimism and hope.

Steve looks out over the birds, dark silhouettes against silver water, with a tranquil smile on his face. We stand waiting.

I fidget a little. I don't know it, but the masses of birds paddling, quacking, honking, fishing, preening, and working the shoreline are only the prelude to the show. With a sudden roar, a thousand birds spring up, beating wings crushing air, and honks and quacks filling every space until it feels as though a solid wall, a physical pressure of sound pushes against me, reverberating in my bones and lifting my heart in exaltation.

Hallelujah! I want to yell at the birds. Because if this is not religion, then what is? This is a pure expression of life and joy. But I stand mute and humbled, awash in sound.

The snows and blues and specks circle around, every bird calling at the top of his or her lungs. Steve leans over and yells, "I don't know what it is that they are saying but it sure must be important because they never stop talking." It's

White-fronted geese aka specklebellies

true, there is an urgency to the snow goose honks and the creaky hinge sound of the specklebellies that ripples through the lines of birds as they form into Vs and stream away into the evening air.

We stand, enthralled by the sight and sound of a thousand geese giving voice as they fly to feed in nearby fields. Not because, as some would believe, I am imagining the perfect shot and roast goose on the table. No, it brings life crashing down around me, where predator, prey, hunter, and protector align in a beautiful juxtaposition. I breathe deep, life and death inhaled and held deep in my chest as one and the same. It is joy that suffuses my heart and limbs. But it is so much more than mere happiness. No, this joy burns through me, leaving a husk behind that I will fill with the honks and quacks of birdsong, of feathers, friends, ducks, and hope.

Epilogue

Andy has a new retriever, Lolo. Scout spent her last days fetching the morning paper, dozing in the sun, and no doubt teaching Lolo the rules of the household.

Jim Weisenhorn is gone, felled by aggressive cancer diagnosed too late. He made the choice to skip his final treatments and spend his remaining days with dignity, fishing and enjoying the company of friends and loved ones. His retriever, Q, has a new home with a South Dakota duck hunter. I hope the hunter's daughters, who dote on Q, take up duck hunting. I had never imagined a friendship built on ducks, much less duck hunting, and I miss Jim. I regret that I'll never get a Duck Report again, watch him work with Q, or sit together in a blind in companionable silence waiting for ducks.

Jim's death speaks to a larger truth about hunters of all kinds in the United States: the average hunter is a white male forty-five years old or older. The number of individual hunting license buyers has dropped from over 14 million in 1991 to around 11.5 million in 2016 (the most recent data). Hunters make up only 4.5 percent of the population, and that number drops every year. Decades of decline seem irreversible.

That is until the novel coronavirus pandemic forced changes on us all. Bill and I had our lives and our hunting plans put on pause as we waited for a vaccine. Yet the pandemic year brought a surge of men, women, and families back to our public lands. People turned to the outdoors and birdwatching, hiking, bicycle riding, fishing, and hunting. Hunting license sales went through the roof as men and women hunted for ducks, geese, doves, deer, turkeys, and hogs, many for the first time. Some did it to feed their families local sustainable protein. Others pursued self-sufficiency, and some hunted purely for the intimate connection to nature. The 12 percent rise in hunting license sales equals over a million more hunters than last season. With the revenues from licenses, states can apply for more grants from the Wildlife Restoration Fund and use those funds for habitat, training, biologists, and education. Will the interest in hunting last? Or, when life returns to a semblance of normal, will hunting begin to fade away again?

As our cities expand and suburbs continue to supplant our rural and wild lands, habitat loss will continue to impact migratory bird populations from ducks to swallows. While there is no substitute for preserving natural habitat, programs encouraging the creation of wildscaping will be ever more important. And not just for wildlife, because as so many of us already know intuitively, even a momentary connection with nature not only feels good; it is good for us. The National Wildlife Federation's Community Wildlife Habitat program is just one of many that encourage planting native plants for birds, butterflies, pollinators, and other wildlife in our yards, parks, public spaces, and schoolyards. Programs like Bird City Americas can help us turn our cities and towns into bird-friendly habitats. With a little work, both urban and suburban habitats can be havens for both wildlife and humans.

I now know that John James Audubon was a deeply flawed man. For over a century, conservation groups have glossed over his often-wasteful hunting and collecting. More importantly, shedding light on his unrepentant racism, and slave ownership is overdue. The National Audubon Society, The Audubon Naturalist Society, and local birding chapters are dissociating from the use of his name in their branding. There is a strong movement to rename birds and other species tied to people with problematic pasts. We cannot erase our history, nor should we, but we can move forward with open minds.

On a piece of Brazos River bottomland that has been in Bill's family for generations, we've paid a bulldozer driver to scrape a shallow catchment basin. While Texas Parks and Wildlife offered general advice, it was frustrating that no one at Ducks Unlimited, or the local USDA Natural Resources Conservation Service, could guide us through the process. In the end, we took a cue from Dr. Ken Sherman and created what we hope will be a seasonal wetland and shallow pond. If you build it, they will come—isn't that the idea? If the birds find our Falls County puddle, will we hunt there? It is a possibility, but we'll likely just enjoy watching the birds. Just knowing that we are attempting to return cattle pasture to some sort of wetland is deeply satisfying. If I'm honest, ducks just make me happy. As do egrets, herons, cranes, shorebirds, frogs, toads, snakes, and the other denizens of the wetland realm.

For now, I will go on my way, quietly determined to make a difference in the world. Whether I hunt or not, I vow to participate by buying a Duck Stamp every year—and a federal songbird stamp if that ever becomes a reality—and continuing to donate my small sums to conservation organizations across the country. I will dream of a disparate alliance of birdwatchers, hunters, ornithologists, biologists, hikers, farmers, artists, and gardeners who will work together to save our wildlife and wild places. Again.

I will be a birdwatcher and a bird hunter.

I will be a conservationist in thought, word, and deed.

Appendix
A Concordance of Common Duck and Goose Names

Birder	Hunter
GEESE	
snow goose	white goose, light goose
snow goose, dark morph	blue goose
greater white-fronted goose	specklebelly, speck, tiger breast
Canada goose	honker, black-headed goose
WHISTLING-DUCKS	
black-bellied whistling-duck	black-bellied tree duck
fulvous whistling-duck	fulvous tree duck
PERCHING DUCKS	
wood duck	woodie, squealer
Muscovy duck	domestic, barnyard
DABBLING DUCKS	
mallard	greenhead, curly-tail
mottled duck	black mallard, Florida duck
gadwall	gray duck, square-headed duck, gad-pig
northern pintail	sprig
American wigeon	baldpate, bald-head
northern shoveler	spoonbill, spoonie, smilin' mallard
cinnamon teal	red teal
blue-winged teal	blue-wing, white-faced teal, summer teal
green-winged teal	greenie
DIVING DUCKS	
canvasback	can or bullneck
redhead	raft duck
ring-necked duck	ringbill, blackjack

Spoonies: roseate spoonbill and northern shoveler

DIVING DUCKS, *continued*	
greater scaup	bluebill, dos gris (grayback)
lesser scaup	broadbill, bluebill, dos gris
common goldeneye	brass-eyed whistler
bufflehead	butterball
hooded merganser	hairyhead, wood shelduck
common merganser	shellduck, shelduck
red-breasted merganser	fish duck, common sawbill
STIFFTAILS	
ruddy duck	stiff-tail, spiketail, clicker-tail
American coot	poule d'eau, waterhen, mudhen

Notes

1. I now believe this is a paraphrase of Swiss painter Paul Klee's quote: "He has found his style, when he cannot do otherwise."

2. Duck Stamp dollars are used only to acquire land through purchase, lease, or easement or the restoration of wetlands. Operations and maintenance (staffing, equipment, facility maintenance, etc.) depend on money allocated in the federal budget.

3. On October 1, 2021 (the beginning of federal fiscal year 2022), the Federal Aid in Wildlife Restoration Fund awarded $1,115,157,974 in grants, an increase of more than 60 percent over 2021. Since 1937, the fund's grants have totaled over $14.6 billion.

4. The term "sporting gun" has changed over the decades. Originally it identified a gun that was not military issue or a commercial large-bore gun for market hunting. Currently the term "modern sporting rifle" includes firearms like the AR-15.

5. In fiscal year 2022, Dingell-Johnson grants totaled $399,661,336. Since its inception in 1952, Sport Fish Restoration grants have totaled more than $10.9 billion.

6. In fiscal year 2021, Pittman-Robertson and Dingell-Johnson grants totaled $1,093,154,901. In fiscal year 2022, the combined grants totaled $1,514,819,310.

7. Shotgun shells, or cartridges, come in high-base or low-base styles (also called high-brass and low-brass). The name refers to the height of the metal base at the bottom of the shell. Typically, high-base shells contain more gunpowder. This results in the pellets traveling at a higher velocity (feet per second, or FPS). Low-base shells, which usually—not always—have less gunpowder, are typically used for sport shooting.

8. Audubon, *Ornithological Biography*, 1:ix.

9. *Ornithological Biography*, 3:83.

10. A number of shorebirds have elliptical routes. For instance, the red knot follows the Central Flyway north in the spring, but its southbound path follows the Atlantic coast of the United States and then the Atlantic coast of South America before arriving in Tierra del Fuego.

11. I later learn that I've bypassed the important playa lakes region of the Texas and Oklahoma Panhandles, eastern New Mexico and Colorado, and western Kansas. The playa lakes are shallow seasonal wetlands that form after rain. They are not only important migratory bird habitat but a critical recharge source for the Ogallala aquifer.

12. A Ramsar site is a wetland site designated to be of international importance under the Ramsar Convention, or the Convention on Wetlands, an intergovernmental environmental treaty established in 1971 by UNESCO, which came into force in 1975. It provides for national action and international cooperation regarding the conservation of wetlands and the wise, sustainable use of their resources.

13. Kansas permits its water according to a "first in time, first in right" basis. Quivira's 1957 surface water right is senior to approximately 95 percent of the total rights in the Rattlesnake Creek drainage. The chief engineer of the Kansas Department of Agriculture determined that Quivira's right is impaired by junior right irrigators.

14. Research by the International Crane Foundation and others demonstrates that a nontoxic coating can be added to corn seed that will deter sandhill cranes from eating sprouted seed and destroying farmers' crops.

15. Sandhill cranes are classified into five subspecies, of which two are migratory (greater and lesser) and three are nonmigratory. While the two migratory populations are stable and the nonmigratory Florida subspecies is doing well, the nonmigratory Mississippi and Cuban subspecies are both listed as endangered. Of the fifteen species of cranes in the world, eleven are considered at risk of extinction.

16. Wendy Koons (formerly Horine) is now the hunter/trapper education and volunteer services coordinator at Idaho Fish and Game.

17. *The Ripple Effect: How Wetlands Are Shoring Up Canada's Environmental and Economic Well-Being*, 2020 annual report, Ducks Unlimited Canada.

18. "The Plowprint Report: 2020," World Wildlife Fund, www.worldwildlife .org/plowprint; www.worldwildlife.org/pages/plowprint-report-map.

19. The payment percentages are different in each state and can change yearly based on acceptance rates by landowners. In North Dakota, 2018 payment percentages were around 35 percent for grassland acreage and 85 percent for wetland acreage. Randy Renner, personal communication, March 29, 2021.

20. The Conservation Reserve Program, or CRP, is managed by the USDA and pays farmers to take marginal or erodible lands out of production. Lands are seeded with native grasses and often become wildlife havens.

21. A genetically modified organism, or GMO, is any living organism whose genetic material has been manipulated or altered using genetic engineering techniques. "Roundup Ready" is the Monsanto trademark for its patented line of genetically modified crop seeds that are resistant to its glyphosate-based herbicide Roundup.

22. There are three North American breeding populations of piping plovers. The northern Great Plains population and the Atlantic coast population are federally listed as threatened. The Great Lakes population is listed as endangered.

23. Audubon, Audubon, and Coues, *Audubon and His Journals*.

24. Marshall Johnson is now chief conservation officer for the National Audubon Society.

25. "Rules and Regulations," 51358 *Federal Register* 82, no. 213 (Monday, November 6, 2017).

26. Northern shovelers are commonly referred to as spoonies by waterfowl hunters. Please see the appendix, "A Concordance of Common Duck and Goose Names."

27. South Dakota Game, Fish and Parks leases private land for hunting access (as do the game departments of many other states). These programs include Walk-In Areas, the Conservation Reserve Enhancement Program, the Controlled Hunting Access Program, Cooperative Management Areas, and the Lower Oahe Waterfowl Access Program.

28. See note 24.

29. At least two national programs are working to conserve urban and suburban birds, both residential and migratory species. The US Fish and Wildlife Service has the Urban Conservation Treaty for Migratory Birds program. The American Bird Conservancy and Environment for the Americas have the Bird City Americas program. Both work with communities at the local level to design and implement bird conservation strategies.

30. Joint Ventures are subunits of the North American Waterfowl Management Plan that work to create, conserve, and sustain waterbird habitats, depending on a network of private and public partnerships, NGOs, and state and federal agencies.

31. Steve Balas passed away April 20, 2021.

Further Reading

Audubon, John James. 1999. *John James Audubon: Writings and Drawings*. New York: Library of America.

———. 2017. *John James Audubon's Journal of 1826: The Voyage to the Birds of America*. Lincoln: University of Nebraska Press.

Audubon, John James, Maria R. Audubon, and Elliott Coues. 1897. *Audubon and His Journals*. Vol. 1. New York: Charles Scribner's Sons. https://www.biodiversitylibrary.org/item/30957.

Audubon, John James, and William MacGillivray. 1831. *Ornithological Biography, or an Account of the Habits of the Birds of the United States of America; Accompanied by Descriptions of the Objects Represented in the Work Entitled* The Birds of America, *and Interspersed with Delineations of American Scenery and Manners*. Vol. 1. Edinburgh: Adam Black. https://www.biodiversitylibrary.org/item/103784.

———. 1834. *Ornithological Biography, or an Account of the Habits of the Birds of the United States of America; Accompanied by Descriptions of the Objects Represented in the Work Entitled* The Birds of America, *and Interspersed with Delineations of American Scenery and Manners*. Vol. 2. Edinburgh: Adam Black. https://www.biodiversitylibrary.org/item/103785.

———. 1835. *Ornithological Biography, or an Account of the Habits of the Birds of the United States of America; Accompanied by Descriptions of the Objects Represented in the Work Entitled* The Birds of America, *and Interspersed with Delineations of American Scenery and Manners*. Vol. 3. Edinburgh: Adam Black. https://www.biodiversitylibrary.org/item/103782.

———. 1838. *Ornithological Biography, or an Account of the Habits of the Birds of the United States of America; Accompanied by Descriptions of the Objects Represented in the Work Entitled* The Birds of America, *and Interspersed with Delineations of American Scenery and Manners*. Vol. 4. Edinburgh: Adam Black. https://www.biodiversitylibrary.org/item/103783.

———. 1839. *Ornithological Biography, or an Account of the Habits of the Birds of the United States of America; Accompanied by Descriptions of the Objects Represented in the Work Entitled* The Birds of America, *and Interspersed with Delineations of American Scenery and Manners*. Vol. 5. Edinburgh: Adam Black. https://www.biodiversitylibrary.org/item/103786.

Audubon, John James, Roger Tory Peterson, Virginia Marie Peterson, and National Audubon Society. 1993. *Audubon's Birds of America*. New York: Artabras.

Audubon, John James, and Richard Rhodes. 2006. *The Audubon Reader*. New York: Everyman.

Beach, Virginia Christian, and Ducks Unlimited. 2014. *Rice & Ducks: The Surprising Convergence That Saved the Carolina Lowcountry*. Charleston, SC: Evening Post Books.

Brinkley, Douglas. 2017. *Rightful Heritage: Franklin D. Roosevelt and the Land of America*. New York: Harper Collins.

Cather, Willa. 1913. *O Pioneers!* Boston: Houghton Mifflin.

———. 1915. *The Song of the Lark*. Boston: Houghton Mifflin.

———. 1918. *My Ántonia*. Boston: Houghton Mifflin.

Dethloff, Henry C. 1989. *A History of the American Rice Industry, 1685–1985*. College Station: Texas A&M University Press.

Doughty, Robin W. 1975. *Feather Fashions and Bird Preservation: A Study in Nature Protection*. Berkeley: University of California Press. https://books.google.com/books?id=sk8gAQAAIAAJ.

———. 1983. *Wildlife and Man in Texas: Environmental Change and Conservation*. College Station: Texas A&M University Press.

———. 1989. *Return of the Whooping Crane*. Austin: University of Texas Press.

Egan, Timothy. 2013. *The Worst Hard Time: The Untold Story of Those Who Survived the Great American Dust Bowl*. Boston: Houghton Mifflin.

Ehrlich, Paul R., David S. Dobkin, and Darryl Wheye. 1988. *The Birder's Handbook: A Field Guide to the Natural History of North American Birds*. New York: Simon and Schuster.

Fackrell, Jason B. 2017. *Hunters against PETA: Why We Hunt & Why Hunting Helps Wildlife*. Hunters Against PETA. CreateSpace Independent Publishing.

Furtman, Michael. 2001. *Duck Country: A Celebration of America's Favorite Waterfowl*. Memphis, TN: Ducks Unlimited.

Grinnell, George Bird. 1918. *American Duck Shooting*. New York: Forest and Stream. http://books.google.com/books?id=p20mAQAAMAAJ.

Hamm, Dale, and David Bakke. 2008. *The Last of the Market Hunters*. Carbondale: Southern Illinois University Press.

Johnson, William P., and Mark Lockwood. 2013. *Texas Waterfowl*. College Station: Texas A&M University Press.

Kastner, Joseph, Miriam T. Gross, and New York Public Library. 1988. *The Bird Illustrated, 1550–1900: From the Collections of the New York Public Library*. New York: H. N. Abrams.

Kortright, Francis H., T. M. Shortt, and American Wildlife Institute. 1967. *The*

Ducks, Geese and Swans of North America: A Vade Mecum for the Naturalist and the Sportsman. Harrisburg, PA: Stackpole.

Koshollek, Alanna, Dan Durbin, and Aldo Leopold Foundation. 2018. *Why Hunt: A Guide for Lovers of Nature, Local Food, and Outdoor Recreation*. Baraboo, WI: Aldo Leopold Foundation.

Leopold, Aldo. 1970. *A Sand County Almanac: With Other Essays on Conservation from Round River*. New York: Ballantine Books.

Lockhart, M. A. 2017. "From Rice Fields to Duck Marshes: Sport Hunters and Environmental Change on the South Carolina Coast, 1890–1950." PhD diss., University of South Carolina. H4p://Scholarcommons.Sc.Edu/Etd/4161.

Manley, Scott W., and Rice Foundation. 2008. *Conservation in Ricelands of North America*. Stuttgart, AR: Rice Foundation.

McCaddin, Joe. 1991. *Duck Stamps and Prints: The Complete Federal and State Editions*. New York: Hugh Lauter Levin Associates.

Miller, Stephen M. 1986. *Early American Waterfowling, 1700's–1930*. Piscataway, NJ: Winchester Press.

Olson, Roberta J. M., Marjorie Shelley, and Alexandra Mazzitelli. 2012. *Audubon's Aviary: The Original Watercolors for the Birds of America*. New York: Rizzoli Electa.

Reiger, John F. 2016. *American Sportsmen and the Origins of Conservation*. 3rd ed. Corvallis: Oregon State University Press.

Roemer, Ferdinand. 1935. *Texas: With Particular Reference to German Immigration and the Physical Appearance of the Country*. Translated by Oswald Mueller. San Antonio: Standard Printing. Reprinted in 1983 (as *Roemer's Texas: 1845 to 1847*), Austin: Eakin Press.

Sawyer, R. K., and Matt Kaminski. 2019. *A Hundred Years of Texas Waterfowl Hunting: The Decoys, Guides, Clubs, and Places, 1870s to 1970s*. College Station: Texas A&M University Press.

Sawyer, R. K., and Rick Pratt. 2013. *Texas Market Hunting: Stories of Waterfowl, Game Laws, and Outlaws*. College Station: Texas A&M University Press.

Sibley, David. 2014. *The Sibley Guide to Birds*. New York: Knopf.

Sibley, David, Chris Elphick, John B. Dunning, and National Audubon Society. 2013. *The Sibley Guide to Bird Life & Behavior*. New York: Knopf.

Souder, William. 2004. *Under a Wild Sky: John James Audubon and the Making of the Birds of America*. New York: North Point Press.

Vileisis, Ann. 1997. *Discovering the Unknown Landscape: A History of America's Wetlands*. Washington, DC: Island Press.

Walsh, Harry M. 1971. *The Outlaw Gunner*. Cambridge, MD: Tidewater Publishers.

Worthen, Amy N., Jay N. Darling, and Brunnier Gallery and Museum. 1991. *The Prints of J. N. Darling*. Ames: Iowa State University Press.

Zimmerman, John L. 1995. *Cheyenne Bottoms: Wetland in Jeopardy*. Lawrence: University Press of Kansas.

Internet Resources

American Bird Conservancy
    https://www.abcbirds.org
American Bird Conservancy, Bird City Americas
    https://abcbirds.org/birds/bird-city-americas/
American Bird Conservancy, Cats Indoors
    https://abcbirds.org/program/cats-indoors/
Audubon Society, History of Audubon and Science-Based Bird Conservation
    https://www.audubon.org/about/history-audubon-and-waterbird-conservation
Birds of the World, Cornell Laboratory of Ornithology
    https://birdsoftheworld.org/
Delta Waterfowl
    https://www.deltawaterfowl.org
Ducks Unlimited
    https://www.ducks.org
Ducks Unlimited Canada
    https://www.ducks.ca
Ducks Unlimited de México
    https://dumac.org/en/
Friends of the Migratory Bird/Duck Stamp
    http://www.friendsofthestamp.org
John J. Audubon's Birds of America
    https://www.audubon.org/birds-of-america
Margie Crisp
https://www.margiecrisp.com
National Audubon Society
    https://www.audubon.org
National Audubon Society, Conservation Ranching
https://www.audubon.org/conservation/ranching
National Fish and Wildlife Foundation
    https://www.nfwf.org
National Wildlife Federation
    https://www.nwf.org

National Wildlife Refuge Association
    https://www.refugeassociation.org
National Wildlife Refuge Friends Organization
    https://www.nfwf.org/programs/national-wildlife-refuge-friends
The Nature Conservancy
    https://www.nature.org
North American Waterfowl Management Plan
    https://nawmp.org
North American Wetlands Conservation Act
    https://www.fws.gov/birds/grants/north-american-wetland-conservation-act.php
Project FeederWatch, Cornell Lab and Birds Canada/Oiseaux Canada
    https://feederwatch.org
Texas Parks and Wildlife Department
    https://tpwd.texas.gov
US Fish and Wildlife Service
    Duck Stamp
        https://www.fws.gov/birds/get-involved/duck-stamp.php
    Flyways
        https://www.fws.gov/birds/management/flyways.php
    Migratory Bird Program
        https://www.fws.gov/birds/
    National Wildlife Refuge System
        https://www.fws.gov/refuges/
    Urban Bird Treaty Program
        https://www.fws.gov/urban/urbanbirdtreaty.php
Western Hemisphere Shorebird Reserve Network
    https://www.whsrn.org
William B. Montgomery, artist
    https://www.williambmontgomery.com
World Migratory Bird Day
    https://www.migratorybirdday.org
World Wildlife Fund Sustainable Ranching Initiative
    https://www.worldwildlife.org/projects/sustainable-ranching-initiative

Northern shovelers

Index

Other titles in the Kathie and Ed Cox Jr. Books on Conservation Leadership, sponsored by The Meadows Center for Water and the Environment, Texas State University

Politics and Parks: People, Places, Politics, Parks
George L. Bristol

Money for the Cause: A Complete Guide to Event Fundraising
Rudolph A. Rosen

Green in Gridlock: Common Goals, Common Ground, and Compromise
Paul W. Hansen

Hillingdon Ranch: Four Seasons, Six Generations
David K. Langford and Lorie Woodward Cantu

*Heads above Water: The Inside Story of the Edwards Aquifer Recovery
    Implementation Program*
Robert L. Gulley

Border Sanctuary: The Conservation Legacy of the Santa Ana Land Grant
M. J. Morgan

Fog at Hillingdon
David K. Langford

Texas Landscape Project: Nature and People
David Todd and Jonathan Ogden

*Discovering Westcave: The Natural and Human History of a Hill Country
    Nature Preserve*
Christopher S. Caran and Elaine Davenport

Rise of Climate Science: A Memoir
Gerald R. North

Wild Lives of Reptiles and Amphibians: A Young Herpetologist's Guide
Michael A. Smith

Wild Focus: Twenty-five Years of Texas Parks & Wildlife Photography
Earl Nottingham

The Art of Texas State Parks: A Centennial Celebration, 1923–2023
Andrew Sansom and Linda J. Reaves